THE P

How MI6 Masterminded Ireland's
Deepest State Crisis

DAVID BURKE

MERCIER PRESS

Dedication

To My Family

MERCIER PRESS
Cork
www.mercierpress.ie

© David Burke, 2024

ISBN: 978-1-78117-865-2

978-1-78117-866-9 eBook

Printed and bound in the EU.

Contents

AUTHOR'S NOTE

The events of 1969–70, which include the Arms Crisis, are the subject of two books I have previously written: *Deception and Lies* (2020) and *An Enemy of the Crown* (2022). The Arms Crisis concerned allegations that two Fianna Fáil politicians, Charles Haughey and Neil Blaney, together with others, broke Irish law in an illegal attempt to import weapons with the assistance of Irish military intelligence, G2, to arm the Provisional IRA. In those books I set out the basis for my belief that the endeavour, while a chaotic shambles, was not an illegal operation.

A quarter of the present book includes new evidence about the role played by Britain's Secret Intelligence Service, MI6, and their mole within garda intelligence, Patrick Crinnion, in the Arms Crisis. Some of the information published in my previous books is revisited here, albeit in summary form. I have included footnotes which direct interested readers to the unabridged versions of these events which are available in my earlier works. The summaries are included in this volume to maintain a coherent narrative.

I enjoyed access to two separate tranches of documents written by Patrick Crinnion during my research for this book. First, a collection of letters Crinnion sent to various parties in 1973. Second, a compilation of memoranda, also from 1973, which were written by Crinnion. The latter was supplied to me by a source who must remain confidential. For clarity and to avoid repetition, I have made some very minor edits to the 1973 memoranda and I have chosen not to place a footnote after each quote from that material. Readers can assume that where Crinnion is quoted without the addition of a footnote, the words emanate from the second tranche of documentation.

Various people quoted in this work have spelled the names of other individuals and organisations differently. In order to avoid confusion, and for consistency, I have amended these.

When Seán MacStíofáin published his memoirs in 1975, he spelled his name as Seán MacStíofáin, which is the form used throughout this book, except in direct quotations. Crinnion, for example, spelled it Sean Mac STIOPHAIN.

DAVID BURKE, DUBLIN, 2024

Dramatis Personae

AINSWORTH, Joseph: Garda intelligence chief.

BERRY, Peter: Secretary-General to the Department of Justice, 1960–70.

BLANEY, Neil: Fianna Fáil politician. Charged along with Charles Haughey for attempting to import arms illegally into the Republic of Ireland in 1970. The charges against him were dropped at an early stage.

CALLAGHAN, James: Home Secretary 1967–1970. British prime minister, 1976–79.

CASEY, Martin: a member of Saor Éire.

COSTELLO, John A: Fine Gael politician who served as Taoiseach, 1948–1951, and 1954–1957.

COSGRAVE, Liam: Leader of Fine Gael, 1966–1977; Taoiseach 1973–77.

CRINNION, Patrick: a member of the special detective unit (SDU) of An Garda Síochána's assigned to C3, garda intelligence division.

CULHANE, Detective Sergeant Patrick: a member of the SDU.

DOOCEY, Detective Inspector Patrick: a member of the SDU.

FITZGERALD, Garret: Leader of Fine Gael, 1977–1987. Taoiseach 1981–1982; 1982–87

FLEMING, Chief Superintendent John: Head of the SDU.

GIBBONS, James: Fianna Fáil politician and Minister for Defence, 1969–70.

GILCHRIST, Andrew: British ambassador to Dublin, 1966–70.

GODFREY, Hyman: Scotland Yard and/or MI6 agent who posed as an arms dealer in London in 1969.

GOULDING, Cathal: Chief-of-Staff of the IRA. Founding member of the Official IRA. Marxist in his political outlook.

GRAHAM, Peter: a member of Saor Éire.

HAUGHEY, Charles: Minister for Finance, November 1966–May 1970. Leader of Fianna Fáil, December 1979–February 1982. Taoiseach, December 1979–June 1981, March 1982–December 1982 and March 1987–February 1992. Arms trial defendant.

HAUGHEY, Pádraig ('Jock'): businessman and brother of Charles Haughey.

HEATH, Edward: Conservative Party Prime Minister of the UK, 1970–74.

HEFFERON, Col Michael: Director of Irish Military Intelligence, G2, 1958–1970.

HILLERY, Patrick: Minister for External Affairs July, 1969–1973.

HUGHES, Detective Garda Michael: a member of the SDU.

KEANE, Frank: a member of Saor Éire.

KELLY, Capt. James: joined the Irish Army in 1949. He went into the intelligence directorate, G2, in 1961. He was posted to the Middle East, 1963–65. He returned to G2 and retired in 1970.

LITTLEJOHN, Keith: criminal and MI6 agent and brother of Kenneth.

LITTLEJOHN, Kenneth: criminal and MI6 agent and brother of Keith.

LYNCH, Jack: Fianna Fáil politician. Taoiseach, 1966–73; 1977–79.

McMAHON, Superintendent Philip: head of Garda Special Branch, 1961-69.

MacSTÍOFÁIN, Seán: IRA Director of Intelligence. Founding member of the Provisional IRA.

MALONE, Patrick: Head of C3 in the late 1960s and early 1970s. Garda Commissioner, 1973–75.

'MARKHAM-RANDALL', Capt.: the *nom de guerre* of a British spy who visited Dublin in November 1969.

MULLEN, Thomas: Garda intelligence officer attached to C3 in the 1950s and early 1960s.

O'BRIEN, Conor Cruise: Irish Labour Party TD, June 1969–June 1977. Minister for Posts and Telegraphs, March 1973–1977.

O'DEA, Detective superintendent Ned: a member of the SDU.

O'MALLEY, Des: Chief Whip, July 1969–May 1970; Minister for Justice, May 1970–March 1973.

OLDFIELD, Maurice: Deputy Chief of MI6, 1964–73; Chief of MI6, 1973–78; director and co-ordinator of intelligence, Northern Ireland, 1979–80.

PECK, John: British ambassador to Dublin, 1970–73. Founding member of the IRD, and director of the IRD, 1952–53/4.

RENNIE, Sir John: Head of the IRD, 1953–58. Chief of MI6, 1968–73.

ROWLEY, Allan: Director and Controller of Intelligence (DCI) Northern Ireland, 1972–73

SMELLIE, Craig: MI6 Head of Station, Lisburn, 1973–75.

STEELE, Frank: MI6 officer stationed in Northern Ireland, 1971–73.

TIMMONS, Richard: a member of Saor Éire.

WALLACE, Colin: Psychological operations officer with the British army at HQNI in the early and mid-1970s.

WALSH, Liam: a member of Saor Éire.

WARD, Andrew: Secretary of the Department of Justice, 1971–86.

WHITELAW, William: Secretary of State for Northern Ireland, 1972–73.

WILSON, Harold: Labour Party Prime Minister of the UK, 1964–70, and 1974–6.

WREN, Larry: Head of C3 in the 1971–79, and Garda Commissioner 1983-87.

WYMAN, John: MI6 officer.

ORGANISATIONS, TERMS, LOCATIONS AND ACRONYMS

B Specials: the auxiliary force of the Royal Ulster Constabulary.

C3: Garda intelligence unit responsible for the analysis and co-ordination of information collected by the SDU.

Citizens' Defence Committees (CDCs): A collective description of the groups which assembled in 1968 and 1969 to defend Nationalist communities in Northern Ireland from attacks by Loyalist extremists, RUC and B Specials.

CDCs: see citizen defence committees.

Dáil Éireann: Irish parliament, located in Dublin.

DoJ: Department of Justice, Dublin, Ireland.

Dublin Castle: Headquarters of the Special Detective Unit (SDU) of An Garda Síochána.

FCO: The Foreign and Commonwealth Office of the United Kingdom.

FDCO: The Foreign, Commonwealth and Development Office (FDCO), formerly the Foreign and Commonwealth Office (FCO) of the United Kingdom.

FO: Foreign Office of the UK.

Fianna Fáil: Irish political party led by Éamon de Valera, 1926–1959, Seán Lemass, 1959–66, Jack Lynch, 1966–79, and Charles Haughey, 1979–92.

Fine Gael: Irish political party led by Liam Cosgrave, 1965–77, who was succeeded by Garret FitzGerald, 1977–87.

G2: Irish Military Intelligence.

Gaeltacht: a region in which the Irish language is spoken.

Garda Síochána: the police force of the Republic of Ireland.

Garda Special Branch: The intelligence gathering apparatus of An Garda Síochána. It is also known as the special detective unit (SDU).

HQNI: British army headquarters NI, based in Thiepval Barracks in Lisburn.

IRD: Information Research Department. A propaganda and forgery department attached to the FCO.

MCR: monthly confidential reports which were prepared by the C3 directorate of An Garda Síochána. They were produced by the gardaí for the Department of Justice.

MI5: Britain's internal security service, active inside the United Kingdom and her overseas colonies. It is attached to the Home Office.

MI6: Britain's overseas intelligence service, also known as the British secret service. It is attached to the Foreign Office. It is often referred to as the Secret Intelligence Service (SIS).

MoD: Britain's Ministry of Defence.

NAI: National Archive Ireland.

NIO: Northern Ireland Office.

OC: Officer-in-command

Official IRA: the Marxist wing of the Republican Movement which emerged after the split in December 1969. Its chief-of-staff in the 1970s was Cathal Goulding.

Partition: a phrase used to describe the division of Ireland pursuant to the Government of Ireland Act 1920 by a border into two separate jurisdictions, whose successor states are the Republic of Ireland and Northern Ireland.

Provisional IRA: the wing of the IRA which emerged after the IRA split in December 1969 with the intention of ending British rule in Northern Ireland.

PSYOPs: Psychological Operations to influence people and events by manipulation and deception.

RTÉ: Radio Telefís Éireann, the national television and radio broadcaster of the Irish state.

RUC: Royal Ulster Constabulary, the police force of Northern Ireland.

Saor Éire: a Republican socialist paramilitary organisation responsible for bank robberies, the killing of Garda Richard Fallon and an arson attack on Fianna Fáil HQ in 1967.

SDU: special detective unit or special branch of An Garda Síochána

TD: Teachta Dála or member of the parliament of the Republic of Ireland.

UDA: Ulster Defence Association.

UPV: Ulster Protestant Volunteers.

UVF: Ulster Volunteer Force.

Introduction

A Fog of Deceit

Detective Garda Patrick Crinnion was a senior member of C3, the intelligence wing of An Garda Síochána (the gardaí), in the 1960s and 1970s. Secretly, he was working for the British secret service, MI6.

Crinnion rose to become C3's leading analyst. One of those who came under his microscope was John Stevenson, an Englishman better known to history as Seán MacStíofáin. The latter was appointed as director of intelligence of the IRA by its chief-of-staff, Cathal Goulding, and his colleagues on the Army Council, in 1966.

MacStíofáin and Goulding were of immense interest to Crinnion and MI6.

Goulding wanted to nudge the Republican movement in the direction of mainstream politics. That entailed recognising the legitimacy of Dáil Éireann, the Irish parliament, and Stormont in Belfast. MacStíofáin was steadfast in his opposition to both of those assemblies. Instead, he wanted to retrieve the pike from the thatch, swap it for a machine gun, and lead another charge at the British empire in order to achieve full Irish independence.

Crinnion watched the IRA through the prism of his spyglass as the power struggle between these two Republicans grew in intensity in the mid-1960s. The clash culminated in the fracture of the IRA, in 1969, into the Officials, supported by Goulding, and the Provisionals, led by MacStíofáin.

Although MacStíofáin and Goulding had been arrested in 1953, after a raid on an armoury in England, and had served six years in prison at Wormwood Scrubs, they ultimately had little in common. Goulding developed a Marxist vision of a united Ireland hoping to make common cause with working-class Loyalists. MacStíofáin, on the other hand, believed that Unionists were a rabble who 'lacked a cultural identity' and would be taught to speak Irish after reunification. 'I don't see this Irish-speaking provoking a reaction from Northern Protestants ... Adopting the Irish language would show them the real difference between being Irish and being English'.[1]

MacStíofáin was conservative in his views; Goulding a liberal. The former saw himself as a family man. He was a non-smoker and professed not to drink alcohol, whereas Goulding was a 'relentlessly cheery' individual who made friends easily and frequented the 'fashionable bars around St Stephen's Green drinking with writers, musicians and painters and became a recognised feature of Dublin Bohemia'.[2] The writer Brendan Behan, an ex-IRA man, featured prominently among Goulding's friends. The pair had been close since childhood. In adulthood, they shared a common trade as decorators and a similar political outlook.

MacStíofáin was a practising Catholic, whereas Goulding's religion was Marxism. Throughout the years that MacStíofáin spent in prison in the 1950s, he was 'sustained' by his 'belief in God and in the practice of our religion, which I have always found to be a great consolation any time I have been in a tight spot'.[3] In jail, Goulding played chess with a God-less Russian spy convicted of attempting to steal atomic secrets.

WHILE HE WAS LIVING in Cork in the 1960s, MacStíofáin once refused to sell the *United Irishman* newspaper because it had published a letter by Dr Roy Johnston which criticised the recital of the rosary at IRA commemorations as 'sectarian'. At one stage he would only attend mass if it was celebrated in Irish. He told Rosita Sweetman, in 1972, that in a united Ireland he saw the Catholic Church 'playing a very important role'. 'I don't see why the educational control should be taken from the Catholic Church. I think people like the Christian Brothers have done great work in promoting the Irish language and Irish games. What I do think though, is that the same educational facilities should be offered to other non-Catholic people to educate their children.'[4] He would eventually move to live in a Gaeltacht in Meath and place a mat at his doorway instructing visitors thus: 'Labhair Gaeilge anseo'. (Speak Irish here).

MacStíofáin had conservative views about divorce and contraception. 'I don't think these things should be [contained in the] written or unwritten laws of any country. They're a matter of conscience. I do think family planning clinics should be set up to help young married couples, but there are other ways of planning a family you know than these artificial contraceptives. I don't agree with divorce, I think it undermines the foundation of marriage, and I wouldn't agree with contraceptives in slot machines on the street like you have in London and America. But I've never had any problems like this myself.'[5] When the IRA discovered condoms could be used to make acid fuse bombs, MacStíofáin refused to smuggle them into the Republic.

When the IRA split in December 1969, MacStíofáin became one of the key architects of the Provisional IRA. At first the dissidents were perceived by many as a splinter group that would fade away, as had so many other offshoots. They maintained a low profile, recruited volunteers, raised funds and armed themselves. Aside from Goulding, who called MacStíofáin a 'petty-minded conspirator', few had an inkling of MacStíofáin's determination, ability and cunning. He became the Provisionals' first chief-of-staff. While the Provisionals engaged in the defence of the Nationalist ghettoes in Northern Ireland in 1970, they did not go on the offensive until early in 1971.

During his career as an IRA leader MacStíofáin kept many secrets from his colleagues, one of which was that he was an informer for the special branch, or special detective unit (SDU) of the gardaí.

But MacStíofáin, in reality, was playing cloak and dagger games with the gardaí. He never wavered from his vision of Republicanism. He was a quasi double agent.

MacStíofáin's masquerade lasted more than a decade during which he benefited from the immunity afforded to him by his role as an apparent 'informer'. He used his influence to deflect garda attention away from himself towards his rivals, especially Goulding. After the creation of the Provisionals, MacStíofáin enjoyed a breathing space which lasted an impressive two and a half years during which he imported arms and trained his recruits, with far less scrutiny and intrusion from the police than he might otherwise have encountered.

A lot has been written about MacStíofáin. The overlapping story of Patrick Crinnion has received minimal attention from historians despite the massive disruption his career as a garda and British spy occasioned to his homeland.

Between them, Crinnion and MacStíofáin would change the course of Irish politics, throw Fianna Fáil into disarray, and create an atmosphere in which the most militant form of Republicanism came to the fore.

1

THE MAN FROM MENSA

Joseph Crinnion and Mary Hogan were married in October 1933 in Monkstown, Co. Dublin. Joseph, a carpenter, lived in Dun Laoghaire. The couple welcomed their first child, Patrick, to the world on 15 November 1934. He was born at the family home at Mill Lane Shanganagh, Co. Dublin. Another boy, Peter, followed on 12 February 1939, and a daughter, Phyllis, after that.[1]

The Crinnions went to work for Mervyn and Sybil Wingfield and, later, his son Mervyn Patrick, the viscounts of Powerscourt, Enniskerry. Mary served as a housekeeper at their magnificent family home. It was originally a thirteenth-century castle, part of the estate of Phelim O'Toole. In 1603, King James I of England granted a lease of the property for twenty-one years to Sir Richard Wingfield, to punish O'Toole for his disloyalty to the crown. The Wingfields murdered O'Toole in the Killing Hollow, near Powerscourt, in May of 1603. The property remained in the Wingfield family for the next four centuries.

Patrick Crinnion grew up in more humble surroundings. The Wingfield family owned a row of cottages on the Boghall Road, Bray, County Wicklow, in which loyal and trusted servants of the family, such as the Crinnions, were allowed to reside.[2]

The Powerscourts went into a decline in the late 1920s and, by the early 1930s, Mervyn was talking about having to sell the estate. The family was saved by Patrick's marriage to the poet Sheila Claude Beddington.

Mervyn and Sybil died in 1947, almost simultaneously, a

double blow that meant that their son Patrick faced dual death duties which took their toll on the wealth of the family.[3]

Crinnion's parents continued to work for the Wingfields. By the 1950s, the mansion had become a 'sombre' place. 'There were no visitors, nobody went out in the evenings, and the gates were locked at half past ten.'[4]

On the positive side, the Wingfields were good employers, certainly to the Crinnions. Patrick Crinnion's father Joseph predeceased his mother, Mary. She spent her retirement years in a pleasant apartment on the second floor of a Georgian house on Vevay Road which the Wingfields kept for their former servants.

Crinnion, a bright student, was educated at the local national school. He went on to become a member of Mensa. The latter is an organisation recognising those who achieve a 98% score in a supervised IQ examination or other approved intelligence test. Mensa boasts many policemen within its elite membership and, in 1955, Crinnion chose a career in An Garda Síochána. Aged twenty, he commenced his service on 10 May of that year. One of his early tasks, while stationed at Donnybrook garda station, was to protect the home of the then Taoiseach, John A. Costello, at 20 Herbert Park in Ballsbridge.

Nancy Lattimore lived in a mews house on Morehampton Lane, Ballsbridge, with her parents. She met Crinnion one day while he was on guard duty at Herbert Park and they became friends.[5] Soon, they were dating. Such was his acceptance by her family that Nancy's mother now found herself preparing meals for Crinnion when he came off duty. The Lattimores had a military background. One of Nancy's family had served in the British army during the First World War and had been gassed in the trenches. Although he survived, he never got over the ordeal. Two of Nancy's brothers joined the British army. One of them, Seamus, rose to become a major. Patrick Crinnion trotted after Seamus like a besotted pup.

One night, shortly after joining the force, Crinnion was walking beside the wall of a school on his beat in Dublin when he noticed a bundle of old newspapers on the footpath. When he prodded them with his boot, bank notes spilled out. Crinnion could have trousered the money but gathered it up and brought it back to his desk sergeant in Donnybrook. The rule was that if no one came looking for money, the finder could claim it after a year. No one staked a claim. When he went to collect the cash, he was told that since he had been on duty the night he stumbled across the notes, they belonged to the Exchequer.

The money meant a lot to Crinnion. He was outraged that the cash was not returned to him. He approached John A. Costello, whom he had befriended while on protection duty outside his house in Donnybrook, about the matter. The passage of time did not dampen his indignation. In 1973, Crinnion wrote to John's son, Declan Costello, the then attorney-general, recalling how:

> … although I know you cannot picture me now, during the I.R.A Border Campaign of 1956/62, I spent about a year on duty outside your home on Herbert Park protecting your father who was then An Taoiseach. It was while on this duty that I met the girl from nearby who is now my wife. As well, in a matter where I found a hoard of money which the State sought to retain, usurping my rights as a citizen, your father took an interest and I brought the then Commissioner [Daniel Costigan][6] to court in a civil action which although it failed on a technicality satisfied honour.[7]

Crinnion was a non-smoker and teetotal. His potential was recognised quickly by his superiors and he was assigned to the special detective unit (SDU) at the end of the 1950s. To aid his finances, he worked many hours overtime, including VIP protection assignments.

With his career moving in the right direction, Patrick purchased a property in his sole name on Rathmore Avenue, on the Lower Kilmacud Road in Stillorgan, Co. Dublin, on 28 August 1959. He and Nancy were married on 12 September 1959.

Crinnion became a part of the garda intelligence machine that extinguished the flickering embers of the IRA's Border Campaign of 1956–62, an offensive that never caught fire.

In a memorandum prepared in 1973, Crinnion recalled how, when:

> married first I was working on shift [duty and] in order to get to the [Dublin] Castle [the HQ of the SDU] at say 5.45 a.m. on my bike, allowing for windy weather or punctures, I had to set my new alarm clock for a 4.30 a.m. early rise, put on the kettle, wash and shave and have a bit of breakfast, pick up my lunch and leave the house no later than 5.05 a.m. for the [cycle] journey a minimum of 30 minutes and during the winter, in the frost and ice, time was critical to me. At that early hour in the morning and at that time there was no radio station on for me to check the time as I had my cup of tea in the kitchen. The money situation was not good either and I confess I had no watch either.

In the late 1950s a brilliant piece of sleuthing and deduction brought Crinnion to the attention of one of the leading figures of garda intelligence, Patrick Carroll, the officer who commanded C3, the brain centre of garda intelligence at the Phoenix Park. Later, Carroll was promoted to oversee all of the departments in C division, and eventually rose to become garda commissioner, 1967–68. In one of his 1973 memoranda, Crinnion recounted how Carroll:

met me once while he was Chief Supt. C3 and I was a D/Gda. in SDU. He summoned me to his office to explain how I had reached a conclusion in a certain case where scurrilous anonymous documents, directed against political office holders were being distributed in the West of Ireland. He may recall that from sheer interest, although not specifically allotted the case; I had shown the culprit to be a particular person. The case had reached a dead end in the routine investigation and as was the custom then in SDU, the file was read [out] to the men, in case anybody might recall or know something to go further.

The young man impressed Carroll. The meeting proved to be Crinnion's big break. According to one of Crinnion's 1973 memoranda, in late December 1960, he was assigned to C3, and entered a world of deception and lies. The department was based at the Phoenix Park, whereas the SDU was spread out across the country with a HQ at Dublin Castle. C3 collected, analysed and co-ordinated the streams of intelligence which flowed into it from the various SDU divisions dotted across the country. Crinnion continued to work at C3 for the rest of his career as a garda. His role 'was to utilise my special knowledge of [subversive organisations] for the benefit of the State'.

This provided him with the opportunity to peer inside the inner workings of the IRA. During the Border Campaign the IRA had been determined to shield their command and coordination network from the gardaí and the RUC. Crinnion recalled in a memorandum in 1973 how a phone tap revealed that 'in the last two years' of the conflict:

the controlling contact for all the ASU (Active Service Units) along the Border was [a] woman here in Dublin, who knew personally at least one man in each unit. This gave her a check on the authenticity of any caller ...

Crinnion, however, had a haughty streak. In a letter he wrote to Garda Commissioner Patrick Malone, who had been his superior at C3 in the late 1960s and early 1970s, he described his work at C3 as 'not just first class but exceptional'.[8] He spoke of his irritation at 'inexperienced officers' whom he believed should not have been 'left to gain experience [in garda intelligence] in a hit and miss fashion'.[9] He criticised the fact that some of them had 'never previously worked exclusively on Special Branch duties' and, damningly, that a number had had to 'be trained by the Staff [at C3] even in such elementary matters as recognition and, according to the SDU timescale, identification of the enemies of the State'.[10] He saw his own role as crucial because 'the basic recognition and correlation of information' which he developed was the 'most profitable [method of] counter-action' against subversives. That work depended 'on the reflexes of the [SDU] Detective in C3'.[11] Narcissus-like, he was clearly referencing himself.

The type of work Crinnion found himself performing at C3 was stimulating, such as the time he concluded that a maverick element of the IRA had tried to kill President Éamon de Valera.

2

THE DE VALERA BOMB PLOT

During the early hours of St Patrick's Day, 17 March 1963, two young men crept into St Finbarr's Cemetery in Cork under the cover of darkness. St Finbarr's is a hallowed place for Republicans. 'Old' IRA men from the War of Independence are buried there. It is the resting place of Terence McSwiney and Tomás Mac Curtain, both former lords mayor. The remains of the hunger striker Joseph Murphy can also be found inside its walls.

The men, Des Swanton and Gerry Madden, found what they were looking for, a platform made of tubular scaffolding and planks of wood beside a memorial. The structure had been erected for a ceremony which was due to take place the next day. They had brought a suitcase with them containing a bomb.

Their target was the memorial, which President Éamon de Valera was due to unveil at the plot, shortly after noon, that day.

Seán MacStíofáin and his colleagues in the Cork IRA were displeased about the forthcoming visit. The IRA had long since parted company with de Valera, a former IRA leader who had become a politician in 1926, when he established the Fianna Fáil political party. The actions his government had taken against the IRA during the Second World War were still fresh in their minds. Many volunteers had been interned. John Joe Kavanagh, an IRA man who had been killed by gardaí in 1940, was buried at St Finbarr's. Some of the younger IRA men wanted to sabotage the ceremony but were told to stand down by the leadership, including MacStíofáin. Swanton and Madden defied the dictate. Madden stated later:

After carefully considering several courses open to us, Volunteer Swanton and myself decided that at this late stage in the proceedings there was only one alternative open to us that was to blow up the memorial to prevent the desecration of our patriots' graves by those who had sold out the Irish Republic.

On the night prior to St Patrick's Day, Volunteer Swanton and myself were engaged in preparing a mine when two members of the Army [IRA] came upon us. They were looking for a useless revolver, which we gave to them. These men were very obviously under most terrific pressure at the time. Members of the Staff were aware of this and had supplied them with a car to collect the weapon. This interruption delayed us an hour and also endangered the security of the operation.[1]

A celebration was taking place that night for Séamus Ó Líonacháin, an IRA volunteer, who had been captured by the RUC at Torr Head, Co. Antrim, on 12 December 1956, and had been in jail in Belfast Prison until March 1963. He was attending a 'welcome home' event at the Thomas Ashe Hall in Cork. Ó Líonacháin recalled that:

In the course of the night I noticed some agitation and heated discussions taking place and eventually I was approached by a tearful Elma O'Connell, [Dáithí Ó Conaill's] sister who asked me if I could intervene and do something to prevent her boyfriend from doing something. She explained that on the following day de Valera was coming to the Republican Plot to unveil a monument and that her boyfriend and another volunteer intended to blow up the monument that night. I immediately approached the local OC and another senior member of the movement and we went upstairs to the library to discuss it and I was amazed at their casual attitude to what I thought could turn into a disaster. They said that they had warned the two lads that if they went ahead with their plan it would be an unofficial action and they would be dismissed from the movement and I felt that the least that should be done was that a group should go down to the house in Blackrock and detain the two lads there until after Dev had departed again.

However, the senior members' response was that he had come to the dance with his wife and no one was going to spoil his night's enjoyment so he went back to the dance hall again.

As it turned out, the two lads went ahead with their plan and at about three a.m. as John and myself were walking up Mount Carmel Road there was a mighty explosion and I prayed that the two lads would be all right.[2]

Patrick Crinnion later analysed the attack. He believed it took place after midnight, not at three in the morning. He recalled in one of the memoranda he prepared in 1973 that the:

two members of the Gardaí on duty in St Finbarr's Cemetery, Cork, [that night] were sheltering near the Caretaker's House and heard the church chimes ringing out for midnight. Within a period of time which I cannot specify now, without access to the file, but certainly far less than 30 minutes, there was a flash and a bomb exploded beside the platform, killing outright a young man who from post mortem and other deductions was clearly bending over the bomb when it exploded. His companion was maimed.

Séamus Ó Líonacháin further recalled:

The next morning as I was returning from Mass I called to the old Fire Station on Sullivan's Quay and the firemen told me that Elma's boyfriend [Des Swanton] had been blown to bits and that they had collected his remains in buckets and that the other volunteer [Gerry Madden] was so badly injured that he wasn't expected to survive. Despite his severe injuries he did in fact survive but he lost a leg and an eye and as a matter of fact the monument wasn't even scratched and if they had succeeded in blowing it up they would have emptied most of the graves in the Plot.[3]

Thereafter, Madden took to wearing an eye patch.[4]

CRINNION WAS AWARE that the IRA was using alarm clocks in their bomb-making:

At that particular period the IRA was training in the manufacture of clock-timed suitcase bombs. Their training leaflet, (and I believe I have one at home still somewhere in my papers) ... was far from being foolproof. The whole concept of the construction was fraught with danger for the operation, as if on a training class or dummy construction the operator had not realised that the wiring as laid out in the training leaflet would in fact sometimes SHORT-CIRCUIT the moment the device was armed. The short-circuiting would also of course fire the bomb instantly.

Crinnion had an overly active and inquisitive mind. The purchase of an alarm clock for his personal use had provided him with an insight, or so he thought, into something he believed would never have occurred to the ordinary citizen – an understanding of the hazards involved in the making of a bomb with such timekeeping devices. In the 1950s, many such devices required regulation and adjustment before they managed to keep good time. He became focused on the possibility of a fault in the regulation of the clock used in the Cork bomb. On his cycle to work, the first opportunity Crinnion found to 'check' the accuracy of his:

new alarm clock was passing the Monument Creamery on the main road. There was a clock inside and they had some kind of light on all night. On several occasions, indeed until we eventually got the clock properly run in and correctly regulated, I found when I arrived at the Monument Creamery/shop that during the night my own new alarm clock had run either slow or fast and in my anxiety to be on time found that my safety margin was considerably shortened. Alarm clocks give a plus or minus error until regulated.

Joe Ainsworth, who would later direct garda intelligence, was asked by the garda commissioner to carry out the investigation into the attack at the cemetery. As Crinnion recalled, Ainsworth and his team discovered that:

during that day these two young men had gone into Roches Stores, Cork, and bought a new alarm clock. (Fragments recovered were identified with similar clocks in the shop). They had during the day constructed the bomb according to the IRA Training leaflet and here lies the one fatal flaw ... The diagram told the constructors to put the clock into the suitcase FACE DOWNWARDS AFTER SELECTING THE TIME FOR THE EXPLOSION WITH THE ALARM HAND. Those young men constructed the bomb following the leaflet available to them and left the final connection or the safety device unconnected until the last moment. In other words as you built the bomb, you selected your time, wound the clock and fixed it in the case, firmly, face downwards. This gave you a selection of anywhere inside a 12-hour period ...

Crinnion concluded that Swanton and Madden had placed the device upside down without noticing that it was running a little behind time. Thus, he decided, although the intention was for the device to explode at 12 noon the following day, or shortly thereafter, it exploded 12 hours prematurely, shortly after 12 midnight, just as they were planting it. The explosion, however, took place at 3 a.m. which renders Crinnion's deduction about the murderous intent of Swanton and Madden entirely hollow.

Crinnion believed that 'only married men like myself [with imprecise alarm clocks] would [have spotted] this fault [as] young single men would not realise, especially if they lived at home and were called for work by their parents' and were not familiar with such devices.

It is universally accepted that the purpose of the enterprise was to damage the monument De Valera was about to unveil. This was a view shared by Joe Ainsworth and his team. Crinnion, however, took a far more extreme view. He was adamant that if:

the suitcase had been successfully placed in position, tied or wedged or propped under the floor of the platform, (or indeed even laid on the ground and covered over with earth or some other material to disguise its presence and prevent it from being seen) it would have exploded while the platform party stood overhead. This is an undeniable and provable fact.

Crinnion indicated to his superiors 'in precise detail how there had been in existence a plot to murder President de Valera'. He believed that 'clearly persons had put into operation a plot to murder the President shortly after noon one day in St Finbarr's Cemetery, Cork'. In support of this, he argued that the 'President and his party [had been] due to stand on a platform there in the cemetery during a ceremony scheduled to commence shortly after noon.'

The bomb could have exploded prematurely for a variety of reasons other than that put forward by Crinnion. In the first instance, the assembly process was interrupted by the IRA men looking for the 'useless revolver', placing Swanton and Madden under greater pressure to assemble the device than would have otherwise been the case. The wires may have been positioned irregularly due to time constraints. The 'safety device' may have been misassembled or inserted incorrectly, or left aside entirely. The hands of the clock may have been adjusted erroneously. Crinnion's conclusion was not, as he claimed, an 'undeniable and provable fact'. It is not credible that Swanton and Madden were intent on murdering de Valera and the dignitaries at his side, including religious figures. It is hardly feasible that they would have exploded a bomb which could have killed and injured the Republicans and their families who were planning to attend the event. Had de Valera been killed, the perpetrators would hardly have evaded detection. The death penalty was still on the statute books for such a crime.[5] It was clearly the intention of the pair to damage the memorial, perhaps a few minutes after it actually exploded at about three a.m., when it would have done no person any harm. Crinnion's analysis of the purpose of the bomb is an early example of his full-bodied self-belief and proclivity to interpret events involving Republicans in the most extreme and alarming manner despite an abundance of evidence to the contrary. While Crinnion was a member of MENSA, he seems to have lacked an abundance of common sense.

Going forward, it is also worth noting, that Crinnion had a habit, when typing, of highlighting a point he wanted to emphasise by tapping out the words in uppercase. The significance of this will become apparent later.

3

THE NERVE CENTRE OF GARDA INTELLIGENCE

The Old Military Road runs north-south across the spine of the Wicklow Mountains. It was built by the British administration in Ireland after the 1798 rebellion to open up the terrain so they could hunt down the rebels who had taken to the hills. Four barracks were built along the route at Glencree, Laragh, Glenmalure, and Aghavannagh. The British army installed a firing range at Cruagh Wood, not far from the Old Military Road. It was used by soldiers and also officers from a nearby Royal Irish Constabulary (RIC) station. Although it had fallen into disuse and had become overgrown, Patrick Crinnion knew its location. He sometimes hiked up there to practice firing his Walther pistol at the old bank left behind by the British army. The practice stood to him. In one official garda shooting test, he achieved a 92% score for accuracy.

C3, based at Garda HQ in the Phoenix Park, was the brain centre of garda intelligence. It processed more paperwork than any other unit at HQ. Crinnion flourished there. He was able to touch type, and his paperwork was always neat and in order. He could lay his hands on any file he wanted with great speed. He was also personable and resourceful. These positive traits drew approval from his superiors at C3.

C3 was housed in a suite of offices in the large two-storey building to the left of the Phoenix Park Garda HQ as one observes the premises from the main entrance. It was next to the Officers' Mess which had been built for the Royal Irish

Constabulary. The unit's offices were sealed off from the rest of the complex. Inside, there was a series of old wooden pigeon holes which accommodated files relating to ongoing investigations and operations. These shelves had been placed there before 1921. The officers called it the 'registry of files'. Once beyond the locked doors, the documents maintained in the pigeon holes were generally open to all. Hence, Crinnion enjoyed access to information on the IRA and, later, splinter groups such as Saor Éire, as did his fellow officers. Particularly sensitive files were held elsewhere and were not accessible by him without permission from his superiors.

Crinnion contributed to the compilation of detailed summaries about the activities of subversive organisations. They were called the 'monthly confidential reports' (MCRs) and were derived from the intelligence supplied by the SDU to C3.

Eleven people worked in C3. It had five telephones and an intercom. There was a main office, a medium-sized room, where three of the phones were located along with the intercom. There were seven typewriters, two photocopying machines and one Gestetner duplicator.

The conditions were less than satisfactory. Crinnion recalled in one of his 1973 memoranda that:

> Facilities are virtually non-existent and the toilets outside, which are used by the C3 staff are the original ones installed by the British, when they built the Garda Depot. There is no place to have a cup of coffee just off the cuff and I recall the improvisation of a quick-thinking Sergeant when confronted by a visiting British Police Woman who wanted to 'powder her nose'. Luckily it was after dark, or a dark evening, so he said 'excuse me one moment, while I slip down and make sure the toilet is unoccupied'. Quick thinking saved the day – he took the light bulb out of the toilet and hid it, then went back to the policewoman and said – 'I'm sorry it's going to be very awkward as the light bulb seems to be

broken, but I'll switch on the light out in the yard and the light through the window is the best we can manage just now'. What a story she would have carried back to England if she had been able to see the vile condition of the place.

At C3 Crinnion served under eight chief superintendents, including Alfred Flood, Patrick Malone and Lawrence Wren. By the early 1970s, he had become the longest serving officer in C3 and possessed an extensive knowledge of the secrets of the IRA, Saor Éire and, after December 1969, the newly formed Provisional and Official wings of the IRA.

The most significant influence on Crinnion at C3 was Sgt Thomas Mullen, a man who lived in Milltown, south Dublin, not far from where Crinnion resided. Mullen became an undue influence over Crinnion. Over time, he divulged to him the best kept secret at C3: a clandestine role he – Mullen – was performing there.

4

Serving Her Majesty

In the early 1960s, Patrick Crinnion fell into the orbit of Britain's external espionage service, MI6 (sometimes referred to as SIS). Crinnion joined the ranks of an unbroken line of British agents who had served inside C3 after the Second World War. His mentor, Sgt Thomas Mullen, was one of them.

When it came to espionage directed against the gardaí, MI6 often preferred to work with second tier officers, not their superiors. The bosses came and went, while their subordinates remained in place far longer.

As Mullen's retirement approached, he chose Crinnion as his replacement. Mullen was born in or about 1902. He enlisted Crinnion in the early 1960s. Mullen later told Mick Hughes of the SDU that he himself had been recruited by a retiring C3 officer. 'There has to be someone to forward [the information]', was Mullen's explanation for his actions.

Crinnion was an intelligent man. He knew that his relationship with MI6 was a breach of his oath as a garda and the provisions of the Official Secrets Act. He was acutely aware that the majority of citizens of the Republic of Ireland viewed British agents as traitors, the most reviled creatures in Irish society. So why did he agree to work for MI6?

Crinnion never divulged his motive for cooperating with MI6. There is not a shred of evidence that he collaborated by reason of being compromised in any way. Money was hardly the motive for his collusion with London, although it was available and the evidence suggests he accepted payment for his service.

Crinnion did not grow up within a Republican family.

On the contrary, he was reared by parents in service to the aristocracy. He joined the gardaí while he was young and impressionable. There, he was absorbed rapidly into intelligence work, an assignment that required him to frustrate the work of Republicans. When he reached C3 at the end of 1960, he was mentored by Thomas Mullen, a man who had been working for London over many years.

Crinnion was in his late twenties when Mullen recruited him. MI6 knew how to manipulate a young and susceptible man like him. Those who knew Crinnion, say he was 'prim and proper' and had a high opinion of himself. Flattery and the massaging of the ego were time-honoured tactics of MI6 which were put to good use with Crinnion. He was made to feel that he was being taken seriously by MI6, and said so later to a friend.[1]

C3 and the SDU had only one real enemy, militant Republicanism. Crinnion had no difficulty operating in an anti-Republican environment. To his mind, MI6 was the enemy of his enemy, the IRA.

Crinnion later attempted to legitimise his engagement with MI6 by claiming the British service was engaged in the same type of work as C3, and therefore it was natural for him to liaise with them. This was not so. In the first instance, MI6 sent spies abroad whereas C3 operated on home soil. Secondly, C3 officers went about their work openly at the Phoenix Park, albeit in a closed section of HQ, whereas MI6 officers often posed as diplomats, journalists or tourists while on foreign soil hiding all clues as to their true identities. Thirdly, C3 officers operated with legal authority whereas MI6 had no legal standing during their covert operations on foreign soil. Fourthly, MI6's work involved a huge level of criminality. The service carried out assassinations on foreign soil such as Egypt, Iran and the Republic of Congo. It penetrated and, sometimes, toppled foreign governments. C3's work was entirely legitimate.

To many of Crinnion's contemporaries, MI6 was a toxic organisation whereas New Scotland Yard, responsible for policing in London, was an entity which the gardaí respected. The Yard had responsibility for thwarting IRA activity in London.

Crinnion has offered conflicting versions of his enrolment with MI6. One account he put forward involved him meeting a man called John Wyman in the belief Wyman was working with New Scotland Yard. The meeting took place 'sometime in the early 1960s'. In reality, Wyman, born to British parents in Bulu, Cameroon, in 1937, was a young MI6 officer who was building a network of spies and agents in the Republic.

By this telling, Crinnion's collaboration with London commenced after some student lodgers who 'were staying with us left for home'. This opened up the possibility for a short trip to the UK. According to one of his 1973 memoranda:

> I planned to go to London for a week to give my wife a break from the house as we had been both working very hard, she with students and I had at the time 300 hrs overtime on night work protection at the British Embassy. I had bought a do-it-yourself central heating kit and *for a month* or more the house was going to be in a state of upheaval while the work was going on. [A contact at Scotland Yard] told me he would be out of London but if I wanted to do a tour of Scotland Yard to phone and ask for a colleague of his, name and phone [number were] supplied. We had been shopping and sightseeing for about three to four days when a phone message was received at our hotel asking me to ring a number, I did this and my Scotland Yard man answered. He was back sooner than he expected, and as I hadn't seen around the Yard he would be glad to give us a conducted tour. But my wife was footsore from walking and I declined his kind invitation. He told me he was finished with the department and

that a young colleague of his would be linking up with people in the Republic. He said this chap had a rudimentary knowledge of Dublin and Ireland and perhaps from time to time I might be able to give him a helping hand and in time he might be able to put some information my way.

He asked me to meet him for a cup of coffee so that I couldn't go back and say I hadn't been offered the smallest hospitality after all the years of co-operation between the two forces; these are not the right words but something in or about the same. It was the least I could do so I accepted.

It was Wyman who turned up for the coffee:

> ... then Wyman and I went to have our coffee. We then exchanged our names and addresses. [The original contact from Scotland Yard] was no stranger, he was someone I had seen and spoken to over the years in C/3. He is now [in 1973] settled in the South of Ireland, his wife is in bad health.

Crinnion cited alleged immaturity as an excuse for falling into MI6's orbit:

> I must confess that I was so immature that it was not until sometime in the early 1960s when I was given the task of discussing and sorting out some point with the second man, while his partner and my C/S were absent elsewhere that I realised the facts which everyone so slovenly acted out. John Wyman is a member of the B/Service [MI6] which is the equivalent of C3. He was introduced to me by a man [from New Scotland Yard] who has done a lot to assist the Garda in the past. [The man from New Scotland Yard] is a man for whom I have great personal respect. In view of the way things are being sordidly regarded I do not wish to name him unless I can get his personal permission to do so. Over the years Scotland Yard, the British Home Office and the regional police college in Scotland and England, have given full use of their excellent facilities to the Garda.

Crinnion's account of his recruitment omitted any reference to Thomas Mullen, the retired C3 officer who had inducted him, and with whom he maintained contact after he retired. On another occasion, however, Crinnion was more forthcoming and conceded that Mullen had indeed enlisted him. The probable truth is that he knew full well what Mullen was doing and agreed to go to London under cover of a short holiday to meet with Mullen's contacts. Simply put, he knew all along that Wyman was an MI6 officer, not someone from New Scotland Yard.

By the 1960s, Crinnion had graduated from a bicycle to a Morris Minor car. Meanwhile, most of his colleagues were still cycling. Crinnion not only purchased the vehicle, but did so at the start of his mortgage. His family did not have the resources to bestow a car on him, nor his in-laws. His wife's family, while providing well for their children's essential requirements, had little disposable income.[2]

One interpretation of these facts is that Crinnion accepted money from MI6; a more benign one is that he worked so much overtime, and engaged in a lot of part-time work outside the force, that he accumulated a fund for the vehicle from his own endeavours.

John Wyman, the spy Crinnion met in London, developed a network in the Republic of which Crinnion must have been the most important figure (until the 1970s).[3] Secrecy was the hallmark of their relationship. One day Nancy Crinnion was about to visit her mother in Donnybrook when an Englishman, probably Wyman, arrived at the house with an envelope for her husband. She put it in the back of the Morris Minor, where her young son, having chewed it, pushed it playfully down the seat out of sight. On her way home, she paid a visit to the home of a relative. A while later, Crinnion, having ascertained where she was, marched into the house. Normally, he was a 'prim and proper' individual. On this occasion, he lost his cool, demanding to know what had happened to the envelope. There was consternation when it could not be found. A frantic search continued until it was eventually discovered between the gap in the seat where the infant had pushed it. This incident took place around 1964. The envelope most likely contained instructions from Wyman, which, if they had fallen into the wrong hands, could have exposed his double role.

While at C3, Crinnion used his influence to forge stronger bonds between garda intelligence and Britain's special branch, the eyes and ears of MI5 in the UK.

5

THE VISITORS FROM LONDON

Crinnion argued that his relationship with John Wyman of MI6 was not that unusual. The gardaí, he contended, had enjoyed a form of quasi-official co-operation with Britain since the Second World War. This analysis was misleading. The 'quasi-official co-operation' involved New Scotland Yard, not MI6.

Crinnion once outlined the type of visitors who were received at Phoenix Park: 'I have on countless occasions known, seen and was sometimes concerned in visits to that office by people from services performing work similar to ours in foreign countries' he once asserted. They were, 'In fact foreign agents as defined under section 10, Official Secrets Acts 1963. People [so] defined [visited C3 at the Phoenix Park] from [the] RUC, British, American, French, Canadian and Australian [security and intelligence] services.'

Not once, as the years rolled by, Crinnion pointed out, did he 'hear of, know of, or see any permission or direction on these matters from the Department of Justice'. In other words, there was an unwritten tolerance of co-operation with the UK.

One of those Crinnion encouraged to meet with British officials was his superior at C3, Patrick Malone. Malone was a police officer with a brilliant memory. While giving lectures to fellow gardaí he was able 'to close his eyes and ... recount an Act from A to Z. He had a remarkably precise mind. He was a tough and very able officer', a garda who attended one of these talks recounted after Malone passed away in 2001.[1] As a chief superintendent, Malone was in charge of C3 when the Troubles began. One day he received an unexpected message: two men from New Scotland Yard's special branch were making their way to the Phoenix Park for 'an informal meeting with him'. The proposed topic was 'matters of mutual interest'. Malone was concerned. He called in Crinnion and told him 'that he had looked through his file of instructions and could find no authority for such [a] liaison'. Crinnion, who appears to have known of the proposed visit, seized the opportunity to push this door ajar. The more it eased open, the less he would need to hide behind it. Crinnion was able to refer to earlier meetings between C3 and New Scotland Yard. In one of his 1973 memoranda, Crinnion recounted how he told Malone that 'as the second longest member serving in the section ... I understood this was an accepted and mutually beneficial arrangement which originated during World War Two'. Crinnion backed his argument up with facts. 'I had seen correspondence', Crinnion told Malone, 'on old files which showed that ex Commissioner Patrick Carroll, BL, Ranelagh, Dublin, who was for many years in charge of C3, had even then dealt with the British and RUC on an informal basis.'

Another detective called Vaughan supported Crinnion, confirming 'his knowledge of the liaison' with Britain.

Crinnion found he was not pushing at an open door. Malone was not assuaged. He left Crinnion and Vaughan standing and 'went out of his office into the office of Deputy/Commissioner Donovan, who himself was Malone's overseer in C3'. He returned 'after a few minutes, smiling and said he was sorry'. Donovan not only knew about the meeting but the names of the visitors. One was Ferguson Smith, the head of Scotland Yard's special branch. Smith, then in his mid-50s, had garnered a wealth of experience working with MI5. Together Smith and MI5 had rounded up the Portland spy ring in 1961; he had assisted in the arrest of the MI6 traitor George Blake and the Admiralty spy John Vassall. He once hid in a cupboard at Brixton prison to eavesdrop on an incriminating telephone call made by Klaus Fuchs, the atom spy.

The meeting with Smith went ahead and, critically, with Crinnion in attendance. 'I recall as this was their first meeting with Chief Super Malone, being called in by Malone to assist with some matters that [Malone] was not familiar with', he wrote in one of his 1973 memoranda. The encounter developed into something more than 'an informal meeting'. During the exchange the British guests took photocopies of documents from files which were handed to the visitors to retain and take away. 'They in turn left us some copies of their own reports. I believe C/S/John Fleming, SDU, Dublin Met/area joined the group when they returned from lunch.'

Crinnion revealed that lines of communication were also maintained with another New Scotland Yard special branch chief, Evan Jones. Two of his colleagues, Arthur Cunningham and Vic Gilbert, participated in exchanges of information with C3 as well. Relations warmed to the point where British officials started coming to Dublin to give lectures.

Crinnion knew some of his other superiors at C3 had enjoyed meetings with figures from New Scotland Yard. He described them as 'officers and men [who were] engaged on countering subversive organisations, on behalf of Britain'. The meetings took place 'in hotels and other places apart from the C3 office'. Some of the visitors were 'known to hold senior posts in the British counter-subversive organisation'. They visited one of Crinnion's superiors in his 'home at Victoria Road, Clontarf'. The guests included Evan Jones and Ferguson Smith.

Crinnion had personal experience of working with the FBI after the Troubles commenced, which he felt was comparable, in terms of benefit, to his liaison with MI6. He also worked with other overseas agencies. One such organisation with whom he maintained contact was 'the Deuxieme Bureau in France'.

There was a degree of interaction with the RUC during the 1950s and early 1960s as well. Others have provided a glimpse of the types of cooperative relationships that existed. Sir John Hermon, chief constable of the RUC, 1980–89, participated in the cautious exchange of information that flowed between his force and Dublin Castle during the Border Campaign. It involved the passing of what Hermon described as 'sound intelligence'.[2] The process 'was given tacit approval by the Irish and British governments, much to the mutual benefit of both forces. This relationship, which strengthened over the years, was quickly and warmly extended beyond policing into other areas, including recreational and social activities.'[3]

Philip McMahon, the head of the SDU, visited his counterparts in the RUC, openly and in an official car. [4]

When Charles Haughey was Minister for Justice, 1961-64, a line of communication opened up between Dublin and Belfast, involving Peter Berry, the secretary of the DoJ.[5] In 1963, William Craig, the Stormont Minister of Home Affairs, pronounced publicly that a 'sizeable splinter-group' of the IRA was active in the Republic before proceeding to criticise what he alleged was the failure of the 'Dublin Authorities' to curtail them.[6] Haughey asked Berry to meet his opposite number in Northern Ireland, William Stout, to restrain any further outbursts by Craig. A consultation took place at Stormont on 4 October 1963, with Craig joining the two civil servants. Berry stated that 'within the previous 48 hours I had seen [Garda] Chief Superintendent Moore and Superintendent [Philip] McMahon of the special branch and I had had the most categoric assurances that the

Gardai were not aware of any activities in Border counties. I told them that the Gardai hadn't a shred of evidence which would lead them to think that a Border campaign would be re-opened this winter.'[7]

Berry explained patiently that publicity was the IRA's life-blood and that 'statements emanating from the Six Counties, such as Mr Craig's, would be precisely what they would want'. Berry then let slip the fact that top intelligence officers from both sides of the Border had met in Dublin. The parties involved were 'Mr. Smith [of the RUC who] had had meetings with Chief Superintendent Moore of the Special Branch in the Depot [in Dublin] and with Superintendent [Philip] McMahon and that at no time had he given them particulars of IRA activities ... Mr Craig (and Stout) was visibly shaken when he heard of Mr Smith's visit to Dublin of 6th September [1963]. He took a note of it. He said that he would very much like to believe that nothing would happen this winter but he didn't see how he would ignore the advice of his own police [about pending IRA violence]. He said that he had already issued instructions for stepping-up police precautions.'[8]

The North-South collegiality was evident long after the collapse of the Border Campaign. On 19 June 1973, Crinnion addressed the relationship with the RUC in a letter thus:

> Every Detective Sergeant of the Garda Siochana stationed along the Border has discreet contacts and liaison with his opposite member of the Royal Ulster Constabulary and is not discouraged by Garda Headquarters from so doing. Much good has resulted from this informal liaison. I at my level was in touch with a person whom I knew [i.e., Wyman] to be friendly disposed towards the organisations of the State.[9]

6

IRA PRINCE, IRA PAUPER

Garda intelligence enjoyed a substantial number of impressive victories over the IRA, INLA and other Republican groups, during the Troubles. The initial stage of the turmoil, however, was not its most glorious hour, primarily as a result of being royally hoodwinked by Seán MacStíofáin. For a period of eleven years, 1961-72, he engaged in the masquerade of being a garda informer. His garda handlers were utterly convinced by his charade. He exploited the goodwill that was forthcoming from the gardaí to further his own ends and create mischief for his opponents inside the IRA.

Crinnion was one of the few people to learn of the pretence. He described MacStíofáin's deceit as a 'brilliant use of subterfuge'.

MacStíofáin was born John Edward Drayton Stephenson in South Leyton, Essex, on 17 February 1928. He was the only child of Edward George Stephenson, a solicitor's clerk, and Lilian Mary Stephenson (formerly Brown, née Newland), of 81 Maryville Road, Leytonstone. Lilian had three daughters by an earlier marriage but they did not live with her.

Lilian was a Protestant with Unionist roots in East Belfast. Despite this, she baptised her son as a Catholic when he reached age seven and later sent him to a Catholic school in Islington.

When he was seven, she told him, 'I'm Irish, therefore you're Irish. You're half Irish anyway. Don't forget it.'[1] She died when he was ten, leaving him in the care of his father, an Englishman, who was a heavy drinker. Father and son never managed to get along. His childhood was blighted by his father's drinking.

Edward had Irish roots but was indifferent towards them.

Cathal Goulding was five years older than MacStíofáin, having been born on 2nd January 1923, at 1 East Arran Street, Dublin, to Charles and Bridget Goulding (née Costello). Unlike MacStíofáin, Goulding could boast 'impeccable Republican antecedents, important in the movement where a good bloodline is appreciated'.[2] His paternal grandfather had been a member of the Invincibles, the revolutionary group responsible for hacking to death Lord Frederick Cavendish, the British Chief Secretary for Ireland, in the Phoenix Park in 1882.

Goulding's father Charles, together with an uncle, participated in the 1916 Easter Rising. During the War of Independence, Charles fought against the Black and Tans. Both of his parents sided with the anti-Treaty faction during the Civil War and were jailed.

Unlike MacStíofáin, who had a lonely childhood, Cathal Goulding was part of a bustling family, consisting of four boys and three girls. When he was eleven, he joined Fianna Éireann, the IRA's youth wing. He left school at fourteen to take up an apprenticeship and became a housepainter and decorator like his father before him.

On the other hand, MacStíofáin knew little of Ireland until he developed an interest in his roots while at school in London. He befriended Irish students and began to study Irish history. His education was disrupted by the Second World War, when he was evacuated to Bedfordshire. Here, he experienced a demeaning 'insight' into the English class system, one which left him feeling – quite literally – like an outsider. 'When we asked if we could hear the news on the radio, they made us stand outside the window to listen to it', he wrote in his memoirs.[3] This incident left an indelible impression on him. It was the 'first clear' example of a social structure he instinctively abhorred.

Goulding's experience of the 'Emergency', as the war was called in Ireland, had its low points too. In December 1939, he served as part of a raiding party on the ammunition stores in the Phoenix Park, Dublin. In November 1941, he was sentenced to a year in prison for IRA membership and possession of IRA documents. On his release in 1942, he was whisked to 'Tintown', an Irish army internment camp in the Curragh, Co. Kildare. At liberty in 1944, he devoted his energies to the Republican movement. This brought him to the attention of the gardaí once more. He was arrested in the company of a dozen Republican leaders in a pub in Dublin, in 1946, and incarcerated again.

Across the Irish Sea, MacStíofáin left school at the age of sixteen, in 1944. He was conscripted into the RAF the following year, where he remained in service until 1948, rising to become a corporal. In 1946, while serving in the RAF, he was stationed in Jamaica, which he remembered for its 'racism and poverty', both of which he perceived as the product of Britain's colonial system. This was the only part of his life during which he openly enjoyed alcohol. His fondness was for Jamaican rum.

Meanwhile, Goulding, free again, was climbing up the IRA ladder. By the late 1940s, he was running training camps in the Wicklow mountains, perhaps not far from where Patrick Crinnion would practice firing his Walther automatic in later years.

There was no green carpet nor an open door to usher MacStíofáin inside the smoke-filled backrooms where the IRA conducted its business. He took his first step towards acceptance by working as a volunteer for the *United Irishmen* in

London after he left the RAF. To make ends meet, he secured employment in the building trade and, later, with British Rail. His real ambition was to become an IRA volunteer. He and a group of like-minded young men approached the IRA in Dublin through an intermediary with a request that it authorise the formation of a unit in London. The young aspirants were left to kick their heels for a time before a representative of the General HQ in Dublin materialised in London to assess them. In a round-table discussion, they explained that they wanted to join the IRA. Failing that they wanted to come out openly in England as its political wing, Sinn Féin.[4]

MacStíofáin's group was informed they would be left to their own devices for three months and warned that if news of their existence reached the authorities in Dublin, they would be cast adrift. MacStíofáin made it his mission to ensure there would be no loose talk. His efforts paid off. After the passage of three months, his unit was absorbed into the IRA. He was appointed as its officer-in-command. Initially, there were six members in the unit. Their number expanded to sixteen before contracting again because of MacStíofáin's concern that word of their existence might circulate.

Incredible as it may seem, MacStíofáin had yet to set foot on Irish soil. His first visit to Ireland was in 1949 in the company of his wife Mary, a Cork woman. The trip was something he described as a deeply 'emotional experience for me from the moment we set out from Paddington station on the boat-train for the journey to Fishguard and Wales. Even at that time of year the train was packed with Irish people returning home from holiday. The carriages were full of happiness and good humour, and it was the same on the boat. Everybody was obviously delighted to be going back, even for a visit'.[5]

MacStíofáin returned to London, however, with 'very mixed feelings. The source of his malcontent was the lack of interest in Republicanism which he encountered among the general population. For this MacStíofáin blamed the politicians in Dublin who had 'led the people up blind alleys, doing as much as the English to maintain Partition themselves'.[6] He was especially scornful of Fianna Fáil, whom he blamed for sabotaging the IRA. That organisation had carried out a bombing campaign in England at the outbreak of the Second World War. It had involved people such as Brendan Behan and Richard Timmons. MacStíofáin believed it had been betrayed by agents of Fianna Fáil who had 'succeeded in feeding information to the Irish Special Branch, who passed it onto their British counterparts. As a result, men and equipment were seized in England, in some cases as soon as they landed'.[7]

As officer-in-command, London, MacStíofáin dutifully carried out the instructions he received from Dublin, most of which focused on the collection of information, scouting for supplies and equipment, and the recruitment of volunteers. His unit also raised money for the IRA from Irish sympathisers in London. He became fascinated with intelligence work. He felt that in a 'revolutionary force' every member should become an intelligence agent. He encouraged his colleagues to report everything of interest they might see or hear. He 'quickly learned how much a shrewd intelligence organisation [could] put together from systemic study of serious newspapers and military magazines, apart from the efforts of its own agents and contacts'. There was a case in the 1930s, he noted, in which one individual had been able to build up the accurate order of battle of the German army by a close 'analysis of the German provincial press down to reports of dinners and even the engagement notices'.[8]

Counter-intelligence became his guiding star. He conducted background checks into potential recruits in London to weed out anyone who might be working for Scotland Yard or Dublin Castle.[9]

He visited Ireland again in June of 1951, this time to attend the annual Republican gathering at Bodenstown. There, he was struck by the number of SDU detectives among the gathering, most of whom were recording what they were hearing in their notebooks.

During this period MacStíofáin delivered to Dublin some of the first walkie-talkies that became commercially available and encouraged his comrades to study and improve their understanding of modern communications so they could monitor police and military broadcasts. He had an abiding interest in technological advancement. In later life, he was involved in the introduction of the car bomb, set with a timer to explode after being left in a city street. 'He seemed to take a child-like pride in this development. The tactic was to cause considerable carnage and material damage over the years.'[10]

In 1953, MacStíofáin was directed by Dublin to assist Cathal Goulding and Manus Canning execute a raid on the armoury at the Officers' Training Corp School at Felsted in Essex. The venture went ahead on 25 July 1953, but proved a shambles. The raiders overloaded their vehicle with so many arms that when they reached the motorway, its undercarriage was all but scraping off the road. Inevitably, this drew the attention of the police and all three were arrested and later imprisoned.

Goulding taught MacStíofáin his first words of Irish while they were behind bars. Goulding later said of MacStíofáin that he was 'continually trying to prove that he [was] as much an

Irish man as anyone else'.[11] Despite this urge, MacStíofáin, never managed to quite shake off his Cockney accent irrespective of years of immersion in Irish culture, especially the language.

During his imprisonment, Goulding read widely and be-friended Klaus Fuchs, the Russian atomic bomb spy. In addition to playing chess they discussed politics. Joe Cahill, a Belfast IRA leader, was 'convinced that [Goulding] developed his Marxism in jail through his association with the [German-born Russian] spy Klaus Fuchs'.[12]

MacStíofáin used his time behind bars to expand his knowledge of guerrilla warfare. He befriended a group of imprisoned Cypriot EOKA fighters, all of whom had been arrested during the revolt against the British in Cyprus. The Cypriots were fresh from engagement with Britain's then most up-to-date counter-insurgency tactics and possessed a great deal of 'insight and experience'. He took detailed notes of their 'revolutionary and guerrilla tactics' and became a student of the type of torture techniques the British army had meted out to Cypriot prisoners.[13]

Beyond the bars and prison walls that confined Goulding and MacStíofáin, the IRA was engaged in Operation Harvest, better known to history as the Border Campaign of 1956–62.

7

CLIMBING THE REPUBLICAN LADDER

On 12 December 1956, the IRA launched the Border Campaign without the benefit of the arms MacStíofáin and Goulding had tried to steal at Felsted. The pair languished behind bars while the campaign got underway. It lasted until February 1962. Observing what was happening through newspaper reports, MacStíofáin experienced a profound sense of disappointment. He would have preferred a full-throttled confrontation with the RUC. Instead, he noted, none 'of the Special Branch in the North had been eliminated'.[1]

In early 1959, before he was due to regain his freedom, an official photographic session was scheduled at Wormwood Scrubs to capture an up-to-date picture of him. In an attempt to frustrate this, he and some other prisoners, who were also due for release, wet their faces so the resulting pictures would emerge as dark and patchy, thus obscuring their features. He hoped the prison authorities would not develop the negatives before they walked free. 'We were well aware of how photographs taken by British authorities appeared in Special Branch files in Dublin. In the opposite direction, police photographs of Republicans taken in Dublin had already appeared outside RUC barracks in the North.' His ruse was thwarted. The shots were printed before his release and he was marched back to face the cameraman, 'this time with a couple of warders keeping a close eye on us'.[2]

MacStíofáin, now in his early thirties, took the boat to Dublin the same day he was freed. Ever vigilant, he 'kept a wary eye for any surveillance, and again when I reached Westland Row station [in Dublin]. But there was no interference'.[3]

Goulding returned home to Dublin where, in 1959, at the age of thirty-six, he was elected to the Army Council, the ruling body of the IRA. He served as quartermaster general until 1962.

MacStíofáin journeyed to Castletownroche, Co. Cork, to live with his wife and family. After a while they moved to Cappoquin, Co. Waterford, where he was offered a job as a garage storeman. Having spent nearly six years in prison, he now enjoyed a high profile as a former political prisoner and the respect that accompanied it in Republican circles. He was invited to speak in favour of the Border Campaign at meetings, rallies and protests throughout Cork and in other parts of Munster.

Upon a subsequent return to Cork, MacStíofáin contacted the local Republican leadership who advised him he would have to wait a while before he could resume active service. He was later offered a command role which he accepted and began to work out 'a proper training program that would retain the interest of the volunteers'. One of his first steps was to provide an outlet for discussion, 'so that any misapprehensions could be cleared up'. This, he felt, worked well and helped his unit develop a 'good, close working relationship'.[4]

According to MacStíofáin, the hierarchy of the IRA in Dublin supported the continuation of the Border Campaign, while Cork wanted to knock it on the head. In the summer of 1961, the Cork leadership was ousted and he was assigned overall charge. At first, he found the task difficult, not least because he was denied a helping hand from his predecessors. Over time he managed to surmount this obstacle. Yet 'because of my unwavering support for HQ policy, some coolness remained'.[5]

This is but one example of the divisions that plagued the

IRA. Cathal Goulding's friend, the playwright Brendan Behan, once quipped that the first thing on the agenda of any Irish organisation is 'the split'. The differences between Cathal Goulding and Seán MacStíofáin, and their associates, are perfect exemplars of the accuracy of Behan's insightful witticism. The conflict between these two men would ultimately end with the split of the Republican movement into the Official and Provisional wings in December 1969.

Before the Border Campaign was wound up, MacStíofáin embarked on a dangerous high-stake gamble, one that had it backfired, could have cost him his life.

8

A Cuckoo in the Garda Nest

Seán MacStíofáin's time in prison had all but impoverished his family. In August 1961, he took a few months' leave of absence from the IRA to stabilise his finances. In his memoirs, he described how, at this time, his financial position 'had been gradually getting worse'. He concluded that he would have to make a 'big effort to put my personal affairs straight once and for all'. After that, he hoped, he would be in a position to return to the IRA without 'unduly neglecting my family responsibilities'. Towards this end, he took on part-time jobs. A local man took over the Cork unit from him during his period of absence.[1]

This was not, however, the complete picture. That same year, MacStíofáin, a driven guileful man, offered his services as an informer to Patrick McLaughlin, a future garda commissioner. According to Crinnion, MacStíofáin 'conducted a brilliant masquerade as a Garda informant and [was] well paid to boot'.[2] As noted earlier, he described the ploy as a 'brilliant use of subterfuge' to 'mislead and thwart Garda intelligence'.[3]

Patrick McLaughlin was not a member of the SDU and passed MacStíofáin over to Philip McMahon, who had recently taken over command of the unit. McMahon hailed from Moynalty, Co. Meath, and had been in the Old IRA. His knowledge of the movement had proved useful during his career in the SDU. He was a ruthless taskmaster who never forgave a mistake, nor gave a young officer a second chance.

The fact that MacStíofáin was 'well paid' eased the financial pressure on his shoulders and helped him advance the cause of the IRA, all at the taxpayers' expense. It was McMahon's habit to pay informers in small denomination notes, normally 10 shillings. Large payments were often quite bulky, thereby conveying the impression that more money was being handed over than might have been the case with a lower number of larger notes.

MacStíofáin was still on leave in February 1962 when the Border Campaign was finally abandoned. He had not been consulted about the decision in advance and only learned of it from a radio broadcast. As Republicans descended on his house to glean his assessment of the situation, he put on a brave face assuring them that 'the national leadership would not have ended the campaign if there had been a chance of carrying on with any hope of success'.[4]

Further dissension in the ranks followed and a new Cork OC was appointed. When MacStíofáin returned to active duty he found that 'pessimists were already saying that it would be at least 15 to 20 years before an armed struggle could be launched again'. Undeterred, he committed himself to 'build things up once more'.[5]

By the end of February, the SDU and C3 had plenty of reasons to congratulate themselves. Not only had they defeated the IRA, they had – they believed – one of its rising stars on their books.

Not every garda, however, was convinced of MacStíofáin's trustworthiness. Joe Ainsworth, who was based in Cork at this time, was aware that MacStíofáin had been recruited, although he was not directly involved in the development.[6] According to Ainsworth, the perception of MacStíofáin was that he 'was not a very intelligent man but had leadership qualities' which had assisted his ascent within the IRA. He also had 'a big mouth' and when he opened it, he would sometimes proceed to 'spout information'.[7] Yet, he was someone who only talked to the gardaí when it suited him and was a 'man who played the violin with two bows'. Later, Ainsworth became suspicious that MacStíofáin was merely engaging with the gardaí 'in the hope it would take some of the heat off him'.[8]

According to Ainsworth, MacStíofáin and McMahon enjoyed a rapport. At one stage 'all communication was made person to person'.[9]

A retired senior SDU officer – 'D' – who is still alive – had dealings with MacStíofáin during his successful masquerade as an informer.

Over time, a number of sergeants in border regions became suspicious that a high-level informer had been recruited. These men had lived under relentless pressure to file monthly reports about local IRA men. One sergeant even lived in the vicinity of a member of the Army Council and had previously been inundated with requests for detailed reports. Gradually, however, the pressure eased and consequently speculation circulated in garda circles, especially along the Border, about the existence of a 'superspy'.[10]

McMahon became notorious for sending young SDU personnel to cut turf and gather hay at his farm in South County Dublin, another indication that there was not much work to do. This fuelled further speculation about the existence of a 'superspy'.

MacStíofáin faced an almost impossible task: what would he do if a military operation was mounted in Cork? How might he string McMahon along without betraying his colleagues? Shortly, he was going to have to master the skill of spinning multiple plates in the air without letting any of them crash to the floor.

9

SAILING CLOSE TO DANGER

Cathal Goulding was appointed chief-of-staff of the IRA in September 1962, succeeding Ruairí Ó Brádaigh. Goulding embarked on an assessment of where he might take the Republican movement. He received advice from left-wing intellectuals such as Dr Roy Johnston and Anthony Coughlan, both of whom were veterans of the Connolly Association, a British-based Marxist group, and latterly lecturers at Trinity College Dublin. The process produced many ideas, one of which was to focus on politics; another was the creation of a 'national liberation front' to fight capitalism which was to consist of Republicans, trade unionists and small farmers' organisations. Whilst Goulding embraced these ideas, MacStíofáin did not.

Des Swanton and Gerry Madden's bombing of the memorial at St Finbarr's cemetery, on 16 February 1963, was at variance with Goulding's reforms. While MacStíofáin was in charge of the IRA in Cork at the time, the attack did not create friction between him and Goulding. This was because the young men had sought the leadership's permission for the operation, only to be rebuffed by them, including MacStíofáin.[1] The IRA denied responsibility for the strike, although they did acknowledge that the pair, who had participated in the Border Campaign, had been members of the organisation. The gardaí had already concluded they were connected to the IRA because Joe Ainsworth had recognised Dáithí Ó Conaill, a veteran of the Border Campaign, loitering at the hospital where Madden was being treated. Ó Conaill sister, Elma, was the girlfriend of Des Swanton. As this was a maverick operation, carried out behind the back of the Cork IRA, McMahon did not lose faith in MacStíofáin for failing to alert him to the plot.

The Irish Republican Publicity Bureau issued a statement which said, 'It is not the Movement's policy to carry out such incidents – as is well known.' To ensure that the IRA was not implicated in the attack in the mind of the public, the uniforms of a Republican pipe band were placed under lock and key so they could not be worn at the funeral.

As an informer, MacStíofáin went on to enjoy more lives than a clowder of cats.

Behind the scenes, tensions simmered before boiling over. Several of Swanton's allies were expelled from the organisation. Undeterred, they set up a new one. MacStíofáin, an aggressive and imposing man, raided the dissidents' HQ with his adjutant, Gerry McCarthy, thereby reinforcing his detachment from the bomb plot. In response to MacStíofáin's clampdown, the mutineers hijacked copies of the latest edition of the *United Irishman* newspaper, before they went on sale in Cork, and put on an armed show of strength at the newspaper's offices in the city.

Cathal Goulding visited Cork where he tried in vain to broker a compromise. By 1964, the breakaway group was styling itself the 'Irish Revolutionary Forces' and, a year later, began publishing a journal of its own. They had access to arms and made it clear to MacStíofáin that they would not be 'stood down' by him. Politically, they declared themselves 'Marxist-Leninists' of the Chinese variety.[2]

There were other young men who were itching for action. An IRA convention, the supreme decision-making body of the IRA, had given the green light for IRA units to attack Royal Navy vessels sent to visit harbours in the Republic.

On Saturday 21 November 1964, *HMS Relentless*, a destroyer which had sailed with Britain's Atlantic convoys during the Second World War, was departing Cork Harbour. She was one mile upstream from Passage West when, at 8.35 a.m., at least two men opened fire on her from a range of about 400 yards using 0.303 or similar calibre rifles. About ten rounds were discharged but there were no casualties. The damage sustained amounted to one bullet hole and a dent. A garda cordon was set up but the shooters slipped away.

Christopher Mayhew, the Labour Minister of Defence for the Royal Navy, told the House of Commons that while London had 'mentioned [the incident] to the Eire Government ... I think that it is too minor an incident to expect a protest [from the British Government] ... The action was outrageous but the Navy has faced more difficult engagements than this ... We must hope that the shooting would be better than missing a ship at 400 yards eight times out of ten.'[3]

Since the Cork IRA claimed the attack, MacStíofáin must have found some way of excusing his failure to warn McMahon about it in advance.

The attack on the *HMS Relentless* is a good illustration of the tricky situation that MacStíofáin faced on an ongoing basis. While he was happy to take McMahon's money and avoid arrest, he had no intention of actually betraying his colleagues.

MacStíofáin's task became even more arduous when, on 5 June 1965, he was elected to the Army Council, the body which oversaw and managed the activities of the IRA, on both sides of the Border.[4] Henceforth, MacStíofáin would learn about all significant IRA operations while they were still at a planning stage. He would have a lot of explaining to do to the SDU if he did not warn them in advance of these actions.

MacStíofáin used his promotion to the Army Council to oppose the politicisation of the Republican movement. As the drift to the left continued, he discovered a means of keeping McMahon satisfied: he began to tell the SDU man about the growing communist influence in the movement.

There was one operation about which MacStíofáin appears to have failed to issue a warning to McMahon. On 10 September 1965, a unit of the South Kilkenny-Waterford IRA attacked the *Brave Borderer*, a Royal Navy gas turbine motor torpedo boat, the fastest of its kind. The assault had been given the go ahead by the Army Council. The strike team included Richard Behal, Walter Dunphy and Edward Kelly. An anti-tank rifle was discharged at the ship as it sailed down the River Suir. One of the rounds pierced the metal exterior and penetrated into the engine room. One engine was put out of commission but a second one whisked the vessel to safe waters. Behal, Dunphy and Kelly were later arrested.

Behal was described by senior Republicans as an 'irresponsible character' in the next edition of the party's newspaper. MacStíofáin probably told McMahon that he shared this view and had somehow not appreciated the operation was in the pipeline. The SDU recovered the rifle used in the attack on the *Brave Borderer* years later after the 'Battle of Dungooly'.[5]

The following month, October 1965, MacStíofáin managed to claw back whatever credibility he had squandered with his silence before the attack on the *Brave Borderer* by telling the SDU about a plan to attack the *HMS Lofoten*, a ship named after a cluster of Norwegian islands. She was due to visit Cork during 12–17 October 1965. The vessel had once been a transport ship and had been deployed during the Suez Crisis. In 1964, she had been transformed into a helicopter support training ship, a glamorous attraction for young men who might join the Royal Navy. The proposed attack was notified to the Army Council. Seán Garland was sent to Cork to help MacStíofáin plan the assault.[6]

The dilemma placed on MacStíofáin's shoulders was greatly eased by a warning delivered to the Harbour Master at Cork by an organisation calling itself the 'Irish Volunteers':

> We warn all concerned – those who have invited the visit, the captain, officers, and men in the ship, the forces who may try to protect [her] while she is in Cork, and finally any civilians who may be foolishly ill-advised to visit her in Cork – that if the *Lofoten* sails into Cork it will be no fault of ours if, before she sails again, they are not very sorry that she ever sailed in. Finally, we warn them that they alone shall be judged responsible for any casualty or any damage to property which may occur as a result of their ignoring this warning.[7]

The *Manchester Guardian* (now *The Guardian*) reported the statement on 21 September 1965.[8]

As one of the key organisers, it follows that MacStíofáin was involved in the issue of the warning, something that brought the proposed attack to the attention of the public and therefore the SDU. In these circumstances, the possible existence of an informer would not become a talking point when the gardaí reacted. Emboldened, behind the backs of his colleagues, MacStíofáin relayed some of the unpublished details of the plan to the SDU. Alfred Flood, the chief superintendent in charge of C3, prepared a report for Peter Berry of the DoJ, which Berry received and stamped on 29 September. It read as follows:

> Further to this [office's] communication of September 22, 1965, I am directed by the Commissioner to inform you that confidential information has been received to the effect that the IRA Army Council has authorised an attack by its members on

HMS 'Lofoten' during its visit to Cork. Full agreement has been reached on the form of attack, which is to consist of three separate ambush parties manned by a total of twelve men. The arms to be used will be a Vickers machine-gun, a Bazooka, a Lewis machine-gun and a number of rifles. Fire is to be concentrated on the control room and bridge. The purpose of the fire is to cause casualties to the crew and damage the ship. It was agreed by the Council that the loss of IRA personnel by way of arrest or the loss of arms is immaterial provided the object is successful.

Arrangements have also been made for the distribution of leaflets prior to and during the ship's visit, and a protest campaign will be carried out before its arrival.[9]

One former SDU officer, familiar with the military capacity of the IRA at this time, has cast doubt on the report that the IRA had access to a Bazooka, or anything similar. 'That is just MacStíofáin spoofing his handler', the former officer has asserted.[10] It was, however, sufficiently convincing to frighten the authorities. On 30 September 1965, Berry wrote to N.S. Ó Nualláin, of the Department of An Taoiseach, as follows:

With reference to our correspondence of 21st and 22nd September (S 16571 H) I enclose for the Taoiseach's information, copy of a Garda report of 29th September on the same subject. I have had discussions with the appropriate Garda Officers, who assure me that their information is reliable.[11]

The 'appropriate' gardaí clearly included McMahon.

Up to now, our information was that the warning notice and any action contemplated could be laid at the door of irresponsible elements in court but, now, the situation has developed and the I.R.A. organisation itself is planning an armed attack. For that purpose, prominent members of I.R.A. H.Q. have visited Cork, surveying possible sites for firing on the *Lofoten*. The Gardai say it would be almost impossible to fully provide against an attack, as the approaches to Cork Harbour on both sides of the river measure over 20 miles and there are innumerable points from which rifle fire could be directed at the vessel. The Gardai would probably effect arrests within a short time after firing commenced but, in that time, loss of life and injury to property might occur.[12]

Like a line of falling dominoes, Ó Nualláin put the frighteners on Hugh McCann of the Department of External Affairs. On 30 September 1965, he wrote:

> ... I have now submitted the matter to the Taoiseach and have suggested to him that, if he agrees that it would be better that the visit should not take place, you might see the British Ambassador; tell him that our information is that, should the visit take place, it will almost certainly create a good deal of trouble; and that we feel that, in the interest of good relations between the two countries, it might be better if the British authorities could find some pretext for cancelling the visit ... The Taoiseach approves the adoption of the suggestion set out above – as the lesser of the two evils.[13]

The pressure paid off. The ship's visit was cancelled. There were no arrests. No one inside the IRA had any reason to suspect the presence of an informer who had provided the SDU with any sort of information. Put simply, MacStíofáin slipped off the hook, once more.

Untainted by the merest hint of suspicion among his colleagues, MacStíofáin was on the verge of securing a substantial promotion within the IRA, to a position for which he was tailor made.

10

THE DIRECTOR OF IRA INTELLIGENCE

Philip McMahon was due to retire as SDU chief in 1967 but such was the esteem in which he was held by Peter Berry that provision was made to extend his tenure by another two years. When that ended, he was retained as a consultant; a cover for his real mission which was to handle MacStíofáin, as he had done since 1961. A stipend was added to his pension.

McMahon had modernised the SDU and left it in apparent good shape for his successor, John Fleming.

Meanwhile, MacStíofáin was promoted to director of intelligence of the IRA. He moved to Navan, County Meath, in July of 1966, so he could be closer to the Border and live in a Gaeltacht community. He was less than impressed with the work of his predecessors. 'I cannot convey my amazement when the intelligence files were handed over to me. It took me about two days to go through them. My comment was, "ninety per cent rubbish, five per cent of historical interest and five per cent useful material". When I stared at the small pile of what had been worth saving, it didn't seem much of a basis for a modern intelligence branch. I had taken on a task that would tax me to the limit if it were done properly.'[1]

In later years, Eamon Mallie and Patrick Bishop interviewed Cathal Goulding for their highly regarded book on the Provisional IRA. He revealed how a bitterness crept into the relationship between them:

The respect that Goulding and MacStíofáin had for each other in prison did not survive long after their release. MacStíofáin's noisy defence of the old Republican traditions against the assaults of 'communist' infiltrators like [Dr Roy] Johnston inspired Goulding's observation that he was 'continually trying to prove that he is as much an Irish man as anyone else', and that he was a 'petty-minded conspirator'.[2]

Relations were strained by MacStíofáin's 'dour and angular personality'. 'Not the sort of fellow I'd look for after a political meeting to have a drink with,' Goulding told Bishop and Mallie.[3]

MacStíofáin grew increasingly concerned that the military capacity of the IRA was being emasculated in favour of what he perceived was left-wing daydreaming. He complained about the decline in the military prowess of the movement to Goulding, who initially failed to respond. According to Goulding's ally, Dr Roy Johnston, MacStíofáin 'took this as the OK to go ahead, and he went around all the Northern units, with military intelligence as top of the agenda'.[4]

When Goulding made an occasional visit to Northern Ireland, more often than not it was to liaise with left-wing trade unionists or activists. He engaged in trips during which he made no attempt to consult the local IRA leadership.

The Joint Intelligence Committee (JIC) at Downing Street, the body which co-ordinates the activities of the various intelligence bureaucracies in Britain, was keeping a weather eye on the IRA with the benefit of its sources in Dublin, including Crinnion in C3. In 1966, one of their concerns was that there might be an outbreak of violence in Northern Ireland in the run-up to the fiftieth anniversary of the 1916 Rising.[5] The IRA in Belfast, however, only managed to fill a single minibus to send to the 1966 Wolfe Tone commemoration at Bodenstown. Billy McKee, who later emerged as a key Provisional IRA leader, felt the IRA 'was dead, completely dead. And it was except in the minds of myself and other old Republicans. We lived in hope.'[6]

The RUC was poorly informed about the intentions of the IRA at this time. If the force had sources inside the IRA, they were little more than opportunists who were feeding them yarns for payment. These 'misinformers' upped the ante by claiming that Goulding and his associates were preparing to carry out a series of assassinations. There was no hard evidence for this. No names, places nor dates were supplied. Undaunted, the JIC reasoned that 'if the threat materialised, intelligence relating to specific targets for attack could only be obtained at short notice owing to the IRA practice of making last minute decisions'.[7]

The British cabinet secretary, Sir Burke Trend, felt it was time once again to don the armour. Intensive security precautions were put in place for the anniversary of the Rising. The Border was sealed off. The B Specials were put on overtime. But nothing happened. After the commemoration date passed without any IRA violence, a smug intelligence community patted itself on the back. MI5 and the RUC were singled out for compliments by the JIC. London attributed the perceived success to the heightened level of security they had put in place in the run-up to the Easter Rising celebrations.

In the south the advice from C3 to the DoJ had been that Goulding planned no more than a few harmless commemorative parades.

Whatever reliable information Crinnion passed to London about the non-violent intentions of the IRA, it was drowned out by the waves of faulty intelligence emanating from the RUC.

While MacStíofáin certainly harboured an ambition to put the IRA back onto the war path, he was moving cautiously. His intelligence officers were directed to spy on RUC special branch personnel. All of the training courses he organised concentrated on what could be found out about them, from their physical appearance and home addresses, to their routines and habits.

He ordered his subordinates to cut down on the number of paper files held at HQ, requiring instead that local volunteers memorise the information they required. Moreover, any files that were to be maintained were to be scrambled in code. MacStíofáin relayed none of the information about his plans for a return to physical force Republicanism to Philip McMahon at Dublin Castle.

Irish military intelligence, G2, was, in turn, monitoring the IRA. On one occasion, Col Michael Hefferon, the Director of G2, was out for a drive in his car with his son while the annual Republican Bodenstown commemoration was taking place. He pulled up and joined the crowd. Some short time later, he told the boy that he had gone in to let them know he was still keeping an eye on them.[8]

11

Northern Ireland, a Garda Blind Spot

The real threat to the stability of the island of Ireland was rising in Northern Ireland. It was posed by the Ulster Volunteer Force (UVF), the Ulster Protestant Volunteers (UPV) and other extreme Loyalist groups, as well as some politicians at Stormont. This diverse alliance was resorting to violence to counter Nationalist demands for civil rights. Soon, the country was pulled into a vortex of violence and bloodshed. The gardaí had no access to intelligence about the Loyalist extremists and no interest in developing a spy network to find out what they were planning. Like most of his colleagues, Patrick Crinnion was focused exclusively on watching Republicans on the southern side of the border.

On the night of 14 August 1969, the RUC took to the streets in Belfast in Shorland semi-armoured vehicles equipped with Browning 0.30 medium machine guns with a two-and-a-half-mile range. One of the RUC men sprayed bullets into the Nationalist Divis flats. A tracer bullet tore into nine-year-old Patrick Rooney's skull in his bedroom, killing him instantly.

Harold Wilson did not blame the upheaval on the IRA. The root cause of the problem was unmistakeable: militant Loyalists led by firebrands like Ian Paisley, John McKeague and William McGrath.[1] Paisley and others preached that Nationalists were 'vermin' in league with Satanists in the Vatican in a fanciful plot with Fianna Fáil and the IRA to destroy the

Protestants of Northern Ireland. Paisley's followers embraced his inflammatory tirades, hook, line and sinker.

B Specials armed with rifles, revolvers and machine guns swelled the Loyalist mobs that night. Together they advanced on the Falls Road where the Nationalists lived, and attacked their homes. Half of the properties on Bombay Street were gutted by arsonists but not before many were looted. 150 houses were burned and another 300 were badly damaged. All told, seven people were killed in Belfast.

Paddy Devlin described quasi-biblical tactics deployed by the Loyalist gangs to identify their victims. Men who knew the streets 'daubed whitewash marks on the doors or windows of Catholic homes. These homes were then emptied of the people and burned. As far as I could tell around 650 Catholic families were burnt out that night ... Police in uniform, covered in civilian coats, were recognised amongst Loyalist attackers in Dover Street ...'[2]

The gardaí had not warned the DoJ about the trouble simmering across the border and which had now exploded. Taoiseach Jack Lynch was taking a break at his holiday home. The officials who ventured out to him, after a series of un-answered phone calls, knocked on his door but were unable to rouse him from a deep sleep caused by probable intoxication and the consumption of a sleeping tablet. The Minister for External Affairs, Patrick Hillery, was on a painting holiday on Achill Island, on the west coast. The response to the turmoil was left to Neil Blaney, who spent the night making telephone calls, including urgent unreciprocated ones to Lynch, while Jerry Jones, a friend and supporter, refreshed him with cups of tea.

Thousands fled their homes. Many crossed the border into the Republic.

MacStíofáin, who had an intelligence network in Northern Ireland, did not share any meaningful data with the SDU. When Lynch and his ministers convened in Dublin on an emergency footing, the Minister for Justice, Micheál Ó Móráin, proved incapable of providing a picture of what was taking place only one hundred miles away.

It emerged that the gardaí did not have a single undercover officer in place in Northern Ireland. Ó Móráin was instructed by his colleagues to 'expand the intelligence services maintained by the Gardaí in the Six Counties'.[3] It then transpired that the SDU did not have within its ranks a single officer who hailed from across the border. The gardaí had to find northern officers from other divisions of the force. Fleming found three, including Owen Corrigan, and sent them across the border on surveillance duties.[4]

Irish military intelligence, G2, however, had an officer on the ground, Capt. James Kelly. He had travelled to Belfast on 11 August in his car, remaining there for a few hours before driving across to Derry. He travelled back to Belfast on the thirteenth. Having arrived there, he was taken on a tour of Nationalist areas by Paddy Kennedy, a Stormont MP who was also a family friend. Capt. Kelly returned to Dublin on the fourteenth. He was the personal staff officer to the man in charge of G2, Col Michael Hefferon. Col Hefferon instructed him to maintain his contacts in Northern Ireland. Some of his reports were passed to the Minister for Defence, James Gibbons, who relayed select parts to his colleagues.

Another source of information for Lynch and his ministers was Neil Blaney, who had contacts in the Derry area and the more westerly part of the Six Counties.

Charles Haughey, the Minister for Finance, had relatives

who lived in Swatragh, County Derry. They were also able to provide him with information about what was taking place behind the barricades. As a boy, Haughey had encountered the B Specials during school holidays in Derry, an intimidating experience he had not forgotten.[5]

A cry for arms – for defensive purposes – went up from Northern Ireland. According to John Kelly, an IRA veteran of the Border Campaign, 'people all around the Twenty-six Counties contributed weapons at this period, and it was not just Fianna Fáil supporters – people aligned to Fine Gael, traditionally seen as strongly anti-IRA, also helped out. Whatever they had, shotguns, old rifles, Mausers going back to the First World War, were handed over.'[6]

There was enormous sympathy among the gardaí for the plight of Nationalists. In the weeks that followed the bloodshed of August 1969, officers at border checkpoints turned a blind eye to gunrunning efforts by northern Nationalists.

A significant amount of the violence directed at the minority Nationalist population in Belfast in August 1969 was instigated by the Shankill Defence Association (SDA). John McKeague, the paedophile leader of the SDA, was proud of what his army of rampaging thugs had accomplished. When he appeared as a witness before the Scarman Tribunal, he boasted that he had given Nationalists 'a lesson which I do not think they will forget'.

The explosion of hostilities in Ireland ignited MI6 operations in the Republic where the service relied upon Patrick Crinnion for information and an insight into what the leadership of the IRA was thinking and planning in response to the upheaval.

12

MI6 IN THE REPUBLIC OF IRELAND

MI5, which is attached to the Home Office, is primarily responsible for security within the UK and her colonies. Hence, MI5 was active in Northern Ireland during the Border Campaign, and re-emerged in Belfast when the Troubles began in the late 1960s.

MI6, the organisation which ran Crinnion, is controlled by what is now known as the FCDO.[1] It was – and remains – responsible for Britain's overseas espionage operations, including those in the Republic of Ireland. A ruthless individual, Sir Dick White, was in charge of MI6, when Crinnion was recruited by Thomas Mullen as one of its agents. White, or 'C' as he was known inside MI6 was a pitiless character.[2] At an early stage in his career, he had become an expert at torture.[3] He was also a sexual blackmailer who had targeted VIP homosexuals such as Archbishop Makarios of Cyprus.[4]

Sir John Rennie succeeded White in 1968. He had once run the Information Research Department (IRD), a propaganda and disinformation machine. White moved to the Cabinet Office where he performed the role of Co-ordinator of Intelligence, 1968–70.

Maurice Oldfield served as Rennie's deputy. Of the pair, it was Oldfield who oversaw MI6's activities in the Republic of Ireland. The late Anthony Verrier, who wrote a book on MI6, based on unattributable interviews with MI6 officers such as Frank Steele, described how:

Sir John Rennie was still 'C' when [British Prime Minister

Edward] Heath turned to SIS [i.e. MI6]. Rennie, however, was not only due to retire in two years, but was unsuited, from lack of experience and inclination, to add Northern Ireland to the Red Book [MI6 reporting mechanism]. His Deputy, Maurice Oldfield, dealt with the requirement – and with a Prime Minister given to command rather than consultation, Rennie signed the directives in the green ink exclusive to 'C' but his Deputy did the work.[5]

When Rennie retired as MI6 chief in 1973, Oldfield succeeded him and steered the organisation until his retirement in early 1978. According to Verrier:

Oldfield, in 1973, became the first 'C' to be appointed from within the Service, a man from whom writers of fiction greatly benefited but, in fact, an interesting enough individual in his own right: 'Moulders' to the Office, Maurice to his intimates – never a large number – a scholar by inclination and training, an intelligence officer through the fortunes of war. The Derbyshire farmer's son who rose from a sergeant in field security to 'C' had, however, no interest for Heath. But he saw in a fellow bachelor a like professionalism. There was no co-ordination of intelligence in Northern Ireland.[6]

While it was natural for MI6 to carry out espionage activities in the Republic of Ireland, strictly speaking Northern Ireland was not part of their jurisdiction. MI5 (attached to the Home Office) bore constitutional responsibility for Northern Ireland as it was part of the UK. Nonetheless, Ted Heath asked Oldfield to establish an MI6 station in that territory. Oldfield resisted at first as it was part of the UK. Heath kept up the pressure and, by the spring of 1971, MI6 was on the ground. Soon, others came. They were:

officers whose intelligence experience was matched by diplomatic gifts. They executed tasks both overtly and covertly within the

'United Kingdom Representative' structure, a further indication that, in the 1970s, the Foreign Office and [MI6] began working as part of the same team.[7]

With the benefit of decades of hindsight, is now clear that Crinnion was but one of a burgeoning number of important agents on Oldfield's Republic of Ireland roster. The MI6 network in the Republic had been run by John Wyman since about 1961. They were a motley crew. By the early 1970s, one of his most important agents, an individual as important as Crinnion, was an international businessman who had once been close to senior Fianna Fáil politicians. Oldfield also had agents in the IRA who communicated with MI6 by dropping reports into milk churns in the Republic from where they were fished out by Oldfield's field operatives and driven across the border to Craig Smellie and others in MI6.[8]

MI6 had a 'station' in the British embassy in Dublin which gathered information from a wide spectrum of sources. The station participated in the running of MI6 agents in the field. One of the MI6 officers at the embassy in the early 1970s was Andrew Johnstone, a first secretary in his late thirties. Johnstone had joined MI6 in 1956 and had been posted to Syria, Cambodia, Yemen, United Arab Emirates and Pakistan.

Oldfield's sexual preference was for young men. He slept with male prostitutes, some of whom were destitute teenagers, and built up a library of pornographic photographs at his flat in London. Bearing this in mind, it is not difficult to understand how he had the stomach to oversee MI6's egregious Kincora Boys' Home child abuse 'honey trap' operation in Belfast.[9] Teenage boys were used as bait for Loyalist politicians and paramilitaries. A series of Loyalist paedophiles were ensnared by the scheme, including members of parliament.

There was no depth to which MI6 would not sink. According to Oldfield's closest friend, Anthony Cavendish, who served in both MI5 and MI6, deceit was the starting point of an officer's career in MI6, because a recruit was destined to lie 'from his first day in the Service.'[10] Cavendish wrote about the use of blackmail to control MI6 agents and also the use of 'threats to the family of valuable informants. An operative member of MI6 cannot automatically rule out such methods of achieving the required result in an intelligence mission. Similarly, theft, deception, lies, mutilation and even murder are considered if and when necessary.'[11]

MI6's Dublin station was located inside the British embassy on Merrion Square. Some ambassadors resented the presence of the spooks under their roof but not Andrew Gilchrist, who served as British ambassador to Dublin, 1967–70.[12] He was a man well able to navigate the murky waters in which he swam. He was a special forces veteran of the Second World War in Siam (now Thailand) who had gone on to hold the position of chair of the JIC in Asia.[13] While he was serving as ambassador to Indonesia, he participated in black propaganda operations, aided and abetted by the Information Research Department (IRD), which aggravated tensions and, according to Amnesty International, led to the slaughter of 500,000 suspected communists. He and Oldfield must have known each other as Oldfield served as deputy head of MI6's Singapore station, 1950–53, and as head, 1956–59. Singapore served as MI6's regional HQ. One of Oldfield's tasks was to monitor the flow of weapons and money to the communist guerrillas fighting the British in Malaya in the 1950s, a good training for his anti-IRA operations.

By the late 1960s, Oldfield and the MI6 head of station in the Dublin embassy were playing their cards close to their chests. Gilchrist came to feel he was being left out of the intelligence loop. On 24 July 1969, he complained to Edward Peck of the JIC about the reports by MI5: 'we have had little more from London than an out-of-date compilation of information mostly already known from the newspapers.'[14] Worse still from his perspective, he felt he was being kept in the dark about developments in the Republic. Gilchrist wanted to know more, in particular about the SDU reports which he knew were reaching London:

> ... If communications from the Irish special branch to London have been suspended, I should like to know. If reports are still coming in, but contain nothing worth passing on to me, I should like to know that too. If there is good stuff available which it is not desirable that I should now see, that is also a matter which it might be useful for me to be aware of ... It is not mere curiosity. If I am to assess correctly the information and gossip I pick up here ... It is important that I should be kept in the picture ... For subversive purposes, Ireland is one island.[15]

One of the likely heads of the Dublin MI6 station in the early 1970s was John Williams, born on 12 November 1921.[16] Before coming to Ireland, he had been posted to the NATO Defence College in Rome. He occupied the position of 'counsellor' at the embassy. John Peck, who served as Britain's ambassador to Dublin, 1970–73, made no reference to Williams in his Dublin memoir despite his ostensible importance as 'counsellor' to the embassy.

One of the most dangerous groups on MI6's radar in the Republic was Saor Éire, an organisation which had even once targeted Ambassador Gilchrist. Patrick Crinnion likewise had his spyglass trained firmly on them.

13

MacStíofáin's Friends in Saor Éire

On a Saturday night in October 1967, George Orr, a Dublin taxi driver, responded to a hail on his radio. Minutes later, as he pulled up along Upper Erne Street to pick up his fare, he was confronted by two men, one of whom thrust a revolver through the window and ordered him to open his door. When he obeyed, he was pulled out of the driver's seat and pushed into the back. The second man, also armed, slid into the front passenger seat. Two more men climbed in either side of Orr while the first gunman sat in behind the steering wheel. 'Don't be smart', one of them warned him.

Having commandeered the vehicle, the hijackers drove to the Furry Glen in the Phoenix Park where Orr's wrists were tied behind his back with his necktie while his jumper was yanked over his face as a blindfold. Having left him, the gang returned to the city. They reached Upper Mount Street at 9.30 p.m. Two of them got out of the car. They each carried a container filled with a mixture of oil and petrol which they hurled through one of the windows of No. 13, the HQ of Fianna Fáil. A flaming rag was lobbed at the window but landed on a sill. It burned for a while before dropping into the basement where it set fire to the coalhouse door. The plan – which failed – had been to raze the building. A second rag might have finished the job but the would-be arsonists gang had not thought to bring one.

The crew fled from the scene. A well-built SDU officer in a red Leyland mini, who had spotted what was going on, gave chase to the taxi as it sped along Mount Street. Two shots were discharged in his direction but missed him. As the taxi fled, two units of the fire brigade rushed towards Upper Mount Street. The aspiring incendiaries got away.

A statement delivered to *The Irish Press* later that night demanded the release from prison of three members of Saor Éire, a militant IRA splinter group. The unit that attacked the Fianna Fáil HQ was led by Frank Keane, a television engineer in his thirties. One of his accomplices was Simon O'Donnell, a twenty-two-year-old fitter from Gardiner Place in the centre of the city. Saor Éire had been set up in 1967 by disgruntled ex-IRA men and young left-wing activists. A number of criminals mingled with the group and proved useful to them as gunrunners and armed robbers.

Keane, who had served as officer-in-command of the Dublin brigade of the IRA, 1963–65, was a founding member of Saor Éire. Liam Walsh, a veteran of the IRA from the 1950s, was another.

If a letter Crinnion sent to Patrick Malone is accurate, a third former IRA man, Richard Timmons, was a member as well. Timmons had participated in the IRA's 1939 bombing campaign in England along with Brendan Behan, both of whom had been arrested. Timmons was sentenced to thirteen years in prison while Behan was sent to borstal. Timmons escaped from Wakefield prison after ten years and linked up with Behan. He managed to stow away on board a coal ship which ferried him safely to Galway.

Fianna Fáil was in government at the time of the petrol bomb attack on its HQ on Upper Mount Street in 1967. The incident was an unmitigated embarrassment for the SDU. It acted quickly, trailing three members of Saor Éire to a pub in the centre of the city where they arrested them. Another man was picked up elsewhere. They were all taken to the Bridewell garda station for questioning.

Ten days after the attack, Keane and O'Donnell pleaded guilty to a series of charges and were sentenced to six months in prison. In later years, Keane described the event as a political 'stunt'.[1] Both men served about four months behind bars. After they regained their freedom, Keane and O'Donnell participated in further Saor Éire operations.

Saor Éire professed to draw its ideological inspiration from Trotsky, Che Guevara, the Tupamaros urban guerrillas in Uruguay, and, closer to home, left-wing Republicans who had been active in the 1930s. Their political convictions justified, for them, the kidnap and abuse of people like George Orr, a working-class man from Dean Swift Road in Dublin, not to mention the gang's habit of pointing loaded weapons at bank employees and customers during raids.

By the end of 1970, the tally of Saor Éire bank heists reached seventeen during which the gang garnered approximately £60–70,000. It was customary for the raiders to keep a share of the takings for their personal use.

Saor Éire was of interest to MI6, not merely because of the threat it posed to the British embassy, but also because Patrick Crinnion believed MacStíofáin was using the gang to carry out operations he could not ask his own men in the IRA to undertake; endeavours which Cathal Goulding would have opposed. A Saor Éire source who spoke to the highly regarded author Seán Boyne, confirmed Crinnion's suspicion. He revealed that one of the group's leaders, Peter Graham:

> had been involved in channelling funds from Saor Éire bank robberies to Republicans in the North who emerged as the

Provisional IRA. There was speculation that some of this money was earmarked for buying arms.[2]

The significant point here is that some of the funds were being channelled to MacStíofáin's faction of the IRA before the movement split in December 1969.

Also, according to a history of Saor Éire:

When the north of Ireland erupted into violence in 1969, Saor Éire provided funds expropriated in the bank raids to the besieged nationalist population.[3]

The gardaí did not detect the relationship between MacStíofáin and Saor Éire for the simple reason that MacStíofáin, their perceived star informer, did not tell them about it. Instead, the SDU and C3 turned their attention to what Lynch and some of his minsters were doing. So too did Crinnion and his masters in London.

Saor Éire had links to other groups at this time and it is not suggested here that it was merely an instrument of MacStíofáin.

14

PLAYING CATCH UP

By August 1969, MI6 had developed a keen interest in what was going on behind all sorts of closed doors in the Republic, especially those inside Leinster House. Patrick Crinnion had access to some information, but no real grasp of what the politicians were actually trying to achieve.

Crinnion was a hard-working officer, often putting in a seventy-hour week. He came to believe that he was the 'most experienced C3 member' in the force, an officer with a vast 'knowledge of subversive personalities, their capabilities and positions within the structure'.[1] He saw himself as a man with an 'ability to advise and guide the force on the many varied problems concerning firearms and explosive devices used by subversives'.

Unfortunately, Crinnion's powers of deduction were not all that he made them out to be, especially as he was dealing with poor quality information which he believed was pure intelligence gold. Crinnion had just reached his twenty-seventh birthday when he was sent to work at C3. That was shortly before Philip McMahon of the SDU began to furnish reports to C3 which were based on the dubious disclosures made to him by MacStíofáin. Hence, from almost the start of his service at C3, Crinnion was being fed a distorted view of what was going on inside Republican circles.

In his new role, Crinnion came to rely on someone he described in his correspondence as his 'Informant'. In one letter – to be discussed in a later chapter – he revealed that this individual was John Wyman of MI6.[2] Wyman spoon-fed Crinnion a confection of deceit which, over time, led him to believe that elements inside Fianna Fáil were in league with the IRA. In Crinnion's mind, this cabal became a threat to the 'peace and well-being of the State'.[3] Wyman, a field operative, was obviously taking his lead on this high-level operation from Maurice Oldfield.

To make matters even worse, the gardaí had neither eyes nor ears inside the Nationalist communities beyond the border. They knew little beyond what the media was reporting about what was going on in places such as Belfast, Derry and Newry. In particular, the gardaí had no reliable source to advise them about the defence committees which had sprung up in Northern Ireland. They consisted of priests, businessmen, solicitors, school teachers, ex-servicemen from various armies and former IRA veterans. They called themselves Citizen Defence Committees (CDCs). They had no agenda beyond the protection of their respective communities, something the gardaí failed to grasp, especially Crinnion.

In his memoirs, MacStíofáin described how 'throughout August [1969] local defence committees sprang up like mushrooms in the North. They were generally not affiliated to the Republican movement and did not even follow a common pattern. In Belfast they were known as the Citizens' Defence Committees. In other places they called themselves defence units.'[4]

Seán Keenan and Paddy Doherty ran the Derry defence committee. Keenan was a veteran IRA leader; Doherty, a civil rights campaigner who was a friend of John Hume and an opponent of the IRA. Doherty joined the defence committee to ensure that it did not fall under the sway of the IRA. The pair visited Dublin on the eve of the eruption of the Loyalist attacks on nationalist communities in August 1969. After a discussion with officials at Leinster House, they visited the HQ of Sinn Féin, a Georgian house on Gardiner Street, where Keenan arranged a meeting with Goulding. 'We are to return in 15 minutes,' he told Doherty. The pair walked a short distance to the Belvedere Hotel. 'We are going to meet the commander-in-chief,' Keenan enthused. 'You'll like him. He has a grown-up daughter but he looks so young and fit we give him the nickname "Peter Pan".'[5] They returned to the Sinn Féin HQ. A car pulled up at the kerb and, as if from a scene in a Harry Palmer movie, they were ordered to get in quickly. Doherty recalled:

> The silence of the car reflected the secrecy of the mission. The man in the passenger seat – our guide – kept glancing back through the rear window. I had no idea where we were going. I might as well have been wearing a blindfold. Finally we stopped in front of a pair of closed gates which looked like the entrance to a builder's yard. As the guide opened the small wicket in the centre, my assumptions were confirmed by the neatly stacked scaffolding, ladders and paint drums. There was an air of organisation in place. As we stepped over the threshold, we were greeted by Peter Pan's daughter. She was small, slender and well-groomed. She said her father would join us shortly.[6]

Doherty was struck by the posters of Marx, Lenin and Mao Tse-tung that 'glowered down from the walls'. They were taken to an office where Goulding joined them and, after a few pleasantries were exchanged, Keenan told Goulding that the 'citizens of Derry call upon the people of Ireland to come to their assistance if the Bogside is attacked'.[7] Goulding was:

> sitting on top of the table, one sandalled foot on the floor, the other swinging freely. I could see his bare toes straining against

the leather straps of the sandals as if they were trying to break out. What we heard next shattered a myth. The commander replied: 'I couldn't defend the Bogside. I have neither the men nor the guns to do it'.[8]

Doherty described how 'Keenan stood there, motionless, as if the message hadn't sunk in yet'. Doherty, however, had had enough and stood up. 'I told you the IRA was only a myth, a fantasy army, with nothing to offer the people of Ireland,' he sneered and sat down. 'The toy soldier, the commander-in-chief of the phantom army,' Doherty added, 'was shaken by my reaction.'[9]

Instead of the IRA, the British army stepped up to the plate. By mid-August 1969, soldiers were safeguarding many, but not all, of the Nationalist communities in Northern Ireland. This became known as the 'honeymoon period' during which the locals provided the troops with tea and sandwiches. On at least one occasion, a group of soldiers left rifles resting against the wall of a church in Belfast before they attended mass inside.

As early as 19 August, London was talking about how Britain's troops would be 'withdrawn from the internal security role at the earliest possible moment'.[10] Dublin was deeply concerned about the intention to pull out the soldiers. A meeting took place behind closed doors in London, on 15 August 1969, between the Minister for External Affairs, Patrick Hillery, and Lord Chalfont of the FCO, at which Chalfont stated: 'I can tell you with the greatest confidence that [the British army] will handle it successfully and with the minimum use of force. They will go when order is restored.'[11] Hillery asked Chalfont: 'But when the troops are withdrawn, what then? Will the minority be exposed once again to repression and be terrorised again?'[12] Lord Stonham, the Minster for State for Home Affairs, who was also in attendance, interjected and said, 'At this stage it is not possible to say more than that we are determined to end the state of terror, and to relinquish control only when we are satisfied there are no other problems.'[13]

In Northern Ireland, the concern of many Nationalists was more immediate: there were too few British troops on the ground. The IRA had not been able to protect their communities because it was no longer a fighting force due to Goulding's neglect. It had only a tiny number of guns and a handful of men trained to use them. Joe Cahill, a veteran IRA leader, told his biographer that the name of the IRA 'was mud' and that walking 'down the Falls Road next day, [Jimmy] Steele and I were called deserters and traitors and people spat at us ... It hurt, it hurt like hell.'[14]

At that time the British army and the RUC were targets of Unionist fury.[15] The first RUC officer to die during the Troubles was Victor Arbuckle. He was shot dead by the UVF amid rioting by Loyalists on the Shankill Road in October 1969. The defence committees were not hostile to the British soldiers, nor intent upon ending partition. They cooperated with the RUC and the British army. In Belfast the various committees rallied together under the banner of the Central Citizens' Defence Committee, or CCDC.

The committees began to place Jack Lynch and his colleagues under pressure to supply them with arms, thereby generating alarm inside Century House, the HQ of MI6 in London.

15

MINISTERS IN DUBLIN HATCH A PLAN

A covert operation was set in motion by three of Jack Lynch's ministers in Dublin to cater for some of the thornier aspects of the urgent situation in Northern Ireland. The undertaking involved the importation of a secret consignment of weapons for the defence committees.

The plan changed shape, if it ever really possessed one, and eventually evolved into a strategy whereby G2, Irish military intelligence, was to import the arms and store them in a monastery in Cavan, near the border. Thus stockpiled, they would be available for distribution to the defence committees if a 'doomsday' emergency erupted.

One of the key figures in the endeavour was James Gibbons, the Minister for Defence, an office that licensed him to import arms. The centrifugal force, however, was Neil Blaney, the Minister for Agriculture. Charles Haughey, the Minister for Finance, was the third strategist.

The weapons were to be purchased with money made available after a vote in Dáil Éireann, which had established a fund for the 'relief of distress' in Northern Ireland. At first, CDC figures tried to acquire arms but failed. Later, Capt. James Kelly of G2 took over. Capt. Kelly's plan was to import and stockpile a consignment of arms. As Seán Boyne has pointed out:

> There was media speculation that the monastery in which the arms were to be hidden was Kilnacrott Abbey in County Cavan, run by the Norbertine order. In recent years a priest, Father

Cataldus McKiernan, who was based at the monastery at the time and who died in October 2002, talked to a journalist about the matter. The journalist gave me an outline of what the priest said. According to Father McKiernan, he was approached by Captain Kelly and another man and asked to hide arms in outbuildings or sheds at the monastery. It was indicated to the priest that the matter had something to do with the government. The priest was horrified – one of his concerns was for the students in a school run by the order at Kilnacrott at the time. He refused point-blank to have anything to do with storing arms.[1]

In light of this rejection, Capt. Kelly made alternative plans for the storage of the weapons at a property in the west of Ireland.

John Kelly, the national coordinator of the defence committees, was involved in the endeavour from the start. Kelly was also a veteran of the Border Campaign and sided with the Provisionals after the split in the IRA in late 1969. This fact, taken out of context, has allowed MI6 and their assets, along with an array of 'useful idiots' and conspiracy theorists, to misrepresent the defence committees as a front for the faction in the IRA that subsequently transformed into the Provisionals.[2] In reality, the CDCs represented the wider Nationalist community. The leadership included legal, religious and other members of the community who were, in many instances, opposed to the IRA. One of them, Tom Conaty, became an adviser to the first secretary of state to Northern Ireland, William Whitelaw. Conaty was the chairman of the organisation. Another, Paddy Devlin, MP, was secretary of the CCDC. He became a SDLP minister in the Sunningdale-inspired power-sharing government of Northern Ireland in 1974. There was another senior IRA man in the organisation – Jim Sullivan – but he joined the Official IRA. Sullivan was the chairman of the CCDC in Belfast. The Officials were the rivals of the

Provisionals, even to the extent of assassinating each other in a feud in the mid-1970s. In Derry, Paddy Doherty, the deputy chairman of the Derry defence committee, the man so derisive of 'Peter Pan', was another opponent of the IRA. The new RUC chief constable, Arthur Young, attended one CCDC meeting in a public house in Belfast without bodyguards. The latter had been drafted in from London by James Callaghan.

The fact that some IRA veterans from the 1940s and 1950s occupied positions of importance on the defence committees was not a red flag for James Callaghan, who pointed out in *A House Divided* that the IRA did not switch from a defensive role to one of attack until the summer of 1970.[3] This shift took place after the eruption of the Arms Crisis. It was also subsequent to the victory of the Conservative party under the leadership of Ted Heath in the June 1970 general election. The new administration was far more disposed towards the Unionist government at Stormont than Labour under Wilson and Callaghan had been. Callaghan argued that were it not for mistakes by the Tories and Unionists, the IRA could have been brought into the political fold.[4] The Provisionals captured 'the support of the majority of the Catholic population' only:

> after insensitive British handling had disenchanted it. If other political courses had been followed in 1970 and 1971, it is possible that the Official IRA would have kept their hold and the Provisionals would never have gained the ground that they did.[5]

While Crinnion and MI6 were focused on the amateurish attempts by the CDCs to run guns to Ireland, Seán MacStíofáin and Dáithí Ó Conaill were building a watertight transatlantic arms-supply pipeline. Suffice it to say, MacStíofáin failed to reveal this endeavour to McMahon. Consequently, the SDU continued to focus its attention on the CDCs.

16

A Man Called Jock

One morning a small girl stumbled across two caps in her parents' wardrobe while searching for clothes to play dress up. Delighted with herself, she grabbed both and marched out onto the street. When her mother realised what she was doing, she ran after her and snatched the headwear back. The child, Caoimhe Haughey, now an eminent Dublin solicitor, recalls that her mother's demeanour was less than calm.[1] One of the caps resembled that of a garda officer. The second one was white with a leather brim, not unlike that of an official of Customs and Excise. Caoimhe was the daughter of Pádraig ('Jock') and Kitty Haughey. Jock was the brother of Charles, the Minister for Finance.

In the haste to supply arms to the Nationalist community for defensive purposes, in August 1969, Jock Haughey had collected money from businessmen which he gave to Cathal Goulding. There are various accounts as to how much Goulding received. What is clear, however, is that Goulding did not use any of the money to purchase weapons. The following day, Haughey gave the small remaining balance of the fund to Joe Cahill for arms, again, for defensive purposes only.

Jock Haughey was involved in the importation of a consignment of arms from London through Dublin Airport the following month, September 1969. The plan, at least insofar as Haughey was concerned, was that the IRA would transport the weapons to Northern Ireland for distribution to the defence committees.

The gardaí discovered the existence of the September consignment, albeit after the event. According to Crinnion:

> During investigations … it was learned that an importation had been cleared through Dublin Airport Customs in such a fashion that it would be reasonable to believe that it consisted of firearms and this cargo was taken away by [Richard] TIMMONS and [Jock] HAUGHEY.[2]

The weapons were delivered to Goulding; however, his real desire was for peace and a left-wing political solution to the problems of Northern Ireland. In particular, he hoped that working-class people on both sides of the religious divide would unite and rise up against those he perceived as their joint oppressors, the capitalist classes who controlled the island. Dr Roy Johnston, a member of the IRA's Army Executive, and a supporter of Goulding, knew about the arms flight ahead of time. Johnston believed Goulding became involved in the venture to keep the weapons out of the hands of the militants under his command, men such as MacStíofáin, and 'as an insurance policy in case he might need [the weapons] later'.[3]

Kevin Boland, the Minister for Local Government, claimed that many of these smuggling endeavours had the effective blessing of his colleagues. In his book, *Up Dev*, he recorded how reports about one importation operation 'became so insistent as to amount to a virtual certainty at least insofar as the members of the Government were concerned'. As far as he could see, 'everyone assumed everyone else knew'. He felt the tactic of turning a blind eye had evolved as a suitable method by which to help Nationalist communities without causing 'a diplomatic breach' with the UK.[4] The odds are high that Boland had in mind the consignment flown from London to Dublin Airport in September 1969. There were other shipments that reached the Republic by a variety of routes, including by sea. The authority on the subject, author Seán Boyne, has described how some arms were brought ashore off the coast of Dublin.

Crinnion stated in his letter to Patrick Malone in 1973 that the Dublin Airport 'cargo was taken away by [Richard] TIMMONS and [Jock] HAUGHEY' but his information was incomplete. He was not aware of the part played by Bobby McKnight. This implies that the information that reached Crinnion was supplied by a Saor Éire informer who heard about the role of Timmons and Haughey, but not that of McKnight. Born in Belfast in 1936, McKnight was a veteran of the Border Campaign, and an unsuccessful candidate in the 1966 Westminster general election. He was loyal to Goulding.

During the Dublin Airport escapade, Jock Haughey masqueraded as a garda or an official of Customs and Excise, or provided the caps from his wardrobe to his accomplices to assist them to move about freely with the headgear.

According to John Kelly of the CDCs, who was not present but spoke to Jock Haughey later, Haughey 'went out to the airport and collected them in a van and delivered them to Cathal [Goulding]. There were two boxes of short arms. Maybe 20 or 50 weapons, something like that'.[5]

McKnight's recollection differed from the account provided by Jock Haughey to John Kelly as far as the size of the consignment was concerned. 'Two of us went down [and] Charlie's brother brought us into the airport, we'd a wee pickup truck we got a loan of, [and] he brought us in, and they put these big boxes on the truck, we had to take it away, the truck was fucking swaying from side to side [but] we had the right of way.'[6]

According to McKnight, they drove to 'a rendezvous nearby where Goulding had assembled a team who divided up the cargo – handguns and automatic weapons – and moved them to separate dumps'.[7]

John Kelly said the guns 'weren't supplied to the North. They certainly weren't supplied to volunteers in the North so I would say that Goulding sat on them … Pádraig [Jock Haughey] told me he gave the guns to Goulding and then we were wondering "where are they".' Joe Cahill also confirmed they never reached Northern Ireland.[8]

In the split that tore the IRA apart, at the end of 1969, McKnight remained loyal to Goulding. A myth spread later, one encouraged by Crinnion and MI6, that Blaney and Haughey backed the importation of arms in 1969 to help those opposed to Goulding set up the Provisional IRA. The fact that a large sum of money and the September consignment of arms were handed over to Goulding personally by the brother of Charles Haughey belies the myth.

It is interesting to note that Crinnion and presumably the SDU knew about the involvement of Dick Timmons in the escapade but not that of McKnight. This is an early indication of something that will become more apparent in later chapters, namely that the SDU – and possibly MI6 – had a source or sources inside Saor Éire. This individual or group knew something, but not everything, about the Dublin importation.

Crinnion once described himself as 'not just first class but exceptional', as if he was a high-flying eagle with an aerial view of all beneath him. In reality, he was more like a pigeon blind in one eye. Instead of focusing his energies on unravelling the transatlantic arms pipeline that would sustain the IRA for the next decade and beyond, or thwarting UVF bomb attacks in the Republic, Crinnion kept his spyglass trained on the efforts of the defence committees to acquire arms.

17

SDU TUNNEL VISION

The old adage that 'a bird never flew on one wing' could well describe the position in which the SDU found itself in 1969, and beyond. It had neither agents nor observers north of the Border. It had no inkling of the bomb campaign which the UVF was about to unleash in the Republic.

On 5 August 1969, a UVF bomber sneaked onto the grounds of RTÉ at Donnybrook, on the south side of Dublin. He made his way to the west wall of the main block and planted a bomb which exploded at 1.30 a.m. The detonation blew out many of the large plate-glass windows and damaged the wardrobe department. No one was injured. The attack was treated by RTÉ in a light-hearted fashion with a news report stating that while rumours had circulated that 'Wanderly Wagon', a colourful caravan that featured in a children's TV programme, had been damaged, it had in fact not lost its 'magical powers' and had survived the blast intact.

On 19 October 1969, the UVF crossed the Border again, this time to bomb the Ballyshannon Power Station in Co. Donegal. The only fatality was that of Thomas McDowell, a member of the UVF who was electrocuted. He died a few days later in a hospital in Donegal. McDowell was a quarry worker who had experience in handling explosives and had participated in earlier UVF bombings including the Silent Valley strike which toppled Capt. Terence O'Neill as Stormont prime minister of Northern Ireland in April 1969. In addition to being a member of the UVF, McDowell was part of the UPV, a body associated with Ian Paisley, and worshipped at Paisley's Free Presbyterian

Church. RUC investigations into McDowell led them to a man called Samuel Stevenson, a forty-six-year-old former B Special who lived in central Belfast. He confessed to having helped McDowell 'scout' the Ballyshannon Power Station and plan the attack. During his confession he implicated John McKeague and others in the campaign.[1]

The Wolfe Tone Memorial in Bodenstown, Co. Kildare, was next. It was attacked on 31 October. On 26 December, the Daniel O'Connell monument in Dublin was the target of another act of UVF aggression. Two days later an explosion occurred near to the HQ of the Central Detective Unit (CDU) of the gardaí at Dublin Castle. On 18 February 1970, the 240-foot radio mast at Mongary Hill, Raphoe, in Co. Donegal was bombed.

The SDU was also blind to what the IRA was doing. This was because MacStíofáin was still leading McMahon a merry dance. One of the secrets he withheld from McMahon was that an IRA man had travelled to America to meet George Harrison in early 1969. Harrison was an IRA veteran, the man who had supplied arms for the Border Campaign. The visitor asked Harrison to revive a supply line he had run from the US back in the 1950s and early 1960s. Harrison readily agreed. He had kept seventy weapons in storage after the end of the Border Campaign which he now dispatched to Dublin Port. MacStíofáin did not expose Harrison or the dockers who smuggled the weapons through customs. According to author Seán Boyne, this:

> first shipment of arms went to the pre-split IRA, and Harrison believed that a small proportion ended up in the hands of the faction that would go with the Officials [i.e. Goulding's Marxist faction] when the split occurred in December 1969. 'It would be wrong for me to say that none of it went to the Officials because I know that some of it did.'

It is interesting to note that Harrison's recollection was that the weapons were sought in early 1969 and delivered in 'mid-1969', which was before the eruption of widespread violence in August of that year. MacStíofáin and Dáithí Ó Conaill were the driving force behind the arms smuggling initiative, not Goulding, who was still trying to transform the Republican movement into a political force. It is equally interesting to note that Harrison appears to have intended all of the arms to go to the faction represented by MacStíofáin and Ó Conaill, not Goulding's group, i.e., not to those who later transformed into the 'Officials'. This indicates an emerging split on the Army Council which, in turn, raises the possibility that MacStíofáin and Ó Conaill were not only dissatisfied with Goulding's leadership, but were waiting for an opportunity to topple him. Alternatively, they might have foreseen the trouble that lay ahead in Northern Ireland, and were planning their strategy, ahead of time, without letting Goulding impede them.

According to Seán Boyne, over the next decade Harrison and his colleagues smuggled tonnes of arms to Ireland. 'The arms were generally bought over the counter in gun shops,' Boyne discovered. 'An informed source, a New York-based Republican familiar with arms procurement activities during this era, told me that in order to increase the numbers of guns purchased, sympathisers would 'lend' their driver's licences as identification to those doing the buying.'[2]

There is no evidence that the SDU was aware in 1969–70 that Ó Conaill and his colleagues had opened up a transatlantic arms supply route. 'We picked up a few American guns all right [later in the early 1970s], but nothing that opened up who was supplying them or how,' a SDU officer has revealed.[3]

Crinnion disclosed in one of his 1973 memoranda that he

sought and received some assistance from the FBI about the source of the American weapons the SDU had found:

> To give some sort of example I was involved in correspondence about firearms detected being smuggled into this country from New York and then from San Francisco, USA. I did not correspond with the police in either New York or San Francisco. I dealt with the FBI, my opposite number to C3 in the USA.

C3 and the SDU's main focus in 1969–1970, however, remained fixed on the amateurish and doomed CDC endeavours. Des O'Malley, who became minister for justice in 1970, stated in his memoirs that in the 'autumn of 1969 the Special Branch received further information that small consignments of arms were being imported through Dublin Airport at times when a sympathetic Customs officer was on duty. The belief in Garda circles was that [Charles] Haughey was involved; there were also suspicions that Blaney was active in this.'[4]

MacStíofáin was now moving into high gear in his deception of Philip McMahon. In early October he told McMahon that Capt. Kelly of G2 had furnished Goulding with £50,000 for arms. That was a downright lie. MacStíofáin's artifice concentrated garda attention on Goulding. If Goulding had been caught in possession of arms – such as those recently delivered to him by Jock Haughey – he would have been arrested, detained and placed on trial. The IRA would then have been rendered ripe for a takeover by Goulding's opponents.

MacStíofáin was engaged in other devious machinations behind Goulding's back:

> … one of the things I had to do, in addition to duties as intelligence chief, was to approach people for subscriptions to the Northern Defence Fund.

Needless to say, I wasn't looking for fivers or tenners. Selecting a list of prospective subscribers with great care, I succeeded in obtaining several large donations.

MacStíofáin attended an Army Council meeting in September 1969, at which a report on the defence fund was discussed. It stood at a 'healthy five-figure sum'. Goulding and his supporters proposed that it should 'all be used for the general finances of the movement'.[5] MacStíofáin jumped out of his chair and walked 'up and down the room protesting at this proposal'. A compromise was reached whereby 'less than half of what had been collected' would be held for the 'defence of the Northern Nationalist districts'. He contacted a number of businessmen who had pledged the IRA substantial sums for 'the defence fund and told them to hold on to their money for the time being, explaining my reasons'.[6] He approached them several months later when they made 'very generous' donations to the Provisional IRA. He wrote that the donors 'were not connected with Fianna Fáil or with Taca, that party's fund-raising group. They were successful businessmen who would not have touched either of those organisations with a barge-pole.'[7]

In his memoirs, MacStíofáin denied he wanted to set up a breakaway organisation. The fact that MacStíofáin advised these benefactors to withhold their donations until a later date, indicates he was hoping to depose Goulding as chief-of-staff. Equally, it is consistent with a scenario whereby he had no intention of setting up a breakaway group at this stage.

Meanwhile, MI6 and Crinnion managed to achieve a significant breakthrough against Saor Éire, the organisation that was sympathetic to many of MacStíofáin's goals. They discovered an arms' smuggling route the organisation was using to import pistols from Birmingham to Dublin.

18

THE PARKER-HALE CONNECTION

A well-known Dublin underworld figure was a key link in the covert passage of arms from Birmingham to Dublin. He had developed a contact at Parker-Hale, a small arms factory in Birmingham. The criminal's contact had the job of testing 9mm Star pistols which were manufactured by the Star munitions factory in Spain and sent to Birmingham. The contact would condemn perfectly good instruments as flawed and smuggle them out of the factory. Subsequently, they entered a clandestine pipeline which wound its way to Ireland. Some of the weapons were taken by him on flights to Dublin Airport; others were shipped on the B&I Dublin to Liverpool car ferry.

The Dublin criminal was responsible for the transport of between 25–35 Star pistols which reached Ireland in late 1969. They were smuggled in small numbers. In more recent times, this criminal has hinted that he gave some of them to the IRA, probably to Dáithí Ó Conaill, who was in the business of procuring arms for the organisation at this time. The criminal was also an associate of Liam Walsh and Martin Casey of Saor Éire.

Crinnion unravelled the Birmingham operation after conducting an inquiry into a member of Saor Éire who shall be called Michael 'W' in these pages. Crinnion believed that a 'considerable number' of weapons were stolen for Saor Éire in Birmingham. 'W' was involved in smuggling Star weapons for Saor Éire to Ireland by sea. According to Crinnion:

> Perhaps you remember the case of Michael [W] ... which illustrates my point about having a flair for the work in C3. [W], described as a Ships Engineer, was found in possession of two

new 'STAR' pistols and SDU reported that he had bought the weapons, as indeed he claimed, while on a voyage with his ship to Spain. Because of my experience I knew that during the Border Campaign of 1956/62 a brother of [W's] had been active with the IRA splinter group, elements of which later re-appeared as part of SAOR ÉIRE. You allowed me to send a letter to special branch, New Scotland Yard, London, requesting a check on PARKER-HALE Birmingham. (The 'STAR' weapons are manufactured in Spain but PARKER-HALE are the British agents). It transpired that the two weapons found with [W] were part of what must have been a considerable number pilfered from the Birmingham works. [W] instead of being a foreign-going sea man [W] was in fact an Electrician on the Dublin-Liverpool B&I Ferry. It's all set out on his file, he was a large-scale smuggler of firearms for SAOR ÉIRE and weapons dropped at the scene of numerous Saor Éire bank raids, or found in their possession from time to time, were shown by the closeness of their serial numbers to have been companion weapons to [W's] pair.[1]

Crinnion undoubtedly had the Parker-Hale factory in mind when he wrote, in one of his 1973 memoranda, how he had been involved in 'a minor success' where the 'matters concerned were in Birmingham'. According to Crinnion, 'Scotland Yard men did assist C3 but, they did so on behalf of another British Service [i.e. MI6] and generally in the company of an officer of that other service'.

The picture that emerges here is one where Crinnion tipped off MI6 about the arms' pipeline and asked MI6 for help but, for the sake of appearances, approached them with Malone's permission through Scotland Yard.

By October 1969, if not before that month, Oldfield had begun to circle Saor Éire. The first individual caught in his net was Frank Keane, a leading figure in Saor Éire. Instead of finding some way of shutting down Saor Éire's operations in Britain, Oldfield let Keane and his comrades roam freely seeking additional arms.

Crinnion knew about the Dublin underworld figure's involvement with Saor Éire. That meant that MI6 and Scotland Yard did too. The criminal was not arrested for any of these activities. In a letter to Patrick Malone, Crinnion asserted that the individual was a member of Saor Éire and :

> … had been a frequent visitor to Birmingham, flying directly from Dublin, prior to this. I recall that even you were sceptical of [the criminal's] role when I described his functions as an Arms Buyer. Regrettably I was too late to prevent unlawful importations of firearms taking place …[2]

The criminal remained close to Saor Éire. A year later, on 13 October 1970, Liam Walsh, Martin Casey and Máirín Keegan, all members of Saor Éire, were transporting a bomb along the railway embankment at the rear of McKee barracks, off Blackhorse Avenue, Dublin, when it exploded. Walsh died while Casey was left deaf in one ear. Keegan, who had survived a bout with cancer, blamed the stress of the explosion for the return of her disease. She died two years later.[3]

As Liam Walsh's funeral cortège wound its way down O'Connell Street on 17 October 1970, the criminal gave an oration and fired a volley of shots from a revolver into the air.

Two individuals involved in the theft of the Star pistols were arrested, but not the men from Saor Éire. Author Liz Walsh has described how the:

> gunrunning line worked perfectly until the contacts in Britain attempted to knock off a container full of ammunition. The British authorities caught them, and two men were sentenced to twenty years apiece.[4]

Craftily, Oldfield now offered Saor Éire an apparent alternative source of weapons. When Oldfield's trap was sprung, it attracted a most unexpected victim.

19

MI6 AND THE ELTHAM FACTORY STING

By October 1969, MI6 and Scotland Yard had made contact with Saor Éire through two men posing as arms dealers. 'Capt. Peter Markham-Randall' and 'Hyman Godfrey', two MI6-Scotland Yard operatives, masqueraded as arms salesmen with access to a factory in Eltham, south London. They made contact with Frank Keane, of Saor Éire, and Martin Casey. Keane was the man who had pleaded guilty to the attempt to burn Fianna Fáil's HQ to the ground in 1967. Keane was the first to meet with the arms dealers. He then introduced them to Casey. Casey was taken to an arms factory in Eltham, by Godfrey, to inspect weapons that were allegedly for sale.

Keane let a third man from Saor Éire, Richard Timmons, know about his relationship with Godfrey in London. Crinnion believed Timmons was a member of Saor Éire, based on his connection to Frank Keane.[1]

Timmons was a veteran Republican. He had been incarcerated after a bombing campaign in England in 1939, but escaped at the end of the 1940s. Timmons was the man Crinnion believed had participated in the successful smuggling of arms through Dublin Airport, in September 1969, with Jock Haughey.

Timmons knew the defence committees in Northern Ireland were still looking for arms and decided to let them know about the contacts Saor Éire had made in London. He put Jock Haughey in touch with Casey. A meeting took place at the Hollybrook hotel in Clontarf, north Dublin. When Timmons introduced Jock Haughey and Martin Casey to each other at the hotel, he did not use their real, or full, names. The meeting took place towards the end of October 1969. Following the meeting, Haughey agreed to go to London with Casey.

Later, Dick Walsh of *The Irish Times* published an article which detailed what transpired in London. His article was most likely based on information supplied to him by Martin Casey, or someone who learned about the event from Casey. Walsh reported that Timmons introduced Jock Haughey and Casey to each other as 'Pádraig Hoey and Casey as Martin'.[2]

Casey might have recognised Jock Haughey as he had been a member of the 1958 Dublin All Ireland winning GAA football team. Assuming he made the connection, it is safe to say that in normal circumstances, he would have distrusted Haughey. For a start, he was the brother of Charles, the minister who had helped bring the IRA's Border Campaign to an end in the early 1960s, and was perceived by people on the left, such as Casey, as a champion of capitalism and big business. But these were not normal circumstances and Casey and his colleagues were prepared to help Jock Haughey acquire weapons for the defence committees. At this juncture, some Fine Gael supporters were furnishing arms to the CDCs, while the gardaí were turning a blind eye to vehicles crossing the Border with guns.[3]

In his 1971 article, Dick Walsh wrote that:

> It seems likely, however improbable it sounds, that neither Haughey nor Casey knew each other at the time the deal was planned [in October 1969]. Casey was known to have been closely associated with Saor Éire activists. Haughey had obvious connections with Fianna Fáil. At best, they would have made uneasy partners.[4]

Jock Haughey must have concluded that the man introduced to him merely as 'Martin' was linked to a subversive organisation as the latter was involved in the purchase of arms. Haughey may have assumed he was in the IRA.

Casey had every reason to conceal his link to Saor Éire from Haughey. It was, after all, the organisation which had tried to burn down the HQ of Fianna Fáil in 1967. If Haughey somehow made the link to Saor Éire, he might simply have chosen to ignore it and got on with the task in hand, acquiring arms for the defence committees.

Casey took a ferry to London on 2 November 1969, while Haughey flew over and met him at the Marble Arch the following day. Dick Walsh described how the:

> two men met at midday at Marble Arch and went immediately to 299 Oxford Street. There Godfrey, smartly dressed and well-spoken, a man who considered himself immensely attractive to women, had an office beside a model academy and agency. His company he called the Savoy Finance Co.

> Haughey and Casey went in the creaking lift, past offices, another model agency and the workroom of a skirt manufacturer to the sixth floor. While they waited for Godfrey, they sat in the agency's changing room. Then Godfrey and Haughey were introduced— Godfrey as Jimmy, a name he frequently used, and Haughey as Paddy.[5]

Capt. Markham-Randall was not present but was available on the phone to discuss the price for the arms allegedly on sale. Haughey paid a deposit later that evening. Casey and Haughey stayed at the Irish Club on Eaton Square. Haughey signed in as 'George Dixon'. Casey used a pseudonym too. Walsh was able to report that they ate ham salad and beef and potatoes, a tiny detail that reinforces Casey, or someone close to him, as the source of Walsh's report.

Jock Haughey flew home from London to Dublin the next day.

Haughey arranged to return to London later in the month and met Markham-Randall in person. John Kelly from Belfast, a leading figure in the CCDC, joined him on the second trip.[6] Dick Walsh did not refer to the return journey in his *Irish Times* article, a fact that reinforces the probability that Martin Casey, or someone close to him, was the source of Walsh's article, as he only knew about the first outing. More importantly, it shows that Casey and his Saor Éire colleagues had dropped by the wayside after the first meeting in London. As far as Haughey was concerned, this was simply an attempt by the defence committees in Northern Ireland to acquire arms.

Crinnion's analysis of these events, however, produced a wholly different conclusion.

CRINNION LOSES THE PLOT

Patrick Crinnion concluded that Jock Haughey had become a Saor Éire godfather, and a collaborator in their arms smuggling efforts. He was encouraged in this thinking by MI6. Shortly thereafter, Crinnion started pressing these alarming views on his colleagues at C3 and the SDU. This was the root of the myth that ministers in Fianna Fáil such as Charles Haughey helped set up the Provisional IRA.

In one of his letters to Patrick Malone, Crinnion wrote:

> I am sure you recall how, acting on my own initiative, I prepared a report setting out my opinions and deductions about unlawful importations of firearms and Saor Éire involvement. A copy of this report is on the Markham-Randall file and also on 38/1941/55. I set out the facts about SAOR ÉIRE and showed that it was not the ramshackle organisation that we had been lulled into tolerating. I pointed out that Richard TIMMONS was acting as their Director of Finance and I advocated certain courses of Garda Action to thwart their activities. I still recall feeling pleased when you thanked me for my report and you called a conference of officers concerned and tried to implement some of my suggestions.[1]

John Wyman of MI6 and his colleagues at New Scotland Yard were clearly the originators of some of the information in the report coded '38/1941/55'. Crinnion added:

> It's a matter of history now that Markham-Randall was visited in London by three Irishmen who were secretly photographed by special branch, New Scotland Yard. Copies of the photographs were supplied to C3.

Crinnion proceeded to state that 'in the course the 3 were identified' as:

1. John KELLY

Director of Finance, Provisional IRA, 121 Anglesea Road, Ballsbridge, Dublin 4, and formerly of Adela St., Belfast.

2. Patrick ('Jock') HAUGHEY,

Accountant, Boland & Haughey, Accountants, Kildare Street, Dublin 2.

3. Martin CASEY,

Saor Éire, Ballymun,

(Casey was deputising for TIMMONS who as an escapee from a British prison was wary of being found within their jurisdiction).

... When I set out my belief about the importance of Timmons in the SAOR ÉIRE organisation he was genuinely being regarded as a non-entity. Even now I am not sure my authorities recognise that the vast bulk of money stolen by SAOR ÉIRE went to TIMMONS to be utilised to further the objects of the organisation.[2]

C3 showed G2 photographs of two of the three men who had gone to London to confer with Godfrey and Markham-Randall, namely Jock Haughey and John Kelly. These pictures were taken during Jock Haughey's second trip to London. The officer from G2 who examined the shots was Capt. Kelly. He described how, during a visit to the Phoenix Park, in February 1970:

... it was brought to my attention that a large file on the attempted arms sale had been sent to Garda Headquarters. I was given sight of the file which had a photograph of John Kelly and Paddy 'Dublin' [i.e. Jock Haughey] as some of the Belfast men referred to him, coming up the steps of the London tube station.

Obviously, the Irish police had been briefed on the affair by their British counterparts. Interestingly, while the Gardai recognised Paddy, they did not identify John Kelly. Presumably, neither did the British. Apart from filing the information, the security agencies here took no action on the matter, but the file confirmed that Markham-Randall was a British agent.[3]

Markham-Randall visited Dublin shortly after the second trip to London by Jock Haughey. While in Dublin, Markham-Randall all but admitted to John Kelly that he was a British spy.[4] In addition, he displayed a depth of knowledge about the ongoing arms importation operation by the defence committees. His information included the name of a secret bank account being used to finance the endeavour, that of the fictitious 'George Dixon' at the Munster and Leinster bank in Baggot Street.[5]

While in Dublin, Markham-Randall also met with two men from Saor Éire in the Shelbourne hotel, one of whom was Liam Walsh who developed the impression Markham-Randall was a spy and considered having him shot.[6]

Hyman Godfrey and Markham-Randall had obviously absorbed some of the details about the Baggot Street bank account from their meeting with Jock Haughey in London. They had discussed payment methods at the meeting which might have revealed the existence of the George Dixon account. New Scotland Yard would have discovered that Haughey had signed in to the Irish club as 'George Dixon'. Crinnion could have supplied some additional information.

Col Hefferon, the director of Irish military intelligence, G2, was ahead of the game. He concluded that Crinnion was the source of Markham-Randall's information.[7] Capt. Kelly of G2 described how:

One aspect of the [Markham-Randall] affair puzzled Colonel Hefferon. How could a British agent be so well acquainted with security details about members of the Irish Government and their attitude to the North, which could not and should not have been officially communicated to the British? For some time, he had a strong suspicion that there was a leak in C3, the security section of the Gardaí at their Dublin Phoenix Park Headquarters. As he saw it, the finger pointed at the chief clerk there, who 'was always creeping around the place, permitted to listen in to even the most confidential conversations and with apparent unrestricted access to information and files'. The Colonel had nothing concrete to back up his suspicion and as the Garda in question [i.e. Crinnion] was obviously a most trusted individual, probably the most trusted and best informed in Garda intelligence circles, there was little the Director of Military Intelligence could do about it. He would very quickly have been told to mind his own business.[8]

A small number of gardaí were uneasy about Crinnion too. One of them was Chief Superintendent Joe Ainsworth, who took over C3 in 1979 and launched a low-key probe into Crinnion's activities while a member of the unit. In the early 1970s, Ainsworth was assigned to work on a project which required him to base himself at C3's suite of offices. As part of his mysterious work, he maintained what Crinnion described as 'a secret file [which] he had locked in C3'. Crinnion was friendly and welcoming to Ainsworth, a little too friendly for the older man's taste. Crinnion repeatedly offered to tidy up his papers at the end of the day. Ainsworth declined, somewhat suspicious that Crinnion was being unduly inquisitive. Ainsworth's ultra-secret file may very well be the only one into which Crinnion failed to break.

As 1969 drew to a close, the strains within the IRA were reaching an almost intolerable level. A split now loomed on the horizon. Gazing from the distance, Crinnion understood little of what was taking place. Hoodwinked by Wyman, he believed that external forces were helping to engineer a fracture in Republicanism. In his mind, the agitators behind the intrigue included Saor Éire activists, treacherous Irish army officers and senior politicians in Fianna Fáil.

21

THE TRUTH ABOUT KNOCKVICAR

Gerry Callanan was known to many of his customers in Donnybrook, the prosperous suburb on the southside of Dublin, as Gerry 'Furlong', as he was the proprietor of Furlong's news agency. He also owned the nearby post office. One of his former customers recalled him fondly as a 'dapper boulevardier' who dressed in smart blazers and was a prominent member of the exclusive Fitzwilliam tennis club. He was an engaging character who would chat with anyone who strolled into his shop.[1]

Callanan was a lifelong friend of Seán MacBride, his son Tiernan and daughter Anna. MacBride served as chief-of-staff of the IRA, 1937–38, but abandoned armed struggle for constitutional politics. MacBride, a lawyer, set up Clann na Poblachta (Family of the Republic) after the Second World War. The new party drew support from people who were tired of the old Civil War politics and wanted to further social issues. It grew rapidly during 1947, attracting many Republicans.

Callanan was a senior activist in the party. He once stood for it at election time, albeit unsuccessfully. The Clann secured ten seats in the 1948 general election and went on to form part of the first interparty coalition government with Fine Gael and Labour, 1948–51, with John A. Costello of Fine Gael at the helm. McBride served as Minister for External Affairs. This was the high point for Clann na Poblachta. The party secured only two seats in the 1951 general election, and three in 1954.

The Clann maintained close links with Republicans in Northern Ireland who, unlike Sinn Féin, were not deterred by its participation in Dáil Éireann. The most prominent connection of this nature was one with Liam Kelly and his Fianna Uladh movement. The latter had a military wing called Saor Uladh. In 1954, the Clann made Liam Kelly's election to Seanad Éireann a condition for supporting Costello's return to power. On this occasion the Clann did not join the coalition parties in government, rather it offered them support from outside.[2]

The Clann supported the new arrangement until early in 1957, when MacBride set down a motion of no confidence in its economic policies. Many believed MacBride was really seething about the reintroduction of internment. In the debate that followed, Costello accused MacBride of gyrating.[3] The motion was passed. Clann na Poblachta secured only one seat in the general election that followed, with MacBride losing his place in the chamber. The Clann continued its decline and dissolved itself in 1965.

Having retired from politics, MacBride and other lawyers founded JUSTICE, a UK-based human-rights and law-reform organisation.[4] In 1961, MacBride co-founded Amnesty International, and served as its chairman until 1975. This brief résumé only touches upon MacBride's later achievements, all of which were very different from his days as IRA chief-of-staff. His work culminated in the award of the Nobel Peace Prize in 1974, when he was lauded as a man who 'mobilised the conscience of the world in the fight against injustice'.[5] He was also the winner of the Lenin Peace Prize.

MacBride's close friend, Gerry Callanan, shared his political views. Callanan had nothing to do with MacStíofáin and the group that later became the Provisional IRA. Gerry Callanan remained close to MacBride and his children after the demise of Clann na Poblachta. In 1963 or 1964, Callanan joined Fianna Fáil.

MacBride retained an interest in the Republican movement. It can safely be presumed that he supported Cathal Goulding's efforts to move the IRA along a similar political path to the one he had taken two decades earlier.

In 1969, Cathal Goulding and his colleagues were looking for a safe venue which could hold upwards of fifty delegates, for an Extraordinary Army Convention at which they hoped to embark on their new left-wing political venture. There were few locations more suitable for a secret meeting than Knockvicar House in Boyle, Co. Roscommon. Knockvicar village was a remote location. The mansion was located at the end of a laneway and not visible from the road off which the path peeled. The mansion was also inaccessible from the other side as it was surrounded by a river. Gerry Callanan owned the building. It was a 'clean' house as Callanan was not involved with the IRA.

A request for the use of Knockvicar House for a few weeks was relayed to Callanan by a friend of his called Anna Barron. It is likely Callanan consulted with MacBride. It is even possible that MacBride was behind the request.[6] In any event, Callanan agreed to relinquish the property for a few weeks. He was taken aback a short while later when a man he did not know came into the shop asking for the keys to the property. Callanan refused to give them to him but made arrangements to have them delivered to Barron.[7]

The property was out of his hands for longer than a few weeks, possibly even a few months. At some stage there was a discussion between Callanan and the gardaí from Donnybrook station as they knew what was going on at Knockvicar. They told Callanan not to go near the place and let them monitor it. Callanan soon realised that he too was under surveillance.

Maurice Oldfield and John Wyman later smeared Callanan

by claiming he, Haughey and Blaney organised the convention to split the IRA and create the Provisionals from those opposed to Goulding's reforms.

Wyman began to paint this preposterous picture in December 1969, by feeding Crinnion falsehoods about the IRA convention that took place at Knockvicar in December 1969.

The truth about Knockvicar is well known. The proceedings at the venue began late on 13 December 1969, and ran into the early hours of the following day. They were dominated by Cathal Goulding's supporters who wanted to implement a series of policy changes, including one to recognise the legitimacy of Dáil Éireann and Stormont. That meant relinquishing the hallowed tradition of parliamentary abstention. If the anti-abstention motion was carried, successful Sinn Féin electoral candidates would be allowed to take their seats in Dáil Éireann and at Stormont. Another initiative was that the Republican movement would become part of what Goulding called the National Liberation Front (NLF). The Communist Party of Ireland was prepared to join the NLF and it was hoped other organisations would sign up too. Goulding's proposals were opposed by traditionalists such as Ruairí Ó Brádaigh, Seán MacStíofáin and Dáithí Ó Conaill.

Crinnion's focus became fixed on Gerry Callanan, the owner of the property. Callanan was then an ordinary rank-and-file member of Fianna Fáil. Crinnion, however, made a meal out of this rather thin gruel. He decreed that 'senior personages in the Fianna Fáil party had literally stage-managed the IRA CONVENTION'.[8] The 'senior personages' he had in mind included Blaney and Haughey.

If one was to follow Crinnion's logic – something that is not recommended – it would mean that Blaney and Haughey were working hand-in-glove with Goulding as it was the latter's faction that 'stage-managed' the convention. Somehow, Wyman convinced Crinnion to reach the polar opposite conclusion, i.e., Blaney, Haughey and Callanan were colluding with the traditionalists who, far from dominating the proceedings, were outfoxed at it by Goulding's faction.

Crinnion asserted in his 1973 letter to Malone that:

> ... I find it necessary to begin back in December 1969 when I handed you a report (the original of which is filed on 30/44/69), which sets out the information I had obtained concerning the circumstances leading up to the IRA GENERAL ARMY CONVENTION of 1969. My report contained information previously unknown to the Garda Siochana, and which at that time seemed almost incredible, as it showed that senior personages in the Fianna Fáil party had literally stage-managed the IRA CONVENTION. I stated how a member of the Fianna Fáil Party had been approached in the party headquarters in Mount Street, Dublin, and requested to give the use of his large country mansion ('Knockvicar', Boyle Co. Roscommon), for use as the venue for the IRA CONVENTION. I set out the dates the house had been so used and that approximately sixty delegates attended. I need hardly remind you that this CONVENTION gave birth to the Provisional IRA and saw the emergence of Seán Mac STIOPHAIN as their Chief-of-Staff.[9]

MacStíofáin recalls the convention was held at 'an isolated country village' on 'a wet, dirty evening'. The proceedings began late that night.[10] Delegates from Clare, Tipperary and Limerick who supported abstentionism, including Paddy Mulcahy, a member of the IRA Army Council, were absent. They had been left stranded in Mullingar waiting for a lift that Séamus Costello was meant to have arranged for them.[11] Dáithí Ó Conaill, who was living in Co. Donegal at the time, and was in command of the Donegal IRA, did not attend either as he had been suspended for walking out of the Donegal unit convention.

He did so because a veteran IRA volunteer, Frank Morris, had not been allowed to attend the Donegal convention.[12] Belfast, which would have sided with the MacStíofáin faction, had decided not to send a delegate. On the other side of the debate, Co. Tyrone was over-represented by persons opposed to abstentionism.

MacStíofáin feared the proposals would 'reduce the IRA to a cog in a Marxist political machine'. He detected an unmistakable 'air of tension' when he reached the meeting:

> Men who were normally good-humoured appeared quiet and strained ... The place was well packed with delegates, and indeed 'packed' is the right word. The leadership had made an all-out effort to drum up maximum support. 'Have you left anyone behind at all?' I asked one of them.

He noticed that several delegates who supported the traditional line were missing, in particular a group from Munster which he had expected to see in attendance. 'It turned out that this was no accident. There were many other irregularities that made the convention unrepresentative of opinion in the Army as a whole.'

The disagreement was a longstanding one. The debate about the direction the IRA should be taking had been ongoing since Goulding had become chief-of-staff in 1962. MacStíofáin had opposed Goulding's initiative at Army Council meetings since 1966. MacStíofáin was dedicated to the achievement of a thirty-two-county republic by force and he was weary from the debate. It had become particularly intense in 1968 and 1969. On the night of the voting at Knockvicar, MacStíofáin said to himself: 'I can't go through another year of this bickering' and let the voting take place.[13] The notion that Gerry Callanan – who was in Dublin oblivious to all this – somehow engineered a split at Knockvicar is preposterous.

If anyone was 'stage-managing' what took place at Knock-vicar, it was Goulding and his associates. MacStíofáin believed that a two-thirds majority would be necessary for changes 'of such a sweeping nature'. After some debate the chairman ruled that a simple majority would be sufficient.[14]

The National Liberation Front was voted into existence. 'Now, to all intents and purposes, there was no longer an IRA. There was an NLF,' MacStíofáin wrote.[15]

The vote to permit participation in the parliaments at Dublin and Stormont was also passed, twenty-eight to twelve.

MacStíofáin's group stayed to the end of the convention. 'Goulding himself showed no hostility,' MacStíofáin wrote. After the convention he asked him what he planned to do in the coming year. MacStíofáin believed he 'knew well enough, but I wasn't forthcoming'. Goulding said that he hoped 'you'll have a talk with me before you do anything'. But for MacStíofáin, 'it was too late for that'.[16] The traditionalists went away and held their own convention. When Dáithí Ó Conaill, then aged thirty-one, rang Ruairí Ó Brádaigh to ask what would happen at it Ó Brádaigh told him, tongue in cheek, that the 'minority is going to expel the majority'.[17] The dissident convention went ahead and the traditionalists set up a seven-man Provisional IRA Army Council. The inaugural meeting consisted of Ó Brádaigh, Patrick Mulcahy, MacStíofáin, Ó Conaill, Joe Cahill, Seán Tracey and Leo Martin.

Crinnion's peculiar take on Knockvicar was that it demon-strated 'Fianna Fáil support and guidance for the IRA faction which emerged as the PROVOS'. In other words, Callanan, Haughey and Blaney were midwives to the birth of the Pro-visionals. According to MI6, these men organised the convention at Knockvicar and split an otherwise unified IRA. Without them, MI6 would have us believe, the IRA would have trundled on under a unified command as before. Crinnion was feeding even more extreme nonsense to Malone. In his May 1973 letter to Patrick Malone, Crinnion alluded to this information:

> My informant [i.e. Wyman] gave me additional information beyond that typed in my report and I discussed the matter with you in your office. Although we were astounded by the implications of my information it was, sadly, only too true and was all confirmed by subsequent events. That short factual report which I handed you that day was a keystone in later police action which was critical to the peace and well-being of the State. It was the first factual report which gave an insight into the extent of Fianna Fáil support and guidance for the IRA faction which emerged as the PROVOS.[18]

The 'subsequent events' Crinnion referred to in his letter to Malone were those associated with the Arms Crisis during which Charles Haughey and Neil Blaney were accused of attempting to import guns illegally. Clearly, Crinnion had no grip on the fact that the arms were being sought by the defence committees which represented the wider Nationalist community, and they were not a front for the traditional faction of the IRA that transformed into the Provisionals in 1970.

In the final analysis, the only connection that Crinnion cites between Fianna Fáil and the Knockvicar convention is that of Gerry Callanan who was merely involved at a local branch level in the constituency of Dublin South (now Dublin Bay). Callanan, a fascinating character, died in 2011.[19]

22

THE RISE OF THE PROVISIONALS

After the split, the leadership of the Provisional IRA decided to give themselves a year to prepare their new organisation before launching a fresh military offensive to end partition. They decided they would start by defending Nationalist communities in Northern Ireland, then retaliate for attacks on those they were protecting and, eventually, go on the offensive.

It was an open question whether they would be able to garner the type of support necessary to sustain their anticipated onslaught. One of the reasons the Border Campaign, 1952–62, had collapsed was because it failed to attract an appreciable level of support from the Nationalist population of the island. The Nationalists in the Catholic enclaves in Belfast, Derry and elsewhere had rallied around the citizens defence committees in 1969 but that was because they were frantic for protection, not more violence. The defence committees did not come into existence to pursue a military offensive against Stormont and London.

Tim Pat Coogan, author and an authority on the IRA, recalls how he met:

> an IRA friend who had been picking up the threads of his family and business life but now appeared to be going downhill again through becoming involved in [Provisional] IRA activities. As he told me both of his hardships in the past and what he was doing at that time, I remember saying to him: 'Eamon, you are mad! You have done your bit for the cause and now you risk wrecking your own happiness and everyone else's to join a splinter of a splinter group.' For that was how most people in Southern Ireland would certainly have described the IRA in the early part of 1970; but as

it happened I was both completely right and totally wrong. My friend did undergo terrible traumas but the IRA blossomed into one of the major guerrilla organisations to emerge since World War II.[1]

Figures in Saor Éire stepped forward to lend a hand to the fledgling Provisionals. In January 1970, MacStíofáin met its leaders in the home of Joe Clarke, a veteran of the 1916 Rising. Clarke was one of the major figures to support the traditional line on abstention. He and Ó Brádaigh had led the walk-out from the Sinn Féin Ard Fheis in January 1970 that resulted in the formation of Provisional Sinn Féin. He had served as a vice-president of the pre-split Sinn Féin and now occupied the same position in Provisional Sinn Féin.[2] There was a discussion of a merger of Saor Éire and the Provisional IRA at Clarke's house but it did not come to fruition. MacStíofáin, however, did not go away empty handed. He was promised 7,000 rounds of ammunition – he received 30,000 rounds, a heavy Vickers machine gun, a medium-wave radio transmitter and other military equipment.[3] They also donated the proceeds of armed robberies.

Jimmy Roe, quartermaster of the 1st battalion of the Provisional IRA Belfast brigade, confirmed that the Provisionals received arms and equipment from Saor Éire.[4] In spy parlance, Saor Éire gave MacStíofáin and the Provisional IRA 'plausible deniability', i.e., Saor Éire would be condemned for the armed robberies, while, secretly, some of the proceeds went, blame free, to the Provisionals.

In 1973, Crinnion described Saor Éire as the 'Financial agents [of the Provisionals] in the Republic so as not to incur the disapproval of the State against the Provos'.[5] This, he felt, preserved the 'immunity' MacStíofáin enjoyed from garda interference. The level of that 'immunity' was described by Crinnion as registering 'at a reasonable level'.[6] Bishop and Mallie, experts on the emergence of the Provisionals, lend credence to Crinnion's claim that Saor Éire gave the Provisionals funds in 1970.[7]

Seán MacStíofáin did not tell Philip McMahon about his dealings with Saor Éire. Hence, he managed to acquire funds for the new body behind his hapless handler's back.

Peter Graham, aged twenty-six, was one of the links between Saor Éire and the IRA. Graham was tortured and killed in a flat at which he was staying on Stephen's Green in Dublin in October 1971. He was beaten with a hammer and shot in the neck. His killers left him to choke on his own blood.

According to Seán Boyne:

> After Graham's funeral, the Provisional IRA issued a statement which spoke of the dead man in eulogistic terms, and said that his 'death had come as a severe blow to the national resurgence'. The statement said that Peter Graham was 'instrumental in providing aid of all forms to the besieged people of the North'. [The aid included] 'funds expropriated in bank raids'.

> A former Saor Éire member, whom I shall call Mr A, gave the impression in an interview in February 2005 that it was more than just 'some weapons' that were supplied. He said the main purpose of the bank raids was to finance the purchase of arms for political purposes, and that after the Troubles broke out in 1969, it was decided that arms would be sent to Belfast and Derry.[8]

During his inquiries into Graham's death, Boyne spoke to a man who had been a close friend and political colleague of Graham who told him that he believed:

> two members of Saor Éire were involved in the killing. The source said that Graham had been involved in channelling funds from Saor Éire bank robberies to republicans in the North who emerged as the Provisional IRA. There was speculation that some of this money was earmarked for buying arms. The source alleged

that two of the more opportunistic elements in Saor Éire were demanding 'legitimate expenses', and a bitter dispute arose which culminated in the fatal shooting when the two men went to confront Graham.

Mr A said members of the group considered taking revenge against the two Saor Éire 'renegades' who allegedly attacked Graham, but decided against it as it would have led to internecine violence, as later happened with the Irish National Liberation Army (INLA), many of whose members died through internal feuds. He said that he believes the dispute which ended the life of Peter Graham was over the control of arms caches, rather than money ...[9]

There were conflicting rumours about the motive for the killing. Detective Sergeant Hugh McNeilis of the SDU, who participated in the 'handling' of MacStíofáin in the 1970s, believed the SDU had a hold over MacStíofáin because they possessed information about his involvement in the killing of a member of Saor Éire. McNeilis must have heard the various accounts of Graham's death which were in circulation, and latched onto one that implicated MacStíofáin. Clearly, McNeilis was not aware that MacStíofáin had been recruited in 1961.

23

MI6's Debt to Saor Éire

The activities of Saor Éire turned a lot of public opinion against Republicanism, a propaganda windfall for Maurice Oldfield of MI6.

The low point of Saor Éire's existence was reached on 3 April 1970, when a gang of three armed Saor Éire bank robbers burst into the Royal Bank of Ireland on Dublin's quays while a fourth member, a driver, waited for them outside in a gold Ford Cortina. At 10.40 a.m., a trio of unarmed gardaí, Richard Fallon, Paul Firth and Patrick Hunter, of 'D' district in Dublin city were on patrol in a garda car. They were contacted by radio and told to go to the bank. Without hesitation, Fallon, who had finished his shift, volunteered to remain on duty and assist his colleagues. Garda Hunter, the driver of the garda car, raced towards the bank. As they arrived, the raiders, all armed with pistols, were making their escape through the front door. Fallon and Firth confronted them along a narrow passageway at the side of the bank only to face into a hail of bullets. Ignoring the shots tearing at him, Fallon ran forward to grab one of the gang. One bullet tore into the left side of his neck, travelled in an upward direction, and severed his spinal-cord, finally exiting from the point adjacent to his right ear. Another bullet, struck the back of his left shoulder and travelled down his arm shattering the bone. He died almost instantly.

The fatal shot was fired from a Star pistol, one of those smuggled from Birmingham. In 2007, Michael McDowell, then Minister for Justice, stated that 'the gardai were aware of the source of the firearms in question … Low-life Dublin gangland people who sourced the weapons in Birmingham'.[1]

Fallon's father later described him as 'fearless'. Fallon was not afforded a state funeral but the nation gave him a *de facto* one nonetheless. Dublin came to a standstill while a procession of 1,000 gardaí accompanied the fallen man's hearse. He was posthumously awarded the Garda Síochána's Scott Medal for heroism in the line of duty.

John Kelly of the CDC and IRA said: 'The killing of Garda Fallon could not have come at a worse time. Saor Éire was out of control, I don't know what they were at, but they certainly were not helping matters.'[2]

Saor Éire later issued a grotesquely crass public statement: 'We deny that Garda Fallon was killed, as the Government and the anti-socialist press suggest, in the course of protecting the public. He died protecting the property of the ruling class, who are too cowardly and clever to do their own dirty work.' If Oldfield had penned the press release himself, he could not have more inflamed the anger of the Irish public against Republicans.

The confrontational and insensitive language of the press release achieved precisely the type of reaction among the Irish public that Maurice Oldfield would later attempt to stimulate in 1972. During that year he and Wyman would direct the criminal activities of Kenneth and Keith Littlejohn, two British bank robbers. They raided banks while masquerading as Republicans, aided and abetted by paramilitaries who had been attached to the Official IRA.

Craig Smellie, the MI6 head of station at Lisburn, 1973–75, asked Fred Holroyd later to rob banks with the same aim in mind. Smellie was a Scottish kilt-wearing MI6 veteran, described by MI6 expert, the late Anthony Verrier, as a 'very large, pipe-smoking Arabist, a veteran of Suez and the Sudan'.[3] Holroyd, an honourable man, declined the sordid mission.

The Star pistols that the Dublin criminal, and others, smuggled from Birmingham reached Ireland, in relays, in late 1969. MI6 had been circling Saor Éire since at least October 1969, when Godfrey and Markham-Randall had begun to talk to Frank Keane. Crinnion claimed in one of his letters to Malone that he had been 'too late to prevent [the] unlawful importations of firearms' by the Dublin criminal, but we cannot take this statement at face value for Crinnion was a puppet of Oldfield, not his partner and confidant.[4] Some of the pistols might have been allowed filter through the criminal's pipeline to Ireland even after the scam at the Parker-Hale factory in Birmingham had been uncovered.

A number of ugly questions arise from these events. Did Oldfield and New Scotland Yard let some of the Star pistols reach Ireland so they could trace and monitor those involved in the smuggling network and the members of Saor Éire to whom they were distributed?

Why was the Dublin criminal not arrested while on his trips to Britain? Again, it is likely MI6 was watching him from a discreet distance to see what they might learn about his contacts.

Markham-Randall certainly tried to infiltrate the IRA with the promise of cheap arms. When he visited Dublin in November 1969, he told John Kelly that he was an expert in guerrilla tactics and had completed many courses in counter-revolutionary warfare. 'I could be a big help to you people,' he declared. 'If I visited one or other of your training camps, I would be very useful: small arms, fire and movement, tactics and that sort of thing.'[5] Had Markham-Randall succeeded in gaining access to the camps he assumed had sprung up, he would have been able to ascertain the identities of those attending them.

What about the weapons at the factory in Eltham? They included Sten guns, self-loading rifles and Browning machine guns. Did MI6 sell any of the weapon at Eltham to their contacts in Saor Éire? Recall that after the Provisional IRA was set up in early 1970, Saor Éire was able to provide MacStíofáin with 30,000 rounds of ammunition, a heavy Vickers machine gun, a medium-wave radio transmitter and other military equipment.

By not stamping down on Saor Éire in Britain, Markham-Randall's cover was preserved and he was able to meet Saor Éire members such as Liam Walsh when he visited Dublin in November 1969, albeit they were suspicious of him.

It is inconceivable that Oldfield did not attempt to recruit agents in Saor Éire through his usual methods: bribery, coercion and blackmail. The SDU had managed to penetrate Saor Éire, so why not MI6? According to one ex-SDU officer, Saor Éire were 'a rabble, a gang of low life criminals. They stole money from banks in the name of Republicanism yet when we raided their flats, we always found them stuffed with fashionable clothes and televisions and things that were very expensive at the time. And these guys were meant to be unemployed.'[6]

Saor Éire was certainly fearful of infiltration by the police and had moved from 'conventional battalion structures into a cell system, each section consisting of five members'.[7] Nonetheless, the organisation was breached. One Saor Éire member was a pederast and was recruited by the gardaí after they found him in bed with an underage male in a flat on Leeson Street, on the southside of the city.[8]

Liz Walsh has described how there 'is little doubt that an informer [in Saor Éire] had been passing high-grade information to the authorities [in Ireland], and they were anxious that he should not be exposed, a fact referred to by the Taoiseach, Jack Lynch, after the murder' of Garda Fallon.[9]

The activities of Saor Éire became so unbearable that Lynch and O'Malley made preparations to introduce internment, i.e., detention without due process, in December 1970. Peter Berry recorded in his diaries that:[10]

Early in November 1970 there was reliable, highly confidential, police information that a hard core of 15 members of Saor Éire, who had already carried out murder and armed robberies, of banks, were plotting to kidnap two persons, of whom I was one, to hold as hostage against the safety of Frank Keane who was awaiting extradition from London for the murder of Garda Fallon.[11]

Des O'Malley's recollection of this event was as follows:

We made it clear to those involved in the kidnap plot that, unless the Government was satisfied that the threat was removed, internment would be introduced. Places of detention were identified. We were determined to act, and those concerned had a final opportunity of drawing back and obviating the need for internment … There was considerable criticism when news of the possible introduction of internment was made public. There was noisy debate in the Dáil, and more than a thousand people protested at the gates of Leinster House.

[The Provisional IRA] were afraid, of course, that internment would apply to them, and they leaned on Saor Éire to desist from certain activities in the South. In that way the Government's actions worked and it was not necessary to introduce internment, which in any event would have been confined to members of Saor Éire.[12]

All this was a far cry from earlier in the year when members of Saor Éire had discussed a possible merger with MacStiofáin at Joe Clarke's house.

In August 1971, London gave the Faulkner government in Belfast the green light to introduce internment in Northern Ireland. Lynch and his party were unhappy about this but had to mute their criticism as they had so recently considered implementing the same strategy to deal with Saor Éire. Yet again, Oldfield benefited from Saor Éire's provocative behaviour.

Saor Éire became the gift that kept on giving to MI6. Oldfield would exploit the Garda Fallon killing for propaganda purposes, a ploy directed at the Haughey brothers, as will become apparent in later chapters.

In one of his letters to Patrick Malone, Crinnion expressed the hope that it did not read 'like the work of a braggart'.[13] This fleeting glimpse of self-awareness does not detract from the fact that his overarching opinion of himself was that he was 'not just first class but exceptional'. This exceptionalism, however, was not sufficient to deter him from covering up a 'clerical error' that he believed led to the death of Garda Fallon.

24

ONE OF CRINNION'S DARKEST SECRETS

Saor Éire carried out robberies in Tallaght, Co. Dublin; Blessington and Baltinglass, Co. Wicklow; Newbridge, Co. Kildare; Kells, Co. Meath; and Rathdrum in the Wicklow mountains, before the killing of Garda Richard Fallon.

According to one of Crinnion's 1973 memoranda concerning the fatal shooting of Garda Fallon, the fingerprints of:

> Patrick Francis Keane, Saor Éire, 2 North Road, Finglas, Dublin, were [found] on a newspaper left behind in the getaway car and at that time he was the leader of Saor Éire.

The gardaí sought out Keane but he fled to London within days of the robbery. He was arrested by the British police and spent a year behind bars in Brixton prison fighting an application for his extradition. Cathal Goulding swore an affidavit which he sent to London to support Keane's claim that his activities had been political in nature, not criminal. Goulding pointed out he had been dismissed from the IRA over 'policy disagreements'.

Keane fought the request for extradition all the way to the House of Lords. He was unsuccessful and was returned to Dublin to face the charge that he had been part of the gang that killed Fallon. Seán MacBride, SC, represented him in his defence. The trial took place in June 1971. Detective Sergeant Edward McGonagle testified that the gardaí had retrieved Keane's fingerprints from a copy of the *Evening Herald* newspaper found in the gold Cortina used by the raiders.[1] Evidence was also provided by a series of witnesses that all the raiders had covered their faces. The one exception to this was a garda officer who said he had seen Keane's face. The jury was not persuaded by the prosecution's evidence and acquitted Keane on 25 June.

The public had no hint of a disreputable occurrence which had taken place behind closed doors at Dublin Castle while Keane had been on the run. After the Fallon killing, a massive garda hunt had been launched to find Keane and other members of Saor Éire. 'I devoted many, many evenings after work looking for the Saor Éire gang', Crinnion wrote later in one of his 1973 memoranda. Upset at the lack of success in finding Keane, Crinnion dropped into Dublin Castle 'a few days after the murder' where he spoke to Chief Superintendent John Fleming, the head of the SDU, in his office. He wanted:

> to ask [Fleming] to do me a favour. I wanted Garda [Joseph] Arrigan, of Rathdrum Station transferred temporarily to Dublin Castle as he had been held at gunpoint [in his car] during the massive armed holdup carried out by Saor Éire, in Rathdrum, Co. Wicklow, prior to the holdup in which Garda Fallon was shot and Arrigan had identified one of the two men who held him at gunpoint as Patrick Keane, Saor Éire. I greeted Super Fleming and asked him to bring Arrigan up for a few days as I wanted him to accompany me to a few Saor Éire hideouts. Although I knew some of the men on sight I never had seen Keane and was afraid I might pass him and not recognise him.

At various times, Saor Éire had hideouts in Wicklow and Dublin. One refuge was a cottage in a cul-de-sac on the Lacken to Valleymount road in Wicklow. Another was on Bayside Boulevard, North Dublin.

Crinnion did not state how he knew where the Saor Éire 'hideouts' he had in mind in April 1970 were located, nor who told him where to find them. The 'hideouts' were obviously 'safe houses' or flats. Crinnion can only have known about them from one of two sources: either John Wyman or SDU reports.

If Crinnion knew about the 'hideouts' from SDU reports, the properties would have been under intensive around-the-clock surveillance by his colleagues from Dublin Castle who not only knew what Frank Keane looked like but had published photographs of him and other members of Saor Éire. In this scenario it would have been pointless for Crinnion to have monitored the properties, whether on his own or with Garda Arrigan. There were, after all, approximately 6,000 gardaí who were already involved in the manhunt for Keane and six other Saor Éire members wanted for questioning.

It is fair then to ask whether Crinnion was given the addresses by Wyman who, in turn, had obtained the information from an informer or informers inside Saor Éire. It was not until 29 April 1970 that the SDU discovered the training camp at Lacken at which they recovered firearms, detonators, combat uniforms and other military equipment.

Crinnion was surprised when John Fleming did not warm to his request to bring Garda Arrigan to Dublin. 'Why go through all this trouble bringing Arrigan up, sure one of my fellows would do just as well,' he said. Crinnion fought his corner arguing that, 'Arrigan was the last man to see Keane and positively identify him because of the circumstances he is unlikely to have forgotten him'.

Fleming then disclosed, 'My lads have seen him a score of times since the Rathdrum raid' of February 1970. Crinnion realised that they should have arrested him on sight to help with their Rathdrum enquiries. Acting on the assumption Keane was involved in the bank raid in Dublin that led to the killing of Garda Fallon, he concluded that if they had done so, Garda Fallon's death might have been avoided. 'We then discussed this as this was the sort of thing which' might result in 'an enquiry, a panic, [a] drawing off [of] men badly needed in the murder hunt'.

A significant problem for C3 was that the department had reports 'dealing with the Rathdrum raid' and 'Keane was positively identified [in them] by Garda Arrigan'. The report had not been circulated to the SDU or the Central Detective Unit (CDU). Crinnion stressed:

> even the newspapers were publishing bits about the friction between the men engaged on the Fallon murder investigation. The two major detective units concerned were based in Dublin Castle (1) SDU (Special Detective Unit) and CDU (Central Detective Unit). SDU is what people call special branch and CDU would be known as CID in Britain. Both Fleming and I were conscious that if CDU and the uniform branch learned that SDU [had been] tipping their hats to Frank Keane [before 3 April, 1970], while the rest of the 6000 men in the force was [now] looking for him, that the morale of the SDU would have disintegrated.

What now troubled Crinnion was that, 'C3 was the co-ordinating office (the counter subversive control centre)' and 'as a first step [the] person dealing with the file should have sent a copy to the area where the named suspect resided.' Keane lived in Finglas and he might have been picked up for the Rathdrum raid by the local gardaí, but was not.

Crinnion proposed to cover C3's tracks by giving Fleming a file to put on record at Dublin Castle, as if it had been there since it came into being. 'I asked Chief Super Fleming to say absolutely nothing, because this discovery would have split the force and caused bad feeling at a time when morale was none too good.' He returned to C3 where he 'took a copy of the offending report off the file [about Rathdrum] and I recall underlining the identification [of Keane] or writing a marginal note on the copy of the report. I then brought this report down to the Castle and handed it to Chief Super Fleming to put on a file.' From that point on, Fleming could pretend that he had a copy of the identification of Keane all along and all that was left to do was to make sure his SDU men did not let it slip they had been 'tipping their hats' to him before the Fallon shooting.

This was a coup for Crinnion. C3 had made the mistake, by failing to report the details of Rathdrum to the SDU. Yet, the SDU was now covering up the error and, to boot, if ever questioned, would look incompetent for not lifting Keane before the Garda Fallon killing.

A lot of the steam went out of this issue after Keane was found not guilty by the jury at his trial but Crinnion's deception took place before that finding – at a time when Crinnion believed Keane would be found guilty.

Having concealed C3's 'clerical error' relating to Keane with such cynicism, Crinnion jumped back on his high horse and set out to unravel a cover-up Jack Lynch was perpetrating on a separate front.

25

THE CAT JUMPS OUT OF THE BAG

The defence committees expended a lot of energy in the last quarter of 1969, in various attempts to acquire arms, but without success. In January 1970, they asked G2 to take over the endeavour. James Gibbons gave this the green light. Capt. Kelly of G2 assumed control of the operation. Capt. Kelly's initial plan was to purchase weapons which were to be stored in Kilnacrott Abbey in Co. Cavan. This would give Jack Lynch and his ministers the option to distribute them to vulnerable Nationalists in Northern Ireland in the event of a 'doomsday' situation. Contrary to the disinformation MI6 circulated later, Gibbons, Blaney, Haughey and G2 were not involved in a plot to split the IRA, create the Provisionals and provide the latter with arms.

In a wholly separate development, in early 1970, after the IRA split, Dáithí Ó Conaill went to New York in his new role as a member of the Provisional IRA Army Council, with special responsibility for arms' procurement. He had a lengthy meeting with George Harrison and Thomas Falvey at the Horn and Hardart Automat near Columbus Circle in Manhattan, where they revived an old arms' smuggling conduit, using tried and trusted volunteers from the 1950s.[1] None of this critical information was relayed by MacStíofáin to McMahon.

In March 1970, Capt. Kelly of G2 believed he had succeeded in organising a shipment of guns to Dublin Port onboard the *MV City of Dublin*. The vessel sailed to Dublin from Antwerp but without the arms. Otto Schlueter, the German arms dealer, who was selling the weapons, had not arranged the required 'end user certificate'. This was not a mistake. Schlueter was helping MI6. Capt. Kelly and the defence committees had no inkling of Schlueter's betrayal. In the 1950s, Schlueter had supplied weapons to the National Liberation Front (NLF) during the Algerian war of independence, something which had drawn down upon him the wrath of the French Secret Service. French agents masquerading as 'La Main Rouge', were assassinating NLF suppliers. Schlueter was put on their death list.[2] On 28 September 1956, French assassins bombed his Hamburg office killing his deputy, a Mr Lorenzi. On 3 June, Schlueter's mother perished when a French bomb exploded in her car.[3] Schlueter, having learned his lesson from the French, was not going to cross MI6. Furthermore, he was obliged to report all arms sales to German intelligence. German intelligence and MI6 were NATO partners and the information would have been shared as a matter of routine.

Capt. Kelly was the victim of another betrayal, this one closer to home. If the arms had been onboard the ship, they would have been hijacked by a group of men sent by MacStíofáin to confiscate them. The four-man Provisional IRA unit MacStíofáin dispatched to hijack the cargo consisted of Billy Kelly, Paddy O'Kane, Michael Kane and Harry Canavan. Billy Kelly was the brother of John Kelly.[4]

MacStíofáin knew about the shipment from John Kelly. MacStíofáin told Justin O'Brien that:

John [Kelly] came to me a few days before Christmas [1969] ... and told me about the arrangements made to bring in arms, and he told me that 'once they come in, I will give them to you.' I said, 'John, I do not want any details. Give me a report now and again through your brother [Billy]. Just give me a list of the weapons you ordered.'[5]

MacStíofáin told an RTÉ interviewer that: 'There was a unit of IRA volunteers from Northern Ireland standing by to take the guns and put them into IRA camps. Certainly, the IRA was going to take the guns for itself.'[6]

John Kelly described the official plan involving Capt. Kelly, and the hijack operation involving the IRA thus: 'We had men in trucks waiting to pick them up under the supervision of [Capt. James] Kelly. They were to be taken to a designated location near the Border for distribution if a doomsday situation developed. There were other plans by Republicans to take the guns directly into the North.'[7]

But there were no weapons on the ship. If, as Crinnion and others have suggested, the arms were destined for the Provisionals, why did MacStíofáin have to send his men to hijack the consignment? The simple truth is that Capt. Kelly's plan for the weapons, had they arrived, was to store them pending the eruption – if ever – of a 'doomsday' situation in Northern Ireland.

Some of Lynch's ministers complained subsequently that the failed importation was illegal because it had not been put to a vote at government level. Cabinet approval, however, is not required for this sort of an operation. Minister James Gibbons had the legal authority to import arms by virtue of his office. Gibbons did not need to consult his colleagues. The ministers would have been consulted at a later stage before any distribution of the arms to the defence committees.

In April 1970, Capt. Kelly renewed his efforts. This time he made arrangements to fly the arms from Vienna to Dublin Airport. Before the flight had a chance to take off, the SDU surrounded Dublin Airport. Brian Lenihan, the Minister for Transport, was informed of the development and rang Col Hefferon, the Director of G2, and the importation was cancelled.

The gardaí knew about the flight for at least three reasons.

First, officials at the airport realised that something suspicious was happening and alerted the authorities.

Second, MacStíofáin told Philip McMahon about it.[8] No doubt he added that the guns were destined for Goulding. After all, MacStíofáin had sought to deceive McMahon the previous October by falsely claiming that Capt. Kelly had given £50,000 to Goulding. The tipoff about the Vienna flight enhanced MacStíofáin's reputation as the SDU's golden intelligence goose while creating havoc for Fianna Fáil, the party he despised, as a bonus. By April 1970, the Provisionals had begun to land high-quality weapons from America and had no pressing need to hijack Schlueter's arms.

Third, MI6 knew about the flight from Schlueter, and passed the information about it to Dublin. One of the remaining secrets of the Arms Crisis is whether MI6 alerted Crinnion covertly, or told the gardaí through official channels, about the flight. The SDU Arms Crisis file – which remains classified – may very well contain the information necessary to answer that question. It is clear, however, even without the benefit of that SDU file, that Wyman sometimes furnished information directly to Crinnion, e.g., when he provided him with his version of what had transpired at Knockvicar, and, as shall be shown in a later chapter, information about Rita O'Hare, a Republican from Belfast who had moved to Dublin. Hence, it is quite likely that Crinnion was told about the Vienna flight and passed the information to his superior, Patrick Malone.

On 20 April 1970, Peter Berry, the secretary to the department of justice, waited outside Jack Lynch's office while a meeting between Lynch and the British ambassador, John Peck, proceeded. When he gained entry, Berry informed Lynch that an attempt had taken place a few days earlier to import the arms from Vienna through Dublin Airport. He identified Blaney and Haughey as the driving force behind the initiative. Lynch pretended he knew nothing of the endeavour and set about covering up the affair. In his book on the Arms Crisis, Michael Heney describes thirty-three lies which Lynch produced during this period. I was able to add a few more in my book which appeared six months after Heney's opus.[9]

Lynch might have wrestled the Arms Crisis genie back into the bottle but for an incendiary note, on headed garda notepaper, which was passed to Liam Cosgrave in early May. Cosgrave was leader of Fine Gael, then in opposition. The note disclosed:

> A plot to bring in arms from Germany worth £80,000 for the North under the guise of the Dept of Defence has been discovered. Those involved are – Captain James Kelly, I.O,[10] Col Hefferon X Director of Intelligence[11] (both held over the weekend in the Bridewell) Gibbons, Haughey, Blaney, and the Jones Brothers of Rathmines Road and Rosapena Hotel, Donegal.[12]
>
> SEE THAT THIS SCANDAL IS NOT HUSHED UP.
>
> GARDA

Cosgrave was sceptical at first about the message and passed it to Ned Murphy, a trusted friend with a military intelligence background.[13] Murphy was now working as the political correspondent of *The Sunday Independent*. He was unable to throw any light on the veracity of the content of the document. The newspaper did not proceed with a report either, and the sheet was returned to Cosgrave.

At some stage Cosgrave spoke to Philip McMahon about the importation attempt. Conor Brady, the former editor of *The Irish Times*, and the author of books on the gardaí, wrote in 2004 that, 'A Special Branch report had McMahon visiting

Cosgrave's home at Rathfarnham in the days leading up to the crisis'. Brady cites an 'author interview with former SDU Detective' as his source for this revelation.[14]

Cosgrave's discussion with McMahon was separate to, and distinct from, his receipt of the 'GARDA' note.

In terms of chronology, it is likely that Cosgrave had possession of the note before he spoke to McMahon. Cosgrave would hardly have doubted its veracity if he had spoken to McMahon first.

On Tuesday, 5 May 1970, Jack Lynch informed the Dáil that Mícheál Ó Moráin, the Minister for Justice, was resigning on grounds of ill health. When Liam Cosgrave asked him whether this would be the only ministerial resignation the House could expect, Lynch replied, 'I don't know what the Deputy is referring to'. It is impossible to believe that Lynch did not know full well to what Cosgrave was alluding. It follows that this was nothing more than an attempt to obfuscate while addressing the Dáil.

Cosgrave responded, 'Is it only the tip of the iceberg?' Cosgrave was then invited by Lynch to enlarge on what was on his mind but he declined.

According to author Stephen Collins, Cosgrave:

> received two tip-offs about the plot to import arms in the days before the news broke on an unsuspecting public. The first came directly from the retired detective Phil McMahon, who played a central role in foiling the arms plot. He was perturbed that Lynch appeared to be taking no action and decided to intervene himself by informing Cosgrave. The second tip-off to the Fine Gael leader came by way of an anonymous note written on Garda headed notepaper.[15]

Collins obtained this information from what he describes as a 'private' source.[16]

There is further confirmation that Cosgrave had two fonts of information. Garret FitzGerald recalls in his memoirs, that on the evening of 5 May:

> I went into Cosgrave's office shortly before 8 o'clock to find a number of members of the front bench talking with him in grave tones. The discussion was clearly confidential; I left them to it. Much later I learned that Cosgrave had been consulting the people present about *two separate reports* [my emphasis] he had received of a plot to import arms for the IRA, which allegedly involved Government Ministers. Fearing that these reports might have been a trap, he hesitated to take action, but Mark Clinton said he should present the information to the Taoiseach. He agreed, returning an hour later to tell his colleagues, 'It's all true'.[17]

When Cosgrave confronted Lynch, he told him that it had come to his attention that some of his ministers were involved in an attempt to bring in arms for Northern Ireland. In the Dáil, Lynch described how Cosgrave 'showed me a document but I will not even tell the House what that document was like because there has been some comment as to whether the information was on headed [garda] paper. I will leave it to Deputy Cosgrave, if he feels like it, to do so.'

The cat was now out of the bag. Within days, Haughey and Blaney were dismissed with another minister, Kevin Boland, resigning in protest at Lynch's actions. Paudge Brennan, a parliamentary secretary, also resigned.[18] Capt. Kelly, Haughey, Blaney and others were arrested later.

Lynch instructed James Gibbons to deny his role in the affair – and therefore that of Lynch too – in the best interests of the Fianna Fáil party. Gibbons went along with the deception. One of the best kept secrets of the Arms Crisis, concealed from the public since 1970, is the name of the author of the 'GARDA' note.

26

THE MIDNIGHT POSTMAN

Liam Cosgrave, the leader of Fine Gael, spent most of his life living at Beech Park, a bungalow located at the end of a private laneway off the Scholarstown Road, Templeogue in south Co. Dublin. A house had stood on the lands there until 1923 when it was burned to the ground during the Civil War. Cosgrave's grandfather, Alderman Michael Flanagan, a successful market-gardener, had purchased the property for Cosgrave's mother. The bungalow was built on the site to replace the burned-out shell. Cosgrave was an intensely private man. He never gave his home phone number to a single one of the ministers in his government from 1973 to 1977. He frequently went home to Beech Park for his lunch, even while running the country.

In 1970, a lone figure made his way up the lane and dropped the 'GARDA' note through Cosgrave's letterbox and left as silently as he had come. The contention of this chapter is that Crinnion was the midnight postman. The note was written on headed garda notepaper. It was delivered after it had become clear to the DoJ that Jack Lynch was intent upon covering up the existence of the importation attempt. On Thursday, 30 April 1970, Jack Lynch had sent for Peter Berry. Lynch told Berry that he had seen:

> Mr Blaney and Mr Haughey and that the matter was ended, that there would be no repetition [of attempts to import arms]. I asked incredulously: 'Does this mean that Mr Haughey remains Minister for Finance? What will my position be? He knows that I've told you of his conversation with me on 18th April [about the

consignment that was due to reach Dublin Airport] and of the earlier police information.' The Taoiseach replied: 'I will protect you'. I felt a very sorry man returning to my Department I told the tale to my usual colleagues.[1]

The note was delivered to Cosgrave approximately four days later, probably late on Monday 4 May or the early hours of the Tuesday. It referred to both Col Hefferon and Capt. Kelly as having been 'held over the weekend in the Bridewell'. This was not so. The colonel was not detained at any time. How could Crinnion have made such a mistake?

Capt. Kelly was arrested on Friday, 1 May 1970, held at the Bridewell garda station, but released the next day.

C3 worked from Monday to Friday, save in exceptional circumstances. All of these facts make it likely that Crinnion returned to work on the morning of Monday 4 May, and caught up with some of the developments, but was relying on gossip. The officers involved in the SDU investigation, such as John Fleming, were based at the Castle and were involved in the unfolding events. There might have been a plan to question both the captain and the colonel but only the former was detained at the Bridewell until the Saturday.

Crinnion was outside the first ring of gossip as he was based at C3 in the Phoenix Park, whereas an officer of the SDU, at Dublin Castle, who was involved in the investigation, would have known that the colonel had not been taken to the Bridewell. This makes it more likely that the author of the 'GARDA' note was knowledgeable but not close to the inquiry.

It is arguable that at some stage on Monday 1 May, Crinnion stole a moment to draft his note and delivered it to Cosgrave's home that night. It contained the erroneous reference to Col Hefferon's detention at the Bridewell.[2]

As stated earlier, one of Crinnion's first assignments in the

1950s had been as part of the security detail at the home of John A. Costello. He lived at 20 Herbert Park in Ballsbridge. Hence, Crinnion knew better than most gardaí the nature of security assigned to protect the homes of senior Irish politicians. He had also spent many overtime hours on protection duty at the US and British embassies.[3] If anyone knew how to deliver a letter undetected to Cosgrave's home it was Patrick Crinnion. Part of the acquired knowledge was that he was aware as leader of the opposition, Cosgrave did not have round-the-clock garda protection, let alone a permanent SDU post at or near the laneway. The local gardaí did little more than keep a weather eye on the access point to the laneway with a perfunctory drive by on occasion.

On 12 June 1973, Crinnion wrote to Garret FitzGerald and Conor Cruise O'Brien, both ministers in the new government. He asserted that he had precipitated the Arms Crisis:

> ... I recklessly crusaded against the IRA and subversives without regard to the double-edged political weapon the IRA is and my personal efforts resulted in a toll which included precipitating the Fianna Fáil Arms Crisis ...[4]

What did Crinnion mean when he claimed that his 'personal efforts ... [precipitated] the Fianna Fáil Arms Crisis'? The interpretation which begs the most scrutiny is that he was responsible for delivering the 'GARDA' note to Cosgrave, the one which had urged the politician in block capital letters thus: 'SEE THAT THIS SCANDAL IS NOT HUSHED UP.'

A major *Magill* magazine investigation in 1980 concluded that McMahon was not the author of the note.[5] It also said that: 'It is absolutely certain that Mr Berry did not cause or inspire the "leak" to Cosgrave.'

A little over a month after the delivery of the note, in June

1970, Ronnie Burroughs, the UKREP in Northern Ireland, wrote to the Foreign Office making reference to a delicate 'source' who had supplied information about G2 activities in Northern Ireland:

> If the function of these [Irish military intelligence] Officers is as innocent as is suggested [their work] can be carried out by ordinary political observers operating quite openly. If there is a clandestine element then I do not see how we can tolerate them. We certainly would not do so in any other part of the UK ... Owing to the delicacy of the source it would of course not be possible to reveal to the Irish their own acknowledgement of the presence of these Officers.[6]

The use of the word 'delicacy' about the source of the information regarding G2 raises the prospect that the individual in question was the holder of a well-informed position within the Irish state security apparatus, possibly Crinnion. It was very much in the interest of MI6 not to expose Crinnion nor any lead that might implicate MI6 in the eruption of the crisis lest it infuriate Lynch, damage Anglo-Irish relations and expose Crinnion as an MI6 agent.

It is clear that:

> {i} Crinnion had access to the bulk of the information in the note from the garda gossip grapevine, not to mention what Wyman was relaying to him;

> {ii} Crinnion stated in writing that he was responsible for 'pre-cipitating' the Arms Crisis;

> {iii} Crinnion had a motive to deliver the information as he was alarmed by his belief that 'senior personages'[7] in Fianna Fáil were involved with Saor Éire and the Provisional IRA in a conspiracy that was a threat 'to the peace and well-being of the State' and that he knew 'the extent of Fianna Fáil support and guidance for the IRA faction which emerged as the PROVOS'.[8]

{iv} Critically, the note used block capital letters to emphasise '... THAT THIS SCANDAL IS NOT HUSHED UP', a style Crinnion used to highlight a point.

Liam Cosgrave died in 2017 without ever having revealed anything in public about his knowledge – if any – of the authorship of the note. Copies of it became public, no doubt as a result of the original being passed to *The Sunday Independent*. It was not submitted to forensic examination by the newspaper. Cosgrave did not allow anyone examine it after it was returned to him.

There was some suspicion that a British spy had dropped the note into Cosgrave's letterbox. Joe Dowling, a Dublin Fianna Fáil TD, raised the issue of a garda traitor in a speech in the Dáil during the Arms Crisis when he said that 'it would appear that there is a double agent in the police ... How much was the man paid for information? ... Whoever was the renegade or traitor who sold the information must be discovered.'[9]

There is another probable reference to the Arms Crisis in Crinnion's correspondence. He wrote a letter to the secretary-general of the United Nations in 1973, in which he stated that his 'endeavours on occasions resulted in distress to the government party of the day'.[10]

Once the Arms Crisis cat was out of the bag, Crinnion and Wyman sought to link Haughey and Blaney to the IRA and Saor Éire.

27

MI6 Links Fianna Fáil to Saor Éire

Charles Haughey and Neil Blaney never conspired with Saor Éire. This fact did not deter Patrick Crinnion from trying to convince his superior, Patrick Malone, otherwise. In fact, this lie became one of the more successful MI6 smears of the Troubles. Irish politicians such as Garret FitzGerald, Des O'Malley and Gerry L'Estrange harnessed and promoted it by raising questions in Dáil Éireann implying there was a link. The root of the smear can be traced back to John Wyman of MI6.

In all the documents that have come to light, Crinnion only ever makes reference to having had a single 'informant'. On 17 May 1973, he wrote to the attorney-general, Declan Costello. The purpose of the letter was to point out, *inter alia*, that certain information Wyman had furnished to him, concerning the IRA, had been beneficial to the security of the state. In the letter, Crinnion stated that 'John Wyman was my Informant'.[1]

Wyman was the source of his report on Knockvicar bearing reference number 30/44/69. Crinnion claimed it 'contained information previously unknown to the Garda Siochana'. Put another way, Wyman's allegations were not corroborated by a single agent, source, journalist nor gossip whom the army of SDU officers encountered.

Wyman's information, according to Crinnion 'seemed almost incredible, as it showed that senior personages in the Fianna Fáil party had literally stage-managed the IRA CONVENTION'.[2] As described earlier, the bigwigs Wyman had in mind were Blaney and Haughey, neither of whom had arranged the IRA convention at Knockvicar.

As already highlighted, the report contained a specific allegation that 'a member of the Fianna Fáil Party had been approached in the party headquarters in Mount Street, Dublin, and requested to give the use of his large country mansion ('Knockvicar', Boyle Co. Roscommon), for use as the venue for the IRA CONVENTION'. For this to be true, it means that a member of the IRA walked into Fianna Fáil's HQ on Mount Street under the gaze of the SDU protection detail, whose members were monitoring the building, and spoke to Gerry Callanan, the owner of Knockvicar. In the real world, the secrecy about the venue, Knockvicar House, was so tight that delegates heading to the convention were not told where the meeting was going to take place. Instead, they were instructed to go to collection points where they were picked up. Those who were not picked up were unable to avail of their own vehicles, or ones they might have borrowed, to reach the venue, as they did not know its whereabouts. The notion that the meeting place was being discussed at Fianna Fáil HQ beggars belief.

Crinnion omitted some details from Report 30/44/69 which he deemed highly sensitive. They had been supplied by his 'informant', i.e., Wyman, and had 'astounded' Malone when Crinnion spoke to Malone in the latter's office. Wyman's allegations 'gave an insight into the extent of Fianna Fáil support and guidance for the IRA faction which emerged as the PROVOS'.[3]

At this time, 1969, Wyman was such a sensitive source that Crinnion was not prepared to commit his name to writing. (As best as can be ascertained, he would not refer to him by name, in writing, until his correspondence in 1973.) Wyman had even more alarming – and deceitful – allegations to make: Saor Éire was supposedly involved in the imaginary Fianna Fáil plot that was underway. Crinnion described how he had been 'puzzled by my informant's assertion that the keys of 'Knockvicar' had been collected before the CONVENTION by Seán DOYLE, Saor Éire, Ballymun, Dublin, but later the inter-relationship between the PROVOS and SAOR ÉIRE (+ Fianna Fáil elements) became clear after the visit to Dublin by Markham-Randall the Arms Dealer ...'

Seán Doyle, known as 'Ructions', was a Saor Éire bank robber. On 3 October 1968, he, Simon O'Donnell, Thomas O'Neill and Pádraig Dwyer had taken part in an attempt to raid the Munster and Leinster bank in Ballyfermot, West Dublin. The heist was thwarted by eagle-eyed gardaí who spotted their car outside the bank. Martin Donnellan, who retired at the rank of assistant commissioner in 2007, was in the patrol car that clocked them. The raiders' car drove off. The gardaí gave chase. Donnellan recounted to author Paul Williams how Pádraig Dwyer:

> ... put his head and shoulders out the back window of the car and fired several shots directly at us. We dived down in the car, as the driver swerved left and right to avoid the gunfire. We continued after them until the getaway car crashed at Cooley Road in Drimnagh and the raiders ran through gardens. They were still armed and shouting at us: 'This is political.' We shouted that we were also armed, which we weren't, and they ran out onto the road, where they encountered two more uniformed guards who managed to disarm and arrest them. One of my colleagues, Kevin Duffin, grabbed Simon O'Donnell around the neck as he raised a rifle to take aim. The weapon was ready to fire. It was pure luck that no one was killed or injured and it was obvious that they had no compunction about shooting a policeman. This was the first time that I have witnessed such violence.[4]

The notion that Goulding would let Doyle, or anyone from Saor Éire, have any sort of an organisational role in the convention lacks credibility. The man who called upon Gerry Callanan, at his shop in Donnybrook, looking for the keys, was rebuffed by him. Thereafter, Callanan made his own arrangements to furnish the keys to Anna Barron. So why did Wyman pass this nonsense to Crinnion?

If we are to accept – as is the contention of this book – that Crinnion was the author of the message sent to Cosgrave, the following chain of events falls into place: MI6 instructed Crinnion to deliver the note, or acquiesced in his decision to alert Cosgrave. In either case, this means that MI6 set out to thwart Jack Lynch's cover-up and precipitated the Arms Crisis. As a supplement to this plot, MI6 attempted to link Haughey and Blaney to Saor Éire.

Who was in control of the MI6 stratagem to link Haughey and Blaney to the IRA and Saor Éire? Did John Wyman entice a gullible Crinnion so deep into the darkness of a rabbit hole dug by MI6 that Crinnion lost sight of what was happening above him on *terra firma*, or was Crinnion a knowing player in a deceitful MI6 plan to deceive his colleagues, the DoJ, ignite the Arms Crisis and link Fianna Fáil to Saor Éire?

The information furnished by Wyman bears the hallmark of a Maurice Oldfield black propaganda exercise, one designed to blight the political careers of Blaney, Gibbons and Haughey. What better way to raise the hackles of the gardaí than to link Blaney and Haughey to the IRA and Saor Éire, particularly Seán Doyle, who had been in the car with Dwyer in 1968 as the latter discharged live rounds at a garda patrol vehicle? The smear linking Fianna Fáil became even more toxic on account of the shooting of Garda Fallon by Saor Éire in April 1970.

Oldfield and his colleagues in the Information Research Department (IRD) of the FCO spent the next decade disseminating black propaganda to the effect that Charles Haughey helped set up the Provisional IRA.[5] It is now clear that the deeply buried roots of this deception began with the lies Wyman relayed to Crinnion in 1969.

It is the contention of this book that Maurice Oldfield, in a masterful sleight of hand, transformed the Blaney-Gibbons-Haughey importation operation into a hammer with which to pound the ruling Fianna Fáil party, thereby committing the most effective MI6 dirty trick of the 1970s. Oldfield succeeded in pushing Blaney and Haughey away from the levers of power because he believed they might otherwise have caused trouble for London.

London was now engaged upon a mutually supportive twin track approach to achieve its aims in the Republic. Overtly, Edward Heath, the FCO, William Whitelaw (the first secretary of state for Northern Ireland) and Ambassador Peck dealt with Lynch, Patrick Hillery and Des O'Malley. Covertly, Oldfield engaged in a series of further dirty tricks to help his masters pressurise Fianna Fáil into enacting tougher anti-IRA legislation.

Oldfield had not, however, looked carefully around the corner. His success would be short-lived and create far greater problems for Britain than if he had not meddled in Irish affairs in the first pace.

Fianna Fáil would stumble through three decades of upheaval as a result of the Arms Crisis. There were two sequels, the Arms Trial and the public accounts committee (PAC) inquiry of 1971 which generated large amounts of political turmoil.

28

THE DOOR SWINGS OPEN FOR THE PROVISIONALS

The Arms Crisis opened the stable door out of which bolted the Provisional IRA. Kevin Boland argued that: 'Prior to [the Arms Crisis] people had placed their faith in the broadly-based Citizens' Defence Committees. These in turn placed their faith in the promises of the Dublin government. When these promises were so dramatically and publicly reneged the Defence Committees were discredited and the threatened people turned to the IRA for defence ...'[1] Paddy Doherty of the Derry defence committee wrote in his memoirs that Jack Lynch 'created a vacuum which the Provisional IRA was only too willing to fill'.[2]

The CDCs held a press conference on Friday, 8 May 1970, at the Gresham Hotel, Dublin. It was organised by Seamus Brady at the request of John Kelly. Brady introduced Kelly in his capacity as organiser for the Citizens' Defence Committees of Belfast, along with his brother James, who was the chairman of St Patrick's Parish Citizens' Defence Committee of Belfast. The speakers described how they felt shocked and betrayed by the events of that week; that they had been promised help in the face of further attacks, but now 'there was only despair for the Northern [Ireland] minority'. According to Brady, the delegation 'cut a sorry picture. They were dismayed and aghast at the sudden turn of events. They were instinctively offering their support to the dismissed Haughey and Blaney, the two members of Jack Lynch's government who had openly given moral assistance to the minority in the North. But they were at this time powerless, removed from the scene of effective action and quite without influence.'[3]

Neil Blaney also blamed Lynch. He recalled in 1990, how, after one of the final meetings between the defence committees and Lynch, two of the Northern representatives went to his office:

[They] were highly confident that they were getting what they wanted. But I said to them 'Don't go overboard on what you believe you have been promised'. And I accuse Lynch and Fianna Fail, if you like, but Lynch specifically, that it was the expectations, real or imaginary, fired in those people and failing to meet those expectations which turned the whole thing on its head. At that point they lost faith in the *bona fide* concern of Dublin and the South re their concerns in the North. And this is why I blame Lynch particularly for helping create the Provisional IRA.[4]

There were, of course, many other factors in the growth and success of the Provisionals. The British general election of June 1970 saw the Tories displace Labour. In July 1970 the director-general of MI5, Martin Furnival Jones, met Edward Heath, the new Tory prime minister, for the first time and told him that there was little the intelligence services could do to solve the problem and that 'no amount of intelligence could cure Northern Ireland's ills. The most intelligence could do was to define the problem and help the security forces to confine the troubles'.[5]

Heath's administration let the Unionist government at Stormont acquire more control over the British army than had Wilson's. Tension between the troops on the ground and people living in Nationalist communities began to simmer. Nationalist youths were becoming involved in confrontations with British troops. Many of the soldiers on the streets were not that much older than the local teenagers. They had little or no idea about what had been happening in Ireland before their arrival. Minor incidents led to overreaction by the military and begat more serious responses. Riots began to break out. The Falls Curfew of 3–5 July 1970, when British troops surrounded the Falls district of Belfast and saturated it with tear gas, was a major factor in this increase in friction. Then, on 18 September 1970, Brigadier Frank Kitson arrived in Belfast to assume command of 39 Airportable Brigade. Kitson was a counter-insurgency guru who had practised his dark arts in Kenya, Malaya, Cyprus and Oman. In Ireland, he instigated the strategy of state collusion with Loyalist paramilitaries, set up MRF death squads, permitted brutal interrogation techniques and manipulated the media.

Kitson was also an advocate of the Maoist dictum that the relationship between insurgents and the population supporting them was akin to that between a fish and water. He later propounded that if a 'fish has got to be destroyed it can be attacked directly by rod or net ... But if rod and net cannot succeed by themselves it may be necessary to do something to the water ...' This could even include 'polluting the water'. In other words, non-combatant members of a community caught up in a conflict could become fair game for strong-arm tactics.

Kitson's indiscreet volume on counter-insurgency, *Low Intensity Operations* (1971) revealed his opinion that the enemy in Ireland was to be found among the Catholic community. He wrote that 'in the historical context it may be of interest to recall that when the regular army was first raised in the 17th century, "Suppression of the Irish" was coupled with "Defence of the Protestant Religion" as one of the two main reasons for its existence'.[6]

The Ballymurphy massacre took place on Kitson's watch

in August 1971. The carnage on Bloody Sunday, in January 1972, was perpetrated by his paratroopers. He was eased out of Northern Ireland by William Whitelaw, the first secretary of state for Northern Ireland, in April 1972, before his two-year tour ended.[7] By the time of his departure, the Official and Provisional wings of the IRA had garnered enormous support within the Nationalist community. Paddy Devlin said of Kitson that he 'probably did more than any other individual to sour relations between the Catholic community and the security forces'.[8]

Crinnion was assigned to the particularly sensitive task of the protection of British diplomats after the burning of the British embassy on Merrion Square in the wake of Bloody Sunday, something that may have enabled him to maintain contact with the MI6 station in Dublin at this particularly sensitive chapter in the Troubles.

29

THE STATE BETRAYS ITS 'CONFIDENTIAL SOURCES'

The Irish public learned of the existence of high-level informers, inside the IRA, in 1971. John Fleming let the cat out of the bag when he spoke about 'confidential sources' at a session of the Public Accounts Committee (PAC). The committee was examining the disbursement of the £100,000 fund created by the Dáil in 1969 for the 'relief of distress' in Northern Ireland. Some of the money was used to finance the CDC-G2 arms purchase in Germany. The nation now discovered that informers had been in place since at least 1969. The agents Fleming had in mind were MacStíofáin and an accomplice, whom he did not name.

At the time, Fleming believed MacStíofáin was a *bona fide* agent. Fleming could have relied upon the Official Secrets Act to avoid providing any information that concerned the SDU's penetration of the IRA but chose not to do so. In the background, Des O'Malley, the then minister for justice, was encouraging Fleming to talk frankly.[1]

At the PAC, Fleming spoke about meetings between Capt. Kelly and Cathal Goulding:

> At the outset I would like to point out that all this information has come from confidential sources and I am not at liberty to reveal the sources from which the information came.[2]

Fleming then proceeded to provide apparent clues which could have helped unmask his sources:

First, in about the last week of September 1969 Captain Kelly met Cathal Goulding, Chief-of-Staff of the IRA, in Virginia, Co. Cavan, and he agreed to get him a regular supply of arms and ammunition for use in Northern Ireland. He also promised to provide training facilities for Northern members of the IRA in Gormanston Camp. Captain Kelly attended an IRA meeting in Cavan in the first week of October 1969 and he then promised the IRA to give them £50,000 by instalments. To prove that he was not bluffing he promised to pay the first instalment within three days. On or about October 7, 1969 he paid over £7,000 at Cavan Town to Cathal Goulding. During the last week of November 1969, he paid over a further sum of £1,000.[3]

When pressed, Fleming was uncertain about his facts:

Chairman: 'To whom [was the payment made] on this occasion?'

Fleming: 'As far as I know it was to Cathal Goulding. I cannot swear to that, though. In the early part of December 1969, he paid over a further £1,500. Again, I am not sure, but I think it was to Cathal Goulding. Those are the sums which as far as I know Captain Kelly paid over.'[4]

Capt. Kelly's barrister, the late Peter Sutherland, has described this evidence as 'complete nonsense'.[5] Capt. Kelly was outraged at Fleming's behaviour at the PAC.

Fleming also alleged that Capt. Kelly had participated in other meetings with the IRA. In his book, *The Thimble Riggers*, Capt. Kelly responded thus:

In answer to Deputy [Garret] Fitzgerald [at the PAC], Fleming said that he knew 'for a fact' of at least one meeting attended by Rory Brady [i.e., Ruairí Ó Brádaigh], a senior colleague of Cathal Goulding's at the time and, later, President of Provisional Sinn Fein.

All the above evidence was false ... As regards giving [Goulding] money, the issue did not arise, because quite simply, and as emerged at the Inquiry, no such money was at my disposal at the time.[6]

Had the meetings in Cavan actually taken place, the IRA's spy catchers would have followed a trail of clues that might have led them to Fleming's sources, and the inevitable torture and death that would have ensued.

In the final analysis, Fleming and O'Malley were prepared to risk the life of the SDU's 'confidential sources' so Fleming could disclose 'hearsay' based on lies to the PAC. His 'evidence' would not have been permitted in a court of law, as he and O'Malley – a solicitor – both knew too well.

While O'Malley was motivated by political opportunism, Fleming's motives are a mystery. What he was doing went against every principle of his profession.

MacStíofáin, of course, survived without a blemish because what he had told the SDU about the payments to Goulding was false and there was therefore no trail leading back to him. If anything, questions might have arisen about what Goulding had done with money he had not, in fact, acquired.

O'Malley took the opposite tack when Jack Lynch's knowledge of the plot threatened to surface. On such an occasion, O'Malley went into cover-up mode. Peter Berry sought to testify to the PAC about a report he had provided to Lynch about the activities of Capt. Kelly at a meeting with the defence committees which had taken place at Baileboro, Co. Cavan, in October 1969. Lynch had received the report from Berry during a visit to see him in hospital that same month. Berry had informed Lynch that CDC officials – some of whom were also known IRA men – were present when guns were sought by the defence committees for the protection of their communities in Northern Ireland. Despite having being appraised of this fact in October 1969, Lynch had done nothing to halt Capt. Kelly's activities. It was this inaction which O'Malley clearly sought to conceal in attempting to silence Berry. *Magill* magazine, which published *The Berry Diaries*, revealed that:

> It emerges from the Berry Papers that [CS John] Fleming [of the SDU] was specifically instructed by Desmond O'Malley, then Minister for Justice, to be totally frank at the Committee of Public Accounts hearing [in 1971]. The instruction to be so was given through Mr Berry. In spite of this Mr O'Malley failed either to defend Mr. Fleming in public or even to inform the Garda Commissioner that he had so instructed Mr. Fleming.
>
> Mr Berry also reveals that when he was invited to appear before the Committee, although he had by then retired from the Civil Service, he wrote a letter to Mr O'Malley enquiring what his response should be. The Minister's private secretary replied saying that the Minister considered that anything which Mr Berry might usefully say would be contrary to the Official Secrets Act and that Mr O'Malley would not agree to release him from his obligations under this act.
>
> He was then invited by the Committee of Public Accounts if he would 'consult' with it and decided to agree, in spite of ministerial objections, and he so informed the Department of Justice. He then enquired of the Minister if he should reveal to the Committee the fact of his meeting with Mr Lynch on October 17, 1969 at Mount Carmel Hospital, where he informed the Taoiseach of information he had received concerning the involvement of Captain Kelly in the arms plot. (As has previously been pointed out in *Magill* this meeting is of crucial importance for it shows that the Taoiseach was informed of the arms plot six months before the date on which he said he was first informed and in the interval, he did nothing to stop the plot.)[7]

Berry, however, refused to let O'Malley muzzle him, and proceeded to tell the PAC about the Baileboro meeting in a private session.[8]

30

HER MAJESTY'S LOYAL CORRESPONDENTS

Patrick Crinnion was far from the only source London had in Dublin. A stream of valuable information drifted from the smoke-filled backrooms occupied by the movers and shakers in the city, along a variety of channels, to Whitehall. Some of these conduits were official, a few treacherous, whilst others lay somewhere in between.

Thomas Mullen, formerly of C3, was still gainfully employed by MI6 as late as 1972. The task assigned to him was to unearth material with which to tarnish Charles Haughey, about which more in a later chapter.

An unidentified 'government' official assisted yet another smear, this one directed at Neil Blaney TD.[1] According to a US embassy cable sent from Dublin to Washington in 1971, an 'authoritative source in the Irish government' claimed that there were three separate wings of the IRA on the island: the Officials, the Provisionals, and a 100-strong underground army he called 'Blaney's Private IRA'. The latter group never existed. Nonetheless, the deceitful 'government' official convinced Virgil Randolph III, the political officer at the US embassy, of its existence. The 'government' official was most likely a civil servant at the DoJ or a police officer, possibly even Crinnion.[2] Whoever the official was, he was singing from the same mud-slinging sheet as MI6.

At this time the Officials were engaged in a war of words with the Provisionals. Cynically, one of Goulding's tactics to bring the

Provisionals into disrepute, in the eyes of their supporters, was to associate them with Fianna Fáil. Towards this end, the Officials produced a pamphlet (1971) and a 68-page booklet (1973) in furtherance of their objective. MI6 and the IRD hijacked this theme. In 1972 the IRD reprinted the Officials' 1971 pamphlet but with the addition of a new paragraph attacking Haughey.[3]

In February 1971, Dick Walsh, Goulding's asset inside *The Irish Times,* published his story about Jock Haughey's visit to London to purchase arms. It fuelled the fiction that Garda Fallon had been shot with one of the guns smuggled to Dublin by Jock Haughey and that Neil Blaney had helped traffic the man responsible for the homicide out of the country in his official car. Oldfield must have been delighted with the timing of Walsh's report.

At least two leading mainstream media outlets were compromised at management level by MI5 and MI6.[4] One of these was Maj. McDowell, the tweedy, monocle-wearing chief executive and director of *The Irish Times*. Born in Belfast in 1923, he had joined the Royal Irish Rifles and, by the end of World War Two, had become a captain. He spent some of his time in the Ministry of Defence at the Judge Advocate's department. While his record showed that he left the army in 1955, that was only half the story. At some stage during the decade after the war ended, he joined MI5 before returning to Civvy Street in 1955.

Cecil King, who owned *The Daily Mirror,* was another MI5 asset who had become a newspaper proprietor.[5] King not only knew McDowell, but was aware that he was a former MI5 officer. King's diary entry for Sunday, 23 January 1972, touched upon McDowell's service with MI5. Having enjoyed a lunch with him and his wife, he recorded that McDowell 'asked us to talk about Irish affairs. He is a man with a very varied background

– a Protestant father from the North, mother from the South, service in the British Army (Ulster rifles), and had served on the Staff in Edinburgh, and in M.I.5.'[6]

In his book *The Irish Times: Past and Present*, author John Martin states that his sources 'within *The Irish Times* have indicated to me that [McDowell] worked for British intelligence in Austria at the end of the war'.[7]

MI6 also exploited the goodwill of many Irish people who attended the British-Irish Association (BIA) to extract information and influence political life in the Republic. John Fleming, the head of the SDU, was one of those who attended the BIA. John Hermon, who rose to become chief constable of the RUC, was another attendee.

David Astor, an asset of MI6 and the owner of *The Observer* newspaper, co-chaired the BIA in the 1970s.[8] Astor provided a platform for the distribution of MI6 propaganda in his paper. Maria Maguire, a Republican activist from south county Dublin, decided to tell her story to *The Observer* in 1972. She had accompanied Dáithí Ó Conaill to the continent to purchase arms from a Czech company the previous year. The operation was foiled by MI6 and exposed in the press. In 1972, Astor took a personal interest in Maguire's story. An extensive account of her year in the Provisionals was published in the paper. She was particularly critical of MacStíofáin. He was astonished when he read the article which presented her as an 'important defector' who had broken with the IRA because she could no longer 'remain silent'. As a piece of propaganda, MacStíofáin felt her 'revelations' were 'not badly done'. He noted:

> One of her Observer pieces was headed I ACCUSE SEAN MACSTIOFAIN. It came to the point fairly quickly. If I were got rid of, the IRA campaign would stop. I was using and abusing the whole Republican movement in my own interests. I had employed

dictatorial methods to gain complete control and remove all opposition ruthlessly. Miss McGuire had seen through all this. Her only aim was to tell it to honest and sincere Republicans who were unaware, and so on.[9]

MacStíofáin alleged that the propaganda in *The Observer*'s series was 'interwoven' with the truth to 'discredit the leadership and encourage disunity in the movement'.[10] The information she disclosed generated dissension within the ranks of the Provisionals, especially an allegation that some of MacStíofáin's colleagues had plotted to kill him:

> ... there was a good deal of fact based on confidential information she had no right to have. There had been a breach of security at the top of the movement, and an inquiry was inevitable. It was long and involved, but inconclusive. Both of the people who had worked closely with her denied passing such information to her, and there was no evidence to prove their responsibility. I, for my part, accepted that neither of them had been involved in a plot to kill me, as the 'revelations' had hinted.[11]

One of Oldfield's closest advisers was Daphne Park. She organised the British-Irish Association in the 1980s. She was responsible for the oft-quoted remark that:

> Once you get really good inside intelligence about any group, you are able to learn where the levers of power are, and what one man fears of another ... You set people discreetly against one another ... They destroy each other, we [in MI6] don't destroy them.[12]

Park could very well have had the Maguire saga in mind when she spoke those words.

In 1973, a memoir by Maguire appeared on the bookshelves. It is impossible to tell what was true and what was invented. Read at face value, it was a highly effective condemnation of the Provisionals, shining more light on internal feuding at the pinnacle of the organisation.

Maguire also described an alleged affair she had conducted with Dáithí Ó Conaill, something she had denied in 1971 after the attempt to buy the Czech arms had been revealed to the public.

Her portrayal of MacStíofáin was not that of a teetotal family man, rather one who made a pass at her in an IRA safe house and sometimes drank wine with his meals.[13] She described how, in the run-up to a meeting in July 1972 (outlined in a later chapter), between a six-man IRA delegation of which MacStíofáin was a member and William Whitelaw, the first secretary of state for Northern Ireland, MacStíofáin became:

a changed man, actually smiling, and obviously feeling expansive. He first wanted some fish and chips — his favourite meal – to celebrate, but the fish and chip shop hadn't yet opened. He told me what a good job I'd done that day, and I hadn't got over the surprise of hearing him compliment me when he asked me out to dinner. I was amazed: never before had he shown such interest in me. I said I didn't think that was a good idea because I thought we might be recognised – even now, of course, he was still in theory on the run. Then I took a gentle rise out of him. saying, 'But of course you're very good at disguises' – I was referring to a Hitler-style moustache he had grown and been photographed in at the Derry press conference on Tuesday. He thought I was serious, and said earnestly that he hadn't liked the photographs published of him afterwards and had decided to shave it off. Then he actually made a very hesitant pass at me, putting his arm round me and asking if I would stay there with him. I suppressed a shudder and left.[14]

The book went on to poke fun at what Maguire portrayed as MacStíofáin's over-reaction to a minor burn he had sustained on his face after the explosion of a letter bomb:

For a long time afterwards MacStíofáin wore a black eyepatch over his slight burn, which I thought made him look like a rather tawdry Moshe Dayan. (The *Irish Press* summed up both the patch and his intransigence by christening him General Die-on.) This was unfortunate at a time when we were trying to persuade the world to take us seriously, I thought ... MacStíofáin's wife Maire was genuinely very shocked by [the explosion of the letter bomb] - it was, she said, 'a terrible thing for anyone to do'. Her opinion seemed ironic - this almost harmless incident coming on the day six men were blown to pieces [in the Abercorn restaurant bombing] in Belfast.[15]

MacStíofáin responded by claiming in his memoirs that he wore the patch on the advice of a doctor.

By early 1972, the activities of the IRA had drawn a plentiful supply of British spies to Ireland. The more senior of the breed established a high-powered HQ at Stormont Castle from where they oversaw operations on both sides of the Border. The era of the British spy scandal in Ireland was now about to begin in earnest.

31

HIGH-PRICED CHAPS

In 1972, Northern Ireland was descending into an abyss of savagery, with the public becoming the grass upon which extremists – on all sides – trampled.

The Stormont parliament was prorogued on 24 March 1972, by London. This introduced 'direct rule' from England's capital. Seán MacStíofáin viewed the demise of the Unionist-dominated legislature as a great victory for the Provisional IRA.

William Whitelaw was appointed by Edward Heath as Northern Ireland's new political overlord. Whitelaw was accompanied by Lord Windlesham; Paul Channon, a millionaire Guinness heir; and David Howell.[1] Their task was to preside over the new institution which would run the Six Counties, the Northern Ireland Office (NIO).

Yet, within a few months of his appointment, Whitelaw would extinguish any hope of a permanent ceasefire with the Provisional IRA, and destroy the Wyman network, due to his inept dealings with an amateurish intelligence community which rose to ascendancy on his watch.

Whitelaw took up residence of Stormont Castle. A feature of the new administration was that the spies occupied the same building as Whitelaw, an indication of their growing power and influence.

When Whitelaw arrived in Belfast, the first person he met after he disembarked from his flight was London's representative to Northern Ireland, Howard Smith, an official of the FCO. Smith's official title was that of 'UK Representative to the Government of Northern Ireland' (UKREP). He was a man well versed in the ways of the intelligence community and became the director-general of MI5 in 1978. In his memoirs, Whitelaw recalled that when he got into the car, Smith handed him a copy of that morning's *Belfast Newsletter* which led with a story claiming he was a prominent English Roman Catholic. He remarked:

> I was amazed, because the only previous religious concern about my appointment had been that many years before, my great-uncle had allowed the grounds of our family home near Glasgow to be used for an Orange function. In fact I was brought up a Scottish Presbyterian and joined the Church of England after we moved to Cumbria in 1959. I gave the facts to Howard Smith and said, 'We must instantly deny the story.' He replied sadly, 'You will find in this community that that is easier said than done.' I had many later opportunities to learn the truth of that statement.[2]

Howard Smith was absorbed into the new Direct Rule structure. Dennis Trevelyan of the Foreign Office took over 'Political Development'.[3]

'Peter', a lieutenant-colonel in the British army was looking forward to returning home after a 'grinding' four-month tour in Northern Ireland.[4] He was expecting an assignment as a teacher at Sandhurst. Instead, he was told that he was to go to Stormont Castle, where he would serve as a military assistant to a senior spy who was to occupy the new position as director and controller of intelligence (DCI) at Stormont. 'Peter' was ordered to find a house, dress in civilian attire and make contact with a certain 'very high-priced chap' on the steps of Stormont Castle the following week.[5]

The 'very high-priced chap' was Allan Rowley, who served as DCI, 1972–73. He was a heavy drinker. So too was his new boss, William Whitelaw. Rowley's successor, Denis Payne of MI5, revealed that Rowley carried out his duties 'in tremendous style …[6] He lived like a king, he entertained like a king, he used to drink with Willie [Whitelaw] all night'.[7]

Oldfield's friend and biographer, Richard Deacon, wrote in 1984 that:

> The appointment of William Whitelaw as Secretary of State for Northern Ireland had not helped what little progress [MI6] had been making not merely in the north, but in the Republic, too. For Whitelaw had turned himself into a kind of supremo on both security and intelligence in Ulster – not at all the role for a politician who hopes to succeed – and he had opened up contacts with the IRA.[8]

Rowley, born in 1922, joined MI6 in November 1948 having won the military cross in Burma at the end of the Second World War. As a spy, he served in Egypt, Ethiopia, Turkey, Burma and Singapore. His résumé also included a three-year secondment to the Australian Secret Intelligence Service. His official designation in Northern Ireland was that of an undersecretary at the Northern Ireland Office (NIO).

Rowley was a man with a cold heart and no moral compass. As DCI, he oversaw the unconscionable Kincora Boys' Home 'honey trap' operation in Belfast. It was designed to create blackmail opportunities for British spies by trafficking young children to Loyalist politicians and paramilitaries for sexual abuse. Rowley's MI6 superior, Sir Maurice Oldfield, was deeply involved in that vile scheme.[9]

Back in London, Whitelaw's boss, Edward Heath, was determined to achieve greater security co-operation between the UK and the Republic as 1972, the worst year of violence in Northern Ireland, dragged on. On 25 April, he wrote to Jack Lynch urging the immediate creation of a system of security co-operation along the Border. When questions were raised in the Dáil about the discussions between Dublin and London, Lynch denied that co-operation had been broached.[10] However, behind closed doors, a rather wily Lynch was telling Ambassador Peck that he agreed that 'discreet collaboration was clearly called for'.[11]

In what must have been music to London's ears, that same month, Lynch gave Peck what he interpreted as 'carte blanche' to pursue the establishment of security co-operation directly with the departments of defence and justice in Dublin. Peck sent a telegram to London stating that the co-operation would be 'mutual and discreet, bearing in mind that it has to be deniable in the Dáil'. Afterwards, there was a meeting to kick start the co-operation between the chief-of-staff of the Irish army and the military attaché at the British embassy.[12]

The point of contact for Peck at the DoJ was Andy Ward, who had taken over from Peter Berry as secretary at the department in January 1971.[13] Ward was forty-four and would remain in place until his sixtieth birthday in 1986. He hailed from Tourard, Co. Cork, was married and lived in Terenure, Co. Dublin. Later, Peck had meetings with Larry Wren of C3.

The Official IRA declared a ceasefire on 30 May 1972. This was spurred by the fury of many of their supporters who were appalled at the atrocity in Aldershot and the killing of a teenage Derry soldier, Ranger Best, who had been on home leave, earlier that month. Some Official IRA activists, unhappy with the ceasefire, joined the Provisionals, yet another windfall for MacStíofáin.

On 31 May, the gardaí arrested Joe Cahill at Sinn Féin's Kevin Street HQ. Warrants were also issued for Dáithí Ó Conaill and MacStíofáin. The SDU, of course, did not want to arrest MacStíofáin but had to pretend otherwise. Maria Maguire sensed that something odd was going on. She commented in her book that Ó Conaill and MacStíofáin:

did go on the run – but it seemed strange that if the Dublin police had really wanted [Ó Conaill], they allowed him to go into the Kevin Street office five minutes after Joe [Cahill] had been arrested and then spend half an hour there. (Ironically [Ó Conaill] and Joe had been due to meet the American religious leader Billy Graham.) [Ó Conaill] also spent a good deal of the subsequent ten days in a flat in the Ballsbridge area of Dublin, and Mac Stíofáin visited it too. It would have been quite easy to trace them there by following me, for I visited them both frequently.[14]

While the SDU in Dublin was letting MacStíofáin go about his business, the new British spy regime at Stormont Castle was contemplating talking to him and his Provisional IRA colleagues. They believed they had an insight into how MacStíofáin would respond to the prospect of talks because they had a spy in Dublin, Patrick Crinnion. Crinnion had access to all the reports from Philip McMahon about MacStíofáin, which reached C3. Little did MI6 realise that the garda intelligence was worthless because MacStíofáin was playing games with the hapless McMahon. It would end in disaster, violence and horror.

32

THE HOUSE ON THE THAMES

On 21 July 1972, Seán MacStíofáin and his colleagues directed a fleet of car bombs onto the streets of Belfast, all set with timers to explode after their drivers' abandoned them. The atrocity that followed, which became known as 'Bloody Friday', brought unparalleled terror to Belfast. Twenty-two cars exploded in the busy city centre in less than two hours, killing nine people and injuring 130 others. MacStíofáin hardly warned Philip McMahon about the planned attack, for the gardaí would surely have alerted the RUC about the threat to the city.

Only two weeks earlier MI6 had been hopeful of a breakthrough with the Provisional IRA. An IRA delegation had flown to London on 7 July 1972, to meet William Whitelaw, at a house in Chelsea. The IRA contingent was made up of MacStíofáin, Dáithí Ó Conaill, Seamus Twomey, Ivor Bell, Gerry Adams and Martin McGuinness.

Dublin had some inkling that this meeting was on the cards. On 19 June, Whitelaw had informed Jack Lynch, through the British embassy in Dublin, that 'it was proposed to him that he should personally meet representatives of the Provisional IRA'.[1] He was, he explained, advised that the Provisionals wanted an assurance that if they declared a ceasefire, it would not be exploited to pick up anyone on a wanted list. Secondly, there was a desire that Republican prisoners would be awarded recognition and the status of 'political prisoners'.[2]

It can fairly be assumed that it was Wyman's job to find out the IRA's bottom line for the talks. Wyman had access, *via* Crinnion, to what appeared to be an intelligence treasure-trove in Dublin. In reality, C3 had collected a mountain of glister but precious little gold. The information Crinnion supplied on this occasion was based, in large part, on what MacStíofáin was relaying to McMahon.

MI6 was optimistic about the talks, as were their colleagues in the Foreign Office, for they hustled Whitelaw precipitously into the negotiations.

If there was a possibility of building a meaningful ceasefire, an overly optimistic MI6 wasted the opportunity by pushing an unwilling and ill-prepared Whitelaw into the Chelsea conference. Their estimation of the willingness of the Provisionals to negotiate was rash. Incredibly, MI6 advised Whitelaw that the IRA was a beaten docket. As noted earlier, in the description of an exchange between Maria Maguire and MacStíofáin, far from feeling defeated, MacStíofáin was elated at the prospect of gaining concessions from the British. The fact that the IRA was able to deploy twenty-two car bombs two weeks later demonstrates they were far from vanquished.

The key MI6 player in this fiasco was a man called Frank Steele who had been assigned as an assistant to UKREP Howard Smith in September 1971. According to Peter Taylor:

> Smith, who was becoming increasingly overwhelmed by the amount of work required to keep abreast of events on the ground and the doings of [Brian] Faulkner's [Stormont] Government, decided he needed a deputy. He knew the man he wanted, a Foreign Office colleague by the name of Frank Steele who worked for the Secret Intelligence Service, MI6. Smith had heard that Steele was at home on leave awaiting his next posting and hoped that he might be enticed to join him in the province.[3]

Steele had served in Basra, Cairo, Tripoli, Beirut, Amman and Nairobi. He brought a team of spooks with him to Belfast. Anthony Verrier, an author who spoke to Steele on an unattributable basis, described the men from MI6 in flattering terms referring to them as experienced and possessed of 'diplomatic gifts'.[4]

Steele freely acknowledged that when he first arrived in 1971, he knew nothing of Ireland's political idiosyncrasies. His value to London derived from his experience of conflict situations in the Middle East – particularly the Lebanon – and Africa. Before direct rule, Steele reported to London, bypassing Stormont, just as Smith did. He was 'horrified' at what he found in Northern Ireland and soon concluded that Faulkner's administration was incapable of reforming that territory. He eventually became an advocate of direct rule.

Robin Ramsay, a former senior Northern Ireland civil servant, described Steele as follows:

> Smith's second-in-command was Frank Steele, a man with a similar CV [to Howard Smith], whose boast was that he brought together in Northern Ireland several of his staff from his earlier posting in Lebanon. He thought that would be 'useful' (a favourite Foreign & Commonwealth Office (FCO) word), since they could draw on their experiences in a country which had achieved an outstanding success in having a trans-communal power-sharing government. Such was the wisdom of Laneside [the office of the UKREP].[5]

Steele came to the conclusion that the IRA was not going to be beaten by military means alone. 'Some of the Army thought they could be beaten, others of us thought they could not be beaten by military means and that it would require political means to beat them.'[6]

A programme was developed during the first part of 1972 to open secret negotiations with the leadership of the IRA, to secure a ceasefire and ease inter-communal tensions. The plan was to use the SDLP as a conduit to the IRA. Steele was adamant that there was no question of trying to penetrate the SDLP, merely to use their knowledge of the Nationalist community to open a few doors to allow MI6 explore the possibility of negotiation with the IRA.[7] Verrier described how the commander of land forces (CLO) in Northern Ireland, Anthony Farrar-Hockley, operated on the principle 'in strange territory it's as well to have guides'.[8] Farrar-Hockley renewed contacts with the Provisionals. Verrier described how:

> Concentrating on Londonderry, meeting at night in safe houses, risking their lives, the parties to this positive conspiracy succeeded, on 22 June [1972] in negotiating a cease fire. The order to MacStíofáin and his fellow commanders came from Dublin. It was not well received, but it was obeyed. The cease fire was a remarkable achievement for all concerned. Yet it led those on the British side to believe that the Provisionals were a totally discredited organisation, its leaders not only rejected by the Catholics in the citadels but of poor quality as revolutionaries.[9]

On 13 June MacStíofáin held a press conference in Derry at which he invited Whitelaw to talk to the IRA. John Hume and Paddy Devlin of the SDLP urged Whitelaw to take up the invitation. Whitelaw came around to the idea. Gerry Adams was released from internment so he could participate in the negotiations. Steele and the number-two man at the NIO, Philip Woodfield, met with Dáithí Ó Conaill and Adams on 20 June 1972, at the home of Col M.W. McCorkell, Ballyarnett House, near the Donegal border for preliminary discussions.[10]

A meeting with Whitehall went ahead on 7 July 1972. MacStíofáin chose the six members of the IRA delegation, including himself. They were collected by the British army and escorted from Derry to Aldergrove Airport. MacStíofáin was armed.[11] On the way, they encountered a herd of cows lumbering along the road ahead of them. MacStíofáin, a man not noted for his sense of humour, quipped that Whitehall could have found a more impressive escort for them.

When they arrived in England, they were taken to the home of Whitelaw's deputy, Paul Channon, at Cheyne Walk, near Chelsea Bridge. The property overlooked the River Thames. Steele and Woodfield were also present.

What Steele revealed to Verrier was that MI6 did not perceive MacStíofáin as an obstacle to progress, at least before the conference commenced. This indicates two things: that MacStíofáin was feeding a line to McMahon that he was in favour of the talks and Crinnion was passing this deceptive information to MI6. MI6 believed Seamus Twomey was likely to be the villain of the piece from their perspective.

MI6 was not on the same page as Whitelaw either. Verrier described how:

> A further barrier to a successful meeting was the attitude of the Secretary of State to negotiations with terrorists. He showed no relish for the encounter. Whitelaw, a man 'whose heart ruled his head' as those about him agree, was prepared to make concessions in order to encourage hopes for a cease fire, but agreed to meet the Provisionals only at their insistence.[12]

A cabal representing what Verrier described as the 'permanent government', made up of the Foreign Office and MI6 officials, was in for a shock. While they had shown 'resolution, imagination and courage', their initiative was virtually dead upon arrival.[13] The coterie had:

> hustled Whitelaw into a premature meeting. No politician likes to be hustled; British politicians loathe it. There was a gap between the permanent government's appreciation of the need for momentum and Heath's refusal to look at Ireland as a whole ... This kind of [meeting had] no appeal to Whitelaw, and he shook hands with the Provisionals on 7 July in a mood of dislike for

the entire proceedings which was apparent to all but himself ...
Lacking a mandate, lacking the temperament for quasi-colonial
horse-trading, Whitelaw dug himself in behind the table.[14]

Foolishly, Oldfield, Rowley, Steele and their associates believed
that 'although suspicious and contemptuous, [MacStíofáin]
had come to accept that his movement had reached the end
of the road'.[15] This hardly seems credible and can only have
been an interpretation of one of the yarns MacStíofáin was
feeding to Philip McMahon. A more accurate appreciation
of MacStíofáin's mood can be discerned from Gerry Adams'
autobiography. Adams describes how, during a break at the
conference, after the IRA had stated their terms, MacStíofáin
was elated and stated: 'Jesus. We have it.'[16]

MI6 did not have a proper grasp of what lay in store for the
British negotiators. Before the conference began, MI6 had not
perceived MacStíofáin as part of the hard core of the delegation.
The latter group, they believed, consisted of Seamus Twomey and
his 'three subordinates – McGuinness and Bell, his commanders
in Londonderry and Belfast, together with Adams [who]
represented intransigence'.[17] Therein lay their error: MacStíofáin
should have been considered as one of the more intransigent
members of the IRA delegation.

In an incredible insight into the errors of MI6's thinking,
Verrier revealed that 'only the leader of this group was committed wholly to terrorism', namely Seamus Twomey, and that
he had travelled to Chelsea 'to keep an eye on O'Connell'.[18]
Yet, MacStíofáin was also a hard liner. Steele believed Ó
Conaill was genuinely interested in a deal 'partly because he
believed in outflanking the SDLP'.[19] Verrier described how
overly expectant 'British officials' hoped that Ó Conaill and
MacStíofáin might 'see a ray of hope in the fact of the meeting

taking place at all, and reckoned, cautiously, that if Whitelaw showed his hand these two Provisionals would use combined authority to exert pressure on their comrades'.[20]

MI6 must have developed their almost comically optimistic opinion of MacStíofáin's flexibility and willingness to compromise from reports emanating from Crinnion. Reading between the lines, the Chelsea conference reveals that MacStíofáin was generally portraying himself to McMahon as someone interested in laying down arms in favour of talks that might result in a long-term ceasefire.

Chelsea would prove to be a wake-up call for MI6. It soon dawned on them that there was 'no love lost between [Ó Conaill] the quiet man and MacStíofáin the hard one'.[21]

Verrier describes how Steele 'nevertheless hoped that a statement from Whitelaw on radical change in Northern Ireland might provide a starting point for rational discussion on wider issues'.[22] This was not to be so.

MacStíofáin adopted a hardline attitude from the start. According to Verrier, MacStíofáin's account in his memoirs, 'although biased, is accurate on the facts, conveying drama about the risks and doubts over the venture. An acid humour etches his picture'.[23]

The British negotiators began to revise their comparatively benign view of MacStíofáin on the morning of the conference, believing he had ordered the IRA to seize a number of soldiers in Derry so they could be held as hostages before the IRA delegation flew to the Royal Air Force Station at Benson in Oxfordshire.[24]

Whitelaw arrived at the conference late. Verrier described how:

Delays and tension made the formal exchanges between Whitelaw and the Provisionals stiff and cold. Whitelaw, 'smooth, well-fed and fleshy' – in MacStíofáin's unkind description – began the proceedings with a general statement. This was anodyne, not positive or specific … there was no mention of those historic issues so dear to an Irishman's heart. Whitelaw summarised the situation in Northern Ireland as if he knew what was best for colonial subjects.[25]

The atmosphere did not improve, 'in fact it deteriorated appreciably'[26] when MacStíofáin read a statement summarising the Provisionals' case which called on Heath's government to declare publicly that it was the 'right of the people of Ireland acting as a unit to decide the future of Ireland'[27] and that Britain should declare its intention to withdraw all British forces from Irish soil, before 1 January 1975. More immediately, he insisted on the withdrawal of British forces from sensitive areas coupled with a general amnesty for all political prisoners in Irish and British jails. The amnesty was to apply to all internees and detainees, and all persons on wanted lists.

In later years Steele told Peter Taylor of the conference that:[28]

It was far worse than I thought it was going to be. I did at least think they'd say, 'Well we're all in a very difficult situation. Fighting each other is getting us nowhere so let's see what we can do by talking and if it doesn't work, Ok we'll go back to fighting.' But there was nothing like that. MacStíofáin behaved like the representative of an army that had fought the British to a standstill, Montgomery at Luneberg Heath telling the German Generals what they should and shouldn't do if they wanted peace. He was in cloud-cuckoo-land.[29]

Despite the lack of progress, the parties agreed to meet again on Friday, 14 July. Unfortunately, the ceasefire collapsed on 9 July, primarily because of an incident in Lenadoon regarding the housing of Nationalist families. After the truce ended, eleven people were killed on 9 July, six of them by the British army, including two youths, a thirteen-year-old girl and a Catholic priest in what came to be known as the Springhill Massacre. The IRA killed five people on the same day, a sixth died two days later. There were no further meetings.

The IRA revealed the existence of the talks on 10 July, whereafter the British government was engulfed by a political crisis. For a while, the conference threatened to destroy Whitelaw's career but, in the end, managed to pull through the storm.

Bloody Friday, which followed on 21 July, infuriated Loyalists, who now began to queue up in great numbers to join the UDA, and other paramilitary groups. This became the era of the Shankill Butcher killings and the romper rooms. The latter consisted of a network of torture chambers where Catholics – some picked up off the street for no reason other than their religion – were beaten, some were peeled of their skin and stabbed to death. Some of those who perpetrated these crimes were British agents such as Albert Baker, John McKeague, Tommy 'Tucker' Lyttle and Tommy Herron.

Ordinary law-abiding citizens were, as always, caught in the crossfire.

The car bomb, controlled by a timer, as deployed on Bloody Friday, was far from the only technological innovation pioneered by MacStíofáin. Before the Troubles began, he had assembled a team of what he called 'Republican technicians'. They were now an integral part of the Provisional IRA's campaign. Wyman and Crinnion set out to thwart them with the aid of a boffin from MI5.

33

Colonel Lee of MI5 lectures the Gardaí

Seán MacStíofáin's interest in the use of technology as a tool of insurrection was a long-standing one. As IRA officer-in-command, London, in the 1950s, he had studied *Guerrilla Days in Ireland* by Tom Barry for what he called 'technical points'. He concluded that, while many of Barry's tactics were still valid, a general overhaul was required to bring them up to date. He foresaw a campaign against heavily fortified transport vehicles, soldiers dressed in protective flak jackets, helicopters, and improved radio communications. After his London unit completed its parade training, he would convene discussion groups to explore how they might further overhaul IRA tactics to reflect the modern era. By 1967, the IRA was busily experimenting with electronics at MacStíofáin's behest. Many of the devices they tried out performed 'very poorly, or were too flimsy and unreliable for active service conditions.[1]

MacStíofáin's 'Republican technicians' made great strides after the Troubles intensified. They discovered that by retuning television coils on sets operating on 'very high frequencies' (VHF), they could eavesdrop on military transmissions. Modified FM radios also served this purpose.[2]

MacStíofáin assigned responsibility for signals intelligence (SIGINT) to the intelligence officers in IRA battalion areas in Northern Ireland. They began to listen to military exchanges, comparing them with reports from observers on the streets, and started to learn the fundamentals. They discovered early on that 'Rucksack' meant 'RUC men', 'Watchdogs' were military policemen and 'Foxhounds' were soldiers, while 'Sunray' meant a military commander.[3]

By late 1970, the Provisionals and Officials were intercepting communication landlines. A number of telephone operators and engineers lent them a hand. The two wings swapped information relating to their strongholds during late 1971 and early 1972.[4]

These operations became more sophisticated with the Provisionals setting up dedicated monitoring posts with access to cables connecting them to phone exchanges. The technicians learnt how to connect and disconnect from the calls they were monitoring without causing clicks or drops in transmission levels. Teleprint communications were also monitored and one interception took place using a test teleprinter which they had acquired.[5]

The Officials were able to find out in advance when houses were going to be raided, often twelve hours ahead of time.

Both wings learned about internment before the swoops on Nationalist communities began, allowing senior IRA figures to flee their homes. No official was safe from IRA snooping. An exchange between UKREP Howard Smith and Philip Woodfield of the Home Office was captured in August 1971, the same month internment was introduced.[6]

MacStíofáin's modernisation of the IRA enabled him to evade capture on at least one occasion 'when IRA monitors in the North one night heard British military wavelengths put out the message: Seán MacStíofáin leaving Belfast by car. Intercept. I was warned and changed my plans.'[7]

MI6 discovered that MacStíofáin had acquired two telephone 'scramblers'. A scrambler is a device which distorts the voice of the user so that only someone with a descrambling apparatus on the other end of the line can understand what is being said. These mechanisms were not commercially available in Ireland. The IRA was able to purchase them in the USA. Others were stolen from government buildings in Northern Ireland. MI6 believed that the IRA would be able to use the devices to listen to calls made by officials in Ireland who believed their conversations were secure.

Wyman told Crinnion about this alarming development and the threat they posed to officials in the Republic. The pair pondered how they might neutralise the danger without exposing their clandestine relationship. If Crinnion shared the information with his superiors, it was inevitable that news of the development would ripple across the Phoenix Park as other departments were consulted. C4, which was based at HQ, had a substantial role in safeguarding official Irish communications. C4 personnel had overseen the installation of scramblers in high-level offices with the help of post office technicians. Another person who would have to be consulted about the threat was Joe Ainsworth. He was 'barracks master', a position which involved keeping up to date with technological advances for the benefit of the force. Ainsworth was already distrustful of Crinnion. G2, based nearby at its Red House HQ in Phoenix Park, would undoubtedly have been informed too. Col Hefferon, who had retired in April 1970, had been suspicious that Crinnion was a British agent and had voiced his concerns to Capt. Kelly and, possibly, others in G2.[8] There were many potential trapdoors through which Crinnion could fall if he was not careful.

Andy Ward, the secretary of the DoJ, was a devotee of his scrambler. It could be switched on and off at will to allow ordinary or secure calls to take place. At the start of a conversation with another government official with a corresponding machine, Ward was prone to say: 'Switch on your scrambler now'.[9]

Crinnion was in no doubt about the threat posed by this development. In one of his 1973 memoranda, he described how:

> All conversations between garda on matters relating to IRA [are] carried out on telephones using identical scrambler unit devices to the ones which were obtained by the IRA. Similarly all telephone calls between garda HQ, section 3 and the RUC, British services, intel/section, Dept of justice/Dept of Defence and a host of other important places use the scrambler device in case of accidental or deliberate eavesdropping by unauthorised persons.

Crinnion appreciated that the technology could enable the IRA 'to gain information by telephone tapping' and that 'the panic which [a] disclosure of this scrambler tech would create', would be 'harmful'. Andy Ward would have been aghast at the possibility the IRA were capable of monitoring his scrambled conversations. He was a deeply cautious and secretive man. After his appointment as secretary at the DoJ, he had dispatched a garda motorcyclist to his golf club to remove a picture which featured him in the company of a group of golfers from one of the walls at the clubhouse.

Wyman and Crinnion found a solution to the problem, one which would 'safeguard and make my authorities more security conscious' while at the same time further normalising relations between the gardaí and British intelligence. Wyman arranged for Detective Sergeants Murphy and McGonagle of C4, the men who looked after the 'technical aspects [of policing] for the garda', to be brought up to speed with the latest advances in technology to safeguard the security of calls. A seminar took place in November 1972 in London. It was attended by the pair from C4. Col Lee of MI5 addressed it, as did some of his colleagues. According to one of Crinnion's 1973 memoranda, Col Lee:

gave the garda a sound verbal briefing and offered them whatever technical assistance they wanted and, if they also wanted, he offered to come to Dublin and go over any problems with them on the spot. D/S/Murphy made a report of what he had learned in MI5 and this report is filed on 3C/181/58 [at C3]. After reading Murphy's reports C/S/Wren asked me if I had seen it and what I made of it. I assured him of the accuracy of the contents and advised him to keep the matters mentioned in view.

Crinnion described how Col Lee:

not alone gave training to S/B, technical bureau and army intelligence personally in London; he often came to Dublin and gave a week long course to selected Special Branch personnel in Dublin. I am glad to say that we paid his hotel bill. The receipt [is] on the file in C3.

Ironically, there were others in MI5 who wanted to follow MacStíofáin's example by intercepting official Irish telecommunications. Peter Wright, a surveillance expert and author of *Spycatcher*, carried out a review of intelligence operations in Ireland in 1972 or 1973, for the director-general of MI5. As he recounted in *Spycatcher*:

The only major recommendation I made was that we should devise a system of tapping the telephone lines of the Irish Republic ... I devised a scheme for intercepting the microwaves from the attic of the British embassy in Dublin using a device no larger than a packing case, but although MI5 endorsed the plan, the Foreign Office vetoed it. This was in the period leading up to what became the Sunningdale Agreement, and the Foreign Office were terrified that news of the plan might leak.[10]

MI6 had – and continued – to deploy other counter-measures against MacStíofáin. As 1972 progressed, the gloves really came off.

34

OLDFIELD'S GLOVES COME OFF

Events continued to churn dangerously on all fronts. Maurice Oldfield decided to send assassins to Ireland to kill Seán MacStíofáin, Séamus Costello and Seán Garland. Costello was the driving force behind the Aldershot atrocity.[1]

One of Oldfield's assassins was Kenneth Littlejohn. John Wyman, the controller of MI6's Irish network, became his handler.[2]

Littlejohn was born in Argyll, Scotland, on 19 October 1940. His younger brother Keith came along in 1946, the year the family moved to Birmingham. Littlejohn joined the British army and served two years with the Parachute Regiment as a lance corporal before being court-martialled for the larceny of a cash box at Warwick in 1959. He was dismissed and became an armed robber, a profession to which he usefully brought his military experience. He was arrested and convicted for the Fisher and Ludlow wages snatch in Ebrington, Birmingham, in 1966. Upon sentencing him, Mr Justice Ashworth, remarked that while the raid was not to be 'compared to the Great Train Robbery in amount, [it] can be compared in execution'.

Littlejohn was released in 1968 and attempted to lead a law-abiding life for the sake of his wife Christine and their two children. There was a sojourn during which he worked as a car dealer but it failed and he reverted to crime. In August 1970, at the age of twenty-nine, he was the driving force behind a wages snatch which netted £38,000, at a factory at Smethwick, near Birmingham. A police manhunt for him was soon underway.

Littlejohn fled to Ireland and made his way to Kerry with his hefty share of the heist. He cut quite a dash speeding around the county in an ostentatious red MGB sports car, flashing a fancy watch. Presenting himself as a playboy businessman, he boasted of his plans to establish a clothes factory to manufacture leather 'hotpants', under the name of Whiz Kids (Ireland) Ltd., in Cahirciveen, Co. Kerry.

Littlejohn, now calling himself Kenneth 'Austen', played the part of a successful property tycoon to the hilt. On one occasion, when he attended a local meeting of the chamber of commerce, he pulled up with a German masseuse and a secretary from Dublin in his sports car. Soon he was telling the chamber that Whizz Kids was Britain's hottest new clothing manufacturer. The attendees lapped up his every word.

It wasn't long before he had frittered away the proceeds of the Smethwick raid. In an audacious move he secured a meeting with Army Minister Geoffrey Johnson-Smith, MP, at 12 Calcutta Street, London, on 21 November 1971, through his brother Keith. During their three-hour encounter, Kenneth bragged that he had established significant contacts with the IRA in Kerry. So close was he to them, he alleged that he had been shown a cache of Russian rifles which had been landed by a Russian submarine.[3]

Another of his boasts was that he knew that John Taylor, a senior Unionist politician, was an Official IRA assassination target. Johnson-Smith was sufficiently impressed with the information that he offered to put Littlejohn in touch with the British special branch, but Littlejohn was adamant that he would only deal with military intelligence. At the end of the meeting Johnson-Smith said he would contact the appropriate authorities. Maurice Oldfield came onboard next and dispatched an MI6 officer to meet and assess Littlejohn at a flat in Cavan Street in London's East End. The man presented himself as 'Douglas Smythe'. His real name was John Wyman.[4] Littlejohn repeated what he had told the minister, and offered to become an agent for MI6. Wyman was more sceptical than Johnson-Smith. He told Littlejohn that he would get back to him.

The following February, an attempt was made on John Taylor's life by Joe McCann of the Official IRA. All of a sudden Littlejohn looked like he really did have the inside track on the Officials. Wyman renewed contact with Littlejohn and the latter's career as an MI6 agent in Ireland commenced.

A deal was struck: the charges against Littlejohn were to be dropped in return for his cooperation with MI6. If this sounds too fantastic to be true, it is worth noting that in August 1973, the Ministry of Defence in London provided a glimpse of what had taken place by issuing the following statement about their relationship with the Littlejohn brothers:

> [it was] arranged that Mr Johnson-Smith, who was then an Under-Secretary of State at the Ministry of Defence, should see [Kenneth] Littlejohn in order to ascertain what kind of information he could, in fact, pass on. This was the only occasion on which Mr Johnson-Smith met any member of the Littlejohn family. Because of what he had to say, the elder Littlejohn was then put in touch with the appropriate authorities.[5]

Kenneth returned to Ireland on a multifaceted mission, one leg of which was to infiltrate the Official IRA. According to MacStíofáin, 'Kenneth Littlejohn, the former British paratrooper with a known criminal record, had made contact with [the Official IRA] with the approval of British intelligence at a high level in London'. The Officials, however, did not fall for Littlejohn's palaver. Hanley and Millar have described how:

> From early 1972 an English criminal, Kenneth Littlejohn, had been

active with a group of Officials in the south Down area. Littlejohn had been introduced through an OIRA member's relative as 'a guy who arranges bank robberies'. He took part in a number of raids in the area during the spring and his brother Keith also became involved. The group carried out a robbery at the Hillgrove Hotel in Monaghan, after which Gardai discovered an arms dump and made arrests. One volunteer became very suspicious of Littlejohn, who incessantly argued for robberies in Dublin, 'as if [he] wanted to make a few waves'. He noticed that Littlejohn and his colleagues were wearing new clothes and socialising a lot. He refused to go on robberies with them, but other local Officials continued to vouch for the Englishman. Littlejohn constantly sought information about OIRA operations and often brought people on drinking sessions while not imbibing himself.[6]

Wyman and Littlejohn met in Dublin, Belfast and Newry during 1972. One of Wyman's haunts in Dublin was Buswell's hotel beside Dáil Éireann where he met the brothers.[7] They devised a scheme to kill MacStíofáin. Littlejohn said later that MI6 was 'convinced that if it had not been for [MacStíofáin] the whole problem could have been solved'.[8]

An attempt on MacStíofáin's life took place on 4 March 1972, when he was sent a letter bomb. It arrived while MacStíofáin was away from home. When MacStíofáin got back, his wife showed him a parcel that had arrived. He and another IRA man took it out of the house where it exploded. The other man's hands suffered burns and his beard and hair were 'badly singed'. MacStíofáin was 'slightly burnt on the face, and had a cut in one eye'. He felt that if the charge had been more powerful, the pair of them might have been killed or badly injured. He attended his local hospital where an optician advised him 'to wear an eyeshade for a while'.[9]

MacStíofáin wrote that although much of Kenneth Littlejohn's story about planning to assassinate him was 'pure cock-and-bull, it is nevertheless interesting that he said one way this was to be tried was by "disintegrating" me. In other words, a bomb.'[10]

When Littlejohn spoke to the press later, he described a more sophisticated plot that involved him driving to the neighbourhood in which MacStíofáin lived, where he waited to see if he might turn up:

> I [Kenneth Littlejohn] was also told to assassinate MacStíofáin in the summer of 1972, just after Operation Motorman.

Operation Motorman took place on 31 July 1972. This was after the collapse of the Chelsea talks between Whitelaw and the IRA and the violence that followed, including Bloody Friday, which took place on 21 July 1972. Littlejohn continued:

> Keith and I waited in a car outside MacStíofáin's house, which is at Navan, Co. Westmeath, but we never saw him. The instructions we were given were that MacStíofáin's body was to be blown up so that it was completely unrecognisable. We should also take his car to Dublin airport, and thereafter money would be sent from Canada to his family so that it would appear that he had absconded with IRA funds. They would also spread rumours to this effect, which they had previously attempted to do so.[11]

This smear was a variation on a slander MI6 and the IRD were circulating in Northern Ireland that Ian Paisley had stolen money from his supporters to purchase farmland in Canada.

MacStíofáin believed he was also the victim of a hostile propaganda campaign which ran in parallel with the plan to kill him. The plot was designed to diminish his reputation in the eyes of his supporters. One of the conduits, he alleged, was the *Daily Telegraph*.[12] He accused one of the paper's former editorial executives of having been in MI6. Another, who had died recently, had been a 'very big wheel in naval intelligence and was a leading authority on intelligence in general'. The cabal at the paper, he alleged, had close ties to the Tories. 'The first inkling of the latest move against me was when Dublin was plastered with posters advertising a forthcoming article in *The Sunday Telegraph*. The posters referred to "the Englishness of Seán MacStíofáin". When the article itself came out, it proved to be merely a personal attack on me. It's essential theme was that my Irish connections were thin ...'[13]

BY MID-1972, JOHN Wyman had instructed the Littlejohns to kill other IRA leaders. Kenneth explained:

> One of my main functions was to assassinate a man called [Séamus] Costello, who was the effective number one of the Officials, and had been trained in Moscow. I was also to assassinate another high-up member in the Officials, Seán Patrick Garland, who I believe was trained in Cuba.[14]

Further attacks were perpetrated against other leading Republicans. A booby-trapped parcel was sent to Cathal Goulding through the Dunleer post office, Co. Louth, not far from 'Smuggler's Cottage', Clogherhead, Co. Louth, where the Littlejohns had made their headquarters. Goulding defused the device.[15]

Tomás MacGiolla, president of Official Sinn Féin, and Ruairí Ó Brádaigh, his counterpart in Provisional Sinn Féin, were sent bombs in the post. Ó Brádaigh's was intercepted by the Roscommon post office.[16]

Tony Ruane, an IRA general in the 1920s, who was now the treasurer of Provisional Sinn Féin, was badly burned when a parcel exploded inside Sinn Féin's head office at Kevin Street.[17]

By now, Wyman was in danger himself. Littlejohn provided him with a warning that the IRA was aware that a man answering to his description had been visiting Belfast pubs and it was their intention to kill him.[18]

Wyman was also directing the Littlejohns to carry out kidnappings. One of the targets was Seán Collins, a Republican from Dundalk. Collins recounted later how:

> On January 13, 1972 shortly before 9 p.m., two men in a car called at my home. My wife told them that I was probably in Mulligan's bar in Crowe Street, Dundalk. Sometime afterwards they arrived at the bar. One of them spoke to me, said he had been sent down from Waterfoot and told to contact me for help. He asked me to go outside with him. When we got outside, he drew a gun at me and forced me into a car which I think was a dark red Fiat 850. I didn't get the number of it but I think that the registration letters were either NZH or MZH. There was a driver in the car. (When the photographs of the Littlejohn brothers were published in the press in July and August of this year – 1973 – I recognised Kenneth Littlejohn as the one who kidnapped me at gunpoint in January 1972).

> We drove to Newry via an unapproved road. They said that they were members of the Official IRA and wanted to have a talk with me. On the way, Kenneth Littlejohn kept the gun on me at all times. In Newry, the driver parked the car in a street diagonally opposite the RUC station. They said: 'The boys are in here'. The driver got out, went over towards the house. Littlejohn was nervous and shaking. Within a few minutes the car was surrounded by soldiers.[19]

The kidnap operation was supervised by someone known to the Littlejohns as 'Captain Van Dorn', the *nom de guerre* of an officer who later became a high-profile Tory politician.

Yet another leg of the Littlejohns' assignment was to carry out bank robberies in the Republic. These were to be blamed on the Officials to provoke public anger.

Subsequently, there were petrol-bomb attacks on garda stations. Two took place, both perpetrated by the Littlejohns, one in Castlebellingham, the other elsewhere in Louth, in September 1972. It can safely be assumed that Wyman did not tell Crinnion that he – Wyman – was overseeing petrol-bomb attacks against garda stations. The Littlejohns also sparked a riot in Dundalk and attempted a bank robbery in Dundalk which was unsuccessful. However, as author Raymond Murray has pointed out:

> After the petrol bombing and a riot in Dundalk, the Minister for Justice, Mr Desmond O'Malley, began to draft his amendment to the Offences Against the State Act. That was the last thing the IRA wanted. In this affair the Littlejohns could claim success.[20]

London denied that the Littlejohns had been cleared to commit bank robberies or any of the other crimes about which they spoke. British spies, it was claimed, simply did not act in such a dishonourable manner. Belying this, Capt. Fred Holroyd a military intelligence officer who worked in the field for MI6, has revealed that he was asked by Craig Smellie, the MI6 officer at Lisburn, to carry out bank robberies. He was warned that if he was caught, he would be abandoned. Holroyd declined the request.[21]

Littlejohn later explained the rationale behind the spate of violence: it was designed to heap pressure on Jack Lynch to get him to enact stronger legislation against the IRA.

During the course of 1972 Wyman handed supervision of the Littlejohns over to a man they came to know as 'Oliver'. According to Littlejohn, Wyman and 'Oliver' were aware of his bank-robbing activities. Neither of them told him to desist 'partly because it might break my cover and also because they were happy for pressure to be brought to bear on the Lynch government to tighten up controls on the IRA'.[22]

A self-righteous Littlejohn added: 'I rowed with Oliver every time I met him. We just didn't get on. His ideas and my ideas were not the same. He wanted the results that would come from illegal acts.'[23]

On 12 October 1972, the Littlejohn brothers and their gang raided a bank on Grafton Street which netted them £67,000, the then largest heist in Irish history. They fled back to Britain immediately after the job. The Littlejohns were far from being the only criminals involved in armed robbery at this time. There were approximately 2,000 incidents on the island, in 1972, netting £800,000. While this statistic could be used to argue that the Littlejohn crime spree was no more than a drop in the ocean, the AIB heist on Grafton Street was the largest in the history of the state, to that point in time and, on its own, made a powerful impact, not least for the fact that the wife of the bank manager, and his children, had been held hostage by the gang. The Littlejohns also attacked garda stations and caused a riot.

As shall be described shortly, Jim Hanna of the UVF was also a British agent. Hanna was responsible for bank raids for which he was not arrested. While Fred Holroyd refused to engage in raids, how many others were asked and agreed to carry out such crimes? Saor Éire had engaged in this activity since the 1960s. After they began to disintegrate as an organisation in the early 1970s, their members continued to target banks. By the last quarter of 1972, all of this violence was adding to the pressure on Lynch, O'Malley, and their colleagues to up their game against the IRA.

Behind closed doors, Lynch was trying to assure the British he was serious about curbing the paramilitaries. On 23 October 1972, he spoke to John Peck, who sent a revealing 'secret' report back to Kelvin White at the FCO the following day:

> … I said we had all been interested in rumours that the Minister for Justice [Des O'Malley] was going to introduce new legislation early in the current session of the Dáil. The Taoiseach replied,

'Well, I don't know about new legislation. Our quarrel is not with the law but with the lawyers. We have a standing group of seven barristers working with us to see how the safeguards in our Constitution need not be used by Ó Dálaigh's boys [*this is a reference to the bench of the Supreme Court*] to block security measures – anyway you have seen that we have shunted Ó Dálaigh into Europe. (It is indeed true that the application of the Offences Against the State Act is indeed subject to the ultimate authority of the judiciary, but this is the first indication I have had that the Chief Justice, who is a dedicated lawyer, historian and exponent of the Irish language, was regarded by the Fianna Fáil Government as an obstacle to internal security measures.)[24]

Chief Justice Ó Dálaigh had felt honoured at being chosen to go to Europe as a judge of the European Court of Justice. At the time no one suspected such a degree of cynicism lurked behind his appointment.

Despite all the promises made by MI6, the Littlejohn brothers were subsequently extradited to Dublin, where they stood trial and were sent to prison. Kenneth escaped in 1974, but was recaptured at the end of that year and reimprisoned. He was released early, in 1981, as one of the first acts of the FitzGerald administration of 1981–82.

35

THE RITA O'HARE WINDFALL

As the Troubles intensified, John Wyman became a wellspring of valuable information for Crinnion. One of the high points of their relationship was reached the day the British spy told Crinnion that a 'particular telephone number in Dublin was a contact number used by the Belfast Provo IRA staff to reach I.R.A., G.H.Q.'[1] G.H.Q meant General Headquarters, the organising hub of Provisional IRA activity. It was located in Dublin. For the gardaí, this was the intelligence equivalent of gaining entry to Aladdin's cave.

Crinnion's superiors, Larry Wren and Michael Fitzgerald, were delighted 'with the prospects and I was instructed to type out an application for a postal warrant to cover all telephone conversations and correspondence to the address'.[2] The property pinpointed by Wyman was in the name of a telephone subscriber on 'Newtown Park Avenue, Blackrock, Co. Dublin'.[3]

The warrant was sent to the DoJ for approval. The following day, Paddy Colwell of the DoJ called Larry Wren to discuss the request. Wren summoned Crinnion to his office and handed the phone over to him:

COLWELL told me the Minister for Justice [Des O'Malley] liked to know a bit about the background to Postal Warrants. I told him that I had received the information from an Informant whom I knew to be reliable as he had given me other information in the past which had been proved accurate by subsequent events.[4]

Detective Sgt Danny Boyle of C3 was standing beside Crinnion during the conversation. He was fully conversant with what was taking place. Crinnion offered to identify his informant. Colwell told him that would not be necessary:

> D/Sergt. BOYLE heard me offering to name my Informant and shook his head in disapproval saying – 'No, No, Never, Never, Never name an Informant'.[5]

Boyle's professionalism is to be admired. However, the fact that Boyle had to urge Crinnion not to name his source, who was, of course, John Wyman, indicates that a slackness had taken root at C3. Crinnion's knowledge that MacStíofáin was talking to Philip McMahon, is another indication of laxity. The identity of McMahon's informers should equally have been a secret McMahon kept to himself.

If Crinnion was prepared to tell Colwell about Wyman over the phone in front of Wren and Boyle, it is difficult to imagine he had not already told Wren about the MI6 spy. If he had not, Wren must have noticed that much of the information provided by Crinnion's 'Informant' concerned overseas activities such as gunrunning and probably originated with MI6.

The postal warrant for the phone tap was duly signed by O'Malley, and surveillance of the Newtown Park Avenue connection, together with postal deliveries thereto, commenced. Crinnion waited anxiously for it to yield the expected bumper harvest of intelligence. When it produced nothing, Crinnion linked up with Wyman:

> [They went] carefully through the information originally at [Wyman's] disposal and discovered that the telephone number shown in the 1972 Directory for the house in Newtown Park Avenue was different to the one shown for the same house in the 1971 Directory. There had also been a change of subscribers and it

seemed to us then that this house might have had three different telephone numbers in a 2-year period.[6]

Crinnion rang Detective Sgt Paddy Shevlin, of the SDU for assistance. Shevlin had contacts at the GPO. Within ten minutes, no less a figure than John Fleming, head of the SDU, rang Crinnion back with news. The phone number was linked to Rita O'Hare who was living at Monaloe, Foxrock, Co. Dublin. O'Hare, originally from Andersonstown in west Belfast, was a significant figure in the Provisional IRA. She was born Rita McCullough to a Protestant socialist father, Billy, and a Catholic mother, Maureen. Her husband was Gerry O'Hare, a fellow member of the IRA. She had been arrested in 1972 for an attempt to kill a British army warrant officer called Frazer Paton in Belfast. Having been granted bail, she absconded to the Republic. She took refuge in a safe house in Goatstown, on the south side of Dublin, for a while. According to one of Crinnion's 1973 memoranda:

> This house was used as a gathering point for the Provos, they all lived together in it. The house was later destroyed as they burned the doors and windows and as the WC'S did not work, the place was in an awful mess. Later on, after this, there was a man shot and nothing much was heard about it as it just fizzled out.

> ... Later [O'Hare] occupied a house, which I can identify from any 1972 telephone directory, at Newtown Park Avenue, Blackrock, Co. Dublin. Then she went to Monaloe, Clonkeen Road, Foxrock, Co. Dublin. It is interesting to notice that the telephone number which had been installed in the house at Newton Park, was transferred to the house at Monaloe and from the subscribers directory – a special directory available to the Garda at the GPO, she is shown as the subscriber and C/S/Fleming confirmed to me verbally that she was at the address. All these houses were in good class residential areas and all three were in the 88 telephone exchange area.

Crinnion's suspicions grew that the Provisionals had a contact inside Post and Telegraphs who was aiding the IRA to jump the queue to obtain telephone lines. In 1972 applicant subscribers endured long waiting periods before they were connected to the phone network. Crinnion, a senior intelligence officer, had waited 'considerably longer for my phone' than had O'Hare:

> Perhaps I should explain that it was obvious at this point that Mrs O'Hare was the subject of preferential treatment from the Telephone Service. Less than a year earlier she had been living in Belfast and came to Dublin on-the-run after being concerned in a shooting incident. [The SDU was] aware that when she first arrived in Dublin she lived in a large detached house at Goatstown, Co. Dublin. Adding my information, it now looked as if she then lived in this house at Newtown Park Avenue before moving to Monaloe, Clonkeen Road. All three houses were in the 88 Telephone Exchange Area. Not alone had the number been taken from Newtown Park Avenue to Monaloe but another number had been installed at the vacated house. I put a Memo on Mrs. O'Hare's file in C3 and explained the confusion to Chief Supt. Wren.[7]

Crinnion 'advised caution to both D/S/Shevlin and C/S/ Fleming, in whatever arrangements they made locally' with officials of the post office to tap O'Hare's line lest they alert O'Hare that she had been rumbled.

Garda intelligence now discovered that O'Hare was a pivotal figure in the Provisional IRA. As Crinnion came to realise, she was performing a similar role to that of one of her predecessors during the Border Campaign:

> Mrs O'Hare was the perfect contact, knowing Belfast and its authentic Provos like her own family. She could readily identify the small number of authorised callers, arrange meetings, delivering points for supplies, know the financial requirements and generally act to the Provo IRA, GHQ staff like a company secretary.

On another occasion, Crinnion explained that O'Hare:

> was [a] fully committed person, her husband was in Long Kesh and with her knowledge of the city and its personalities, from a security angle, she would be a difficult person to deceive. All incoming messages from Belfast, all requests for Arms, Explosives and Meetings would first have to reach her from known Staff Officers, get approval and then be dealt with by GHQ. In the world of commerce she might be described as an Aide to the General Manager.

The SDU continued to monitor her phone over the next few years. O'Hare went on to serve a three-year jail sentence in 1976 for endeavouring to smuggle explosives into Limerick prison while on a visit.

An attempt to extradite O'Hare to Northern Ireland failed after the High Court in Dublin ruled in 1978 that she was wanted for political offences.

She went on to hold several leadership positions in Provisional Sinn Féin, including editor of *An Phoblacht*, the party's newspaper; director of publicity; general secretary; and the party's representative to Washington, 1998–2023. After her death in 2023, aged eighty, Mary Lou McDonald, leader of Sinn Féin, paid tribute to her, describing her as a 'genuine patriot' and a 'powerhouse'.

O'Hare died without knowing that MI6 had organised for her phone to be tapped after the tipoff by Wyman to Crinnion and oblivious to the fact that the tap on her line had been the undoing of Seán MacStíofáin.

36

THE STRAW THAT BROKE THE CAMEL'S BACK

Between 1969 and 1972, Patrick Crinnion and John Wyman enjoyed several coups against the IRA. Crinnion claimed that Wyman's information thwarted a series of arms importations bound for Saor Éire and the IRA. 'I cannot give even an approximate tally but the number of weapons lost on abortive smuggling attempts must be somewhere in the 2,000 region. There was also considerable loss to IRA prestige and important sums of cash were uselessly spent.'[1]

During the same period, the SDU maintained their faith in MacStíofáin as a reliable informer despite his conduct at the Chelsea conference, and the intensification of Provisional IRA operations such as Bloody Friday. Somehow, MacStíofáin managed to convince them that he was doing his best to curtail the violent impulses of his colleagues, and they believed him.

In July 1972, the SDU raided a Provisional IRA safe house occupied by James Conaty, a veteran of the 1916 Rising. Conaty had gone to the US but had returned home in later years. The SDU uncovered a cache of documents at the residence. They revealed a wealth of material about the Provisionals which MacStíofáin had withheld from the SDU. The documents included the names of all of the members of the Provisional IRA.[2] Only now did the full extent of the threat posed by the Provisionals become apparent. The shocking truth finally dawned on them: MacStíofáin had been pulling the wool over their eyes for over a decade. Latterly, he had deflected garda attention toward the Official IRA while creating a breathing space for himself to build up the Provisional IRA. As Crinnion put it, MacStíofáin's 'status' as an informer:

> would in all probability have continued but for documents found in the home of a retired Irish/American and a former Clann na Gael Treasurer, James CONATY, Drumhirk, Stradons. These documents were such that they were brought to the Minister for Justice [Des O'Malley] for his personal perusal.[3]

The SDU had a string of compelling reasons to conceal the entire MacStíofáin fiasco: {i} the abject humiliation that they had been strung along by MacStíofáin for over a decade; {ii} MacStíofáin had been 'well paid'; {iii} a lot of political blood had been spilt.[4] Notably, Lynch had lost three senior and one junior ministers as a result of the Arms Crisis. His party had split and was still engaged in internecine feuding.

A manhunt was set in motion to find MacStíofáin. During the pursuit, a phone call was made from Belfast to Rita O'Hare's house in Foxrock. The caller introduced O'Hare 'to Kevin O'Kelly, the R.T.E. journalist, who arranged with her for an interview with the Provo Chief-of-Staff, Seán Mac-STIOPHAIN, to take place at [O'Kelly's] Rathmines home. What transpired afterwards is now history.'[5]

The encounter with MacStíofáin went ahead at O'Kelly's home on 19 November 1972, while, out of sight, armed SDU officers scruitinised the house closely. After the interview, Mac-Stíofáin was taken away in a car but arrested a short while later by the SDU officers.

Some officers who were unaware of MacStíofáin's duplicity were still labouring under the impression he was a *bona fide* informer. They were taken aback when they learned the SDU had arrested him.

Crinnion kept his head low. He 'made no comment to C/S/Wren nor sought [any] credit for my part in the eventual arrest of MacStiophain, neither did I request at any time any cash [as a] reward for my informant, which would have been forthcoming had I so requested. I did however give John Wyman a small personal gift – an item of small value.'

Crinnion was delighted:

> Wyman's tip to me [about the phone call to monitor] took the Chief-of-Staff out of circulation, complete with all the data and schemes he had in his head and his imprisonment disrupted the Provo Campaign to an appreciable extent.

> Although one can never say it resulted in a saving of this number or that number of lives, the setback to IRA Operations was considerable and it was a milestone along the road towards peace.

Crinnion told Det. Sgt Boyle that MacStíofáin's arrest had come about 'through the data supplied by my Informant'.[6]

After his arrest MacStíofáin was taken to the Bridewell garda station and charged with membership of the IRA. He responded by embarking on a hunger and thirst strike that same night. He persisted with his fast during a number of court appearances which followed each other in quick succession and a trial which ended on 25 November 1972. He received a six-month prison sentence for membership of the IRA.

While the top echelons of the gardaí were aware of the fraud MacStíofáin had perpetrated on them, Des O'Malley was not apprised of the secret. In 2020, O'Malley stated that he was '99% certain' that MacStíofáin had not been an informer.[7]

As fate would have it, Crinnion was about to come face-to-face with MacStíofáin for the first and only time. When the encounter took place, Crinnion was dressed as a doctor and it culminated in the pair wrestling on MacStíofáin's hospital bed.

37

CRINNION'S BEDSIDE MANNER

At about 4.30 p.m. on the afternoon of Sunday, 26 November 1972, four men entered the front entrance of the Mater Hospital in Dublin. Outside, a mob was chanting for the release of Seán MacStíofáin, who was in the eighth day of his hunger and thirst strike. Two men emerged from the crowd dressed as clerics but, in reality, were armed IRA volunteers. Additional IRA men sneaked into the hospital unnoticed at approximately the same time. The 'clerics' headed for St Gabriel's ward where they knew their commander was being confined. They were confronted by a small party of SDU men on the corridor. Eight to ten shots were discharged. Three of the would-be rescuers ran up a flight of stairs, out of sight.

By Crinnion's telling, MacStíofáin heard the commotion outside his room and became excited at the prospect of escape. Sgt Denis Hurley, who was on guard duty inside the room, restrained him from climbing out of his bed. Outside, a sergeant called Madigan was nursing a bleeding hand while a colleague pinned one of the intruders to the floor with his knee.

There were at least two other aspiring liberators on the hospital premises. They scarpered across a flat roof after the shooting began. Garda Owen Sheelin, who was on duty at the Berkeley Road entrance to the hospital, spotted them. As they drew closer, one of the men pulled out a revolver and warned the garda to back off. The gunman held onto his weapon as he scurried down a drainpipe. This pair escaped.

A short while later Fr Seán McManus, an authentic priest, entered the hospital to visit MacStíofáin.[1] As he walked towards St Gabriel's, a group of SDU men grabbed and pinned him to the wall. One was in a rage and cursed at him: 'One of you fuckers tried to shoot me.' The priest was shocked. It took a while for the SDU men to calm down. Reflecting on their behaviour in 2023, Fr McManus said, 'They were young men and frightened.'[2] After the encounter, Fr McManus was left with a bruised neck but was allowed inside to see MacStíofáin. He was stunned at how 'terrible he looked'.[3]

A search was conducted to find the three men who had escaped. Between 6.30 p.m. and 7.00 p.m., Detective Garda Albert McFarland found the three together hiding in an alcove. One of them was dressed as a priest. McFarland ordered them to put their hands up, which they did, and he searched them. One had a loaded gun in his pocket. They were arrested and conveyed to the Bridewell.

Inside the ward room, MacStíofáin was surrounded by an array of people: his wife Mary, one of his daughters, Sr Dolores, Fr Farrell, the chaplain of Mountjoy prison, two staff nurses, a man called Collins from Navan as well as Sgt Denis Hurley.

Alarmed by the drama unfolding at the hospital, the SDU decided to move MacStíofáin from the Mater back to Mountjoy and from there, by helicopter, to a military hospital in the Curragh, Co Kildare. The presence of the protesters posed a problem. The solution they arrived at was to remove MacStíofáin *incognito* in an ambulance. Rather than borrow one from a hospital, they decided to use one of their own. It bore garda markings which were removed.

Crinnion's unit, C3, worked in a standard Monday-to-Friday fashion. It was unusual for C3 officers to find themselves working outside of normal office hours, especially on a Sunday. Nevertheless, Crinnion managed to place himself at the centre of these fast-unfolding events. He volunteered for the mission. Late that night, he and a colleague, both dressed as doctors, drove to the hospital with other SDU officers and made for St Gabriel's ward. His companion coaxed Mary MacStíofáin, wife of the patient, away from his bedside by pretending they were moving him to another room.

MacStíofáin's account of what happened does not include any reference to an attempt by him to jump from his bed. While he may have forgotten some details of the night due to his condition, he was able to describe the presence of a 'doctor'. Unbeknownst to him, there were two 'doctors', one of whom was Crinnion. MacStíofáin's recollection was that:

> ... a strange doctor came in and very abruptly asked my wife to wait outside. Mary said she was usually allowed to stand behind a screen while I was examined. But a detective came and told her she was wanted outside.
>
> This doctor checked me over, saying very little. As soon as he finished, five or six men in plainclothes came quickly into the ward.
>
> 'You're going out of here,' someone said. They just lifted me out of the bed and carried me out into the corridor, none too gently.[4]

Mary MacStíofáin realised swiftly that the doctor who had 'examined' her husband was a garda. She described him later as 'O'Malley's henchman', a reference to Des O'Malley.

CRINNION'S ACCOUNT, RECORDED in one of his 1973 memoranda, is that:

> When MacStiophain was moved from the Mater hospital to Mountjoy prison for his helicopter flight to the Curragh [military hospital], I came with another garda in the Garda ambulance from which all the Garda signs had been removed and after Mrs [Mary] MacStiophain had been decoyed away from his bedside

I entered his ward and told Sean MacStiophain in answer to his query that we were moving him to another place for treatment.

MacStiophain attempted to spring from his bed towards me and when I grasped his arms to force him back I was amazed at his strength.

It took more than just Crinnion to subdue MacStíofáin. Sgt Hurley had to lie across his chest too:

About 8 men kept him on the stretcher in the ambulance and [the] protesters in the street vicinity of the hospital were deceived into thinking we were an ordinary case coming out of the hospital and the transfer [to Mountjoy] went off better than anticipated.

Crinnion did not join the helicopter flight to the Curragh but learned that as it:

lifted over Mountjoy buildings that MacStiophain succeeded in getting a foot loose of the restraining strap on his stretcher and he kicked the controls from the pilots' hand. For a split second the helicopter was out of control and the co-pilot had to fling himself from his seat and keep hold of MacStiophain's feet until they landed in the Curragh.

Crinnion's masquerade as a doctor caused some mirth inside C3:

Super [Michael] Fitzgerald had thought the [media] reports very funny as MacStiophain made some references to me (having lifted him out of his bed in the Mater hospital) and Super Fitzgerald told me that I would be glad to know MacStiophain had forgiven me and was getting the Pope to say prayers for me. Mrs MacStiophain had referred to me according to the newspapers as O'Malley's henchman (O'Malley the minister of Justice), for whisking her husband away while her back was turned. This was a source of amusement for a few days in the office and I was getting a bit of teasing, taking a dying man from his sick bed. I hadn't a chance to read the army comments but, threw a copy in to the tray to read later. No special purpose (vanity I now realise).

Fr McManus went to see MacStíofáin at the Curragh:

I drove down to visit him at the military hospital the following morning. His wife and daughter were outside the hospital block. I joined them there for a while. They were eventually allowed in, but I wasn't. I got an indication of just how tight the security was when I approached a soldier on duty to ask if I could use the bathroom inside the hospital block. When he refused, I told him it was an emergency and that if I could not use the bathroom, I would have to go behind the trees at the bottom of the field. 'Father, please don't,' he implored me. 'We have orders to shoot anything that moves down there.'

Sometime later, the military sent out for me. An emergency had developed and I was going to be let in after all. They escorted me in a great hurry to where MacStíofáin was being held in a cage – literally: his bed was inside a large cage with bars. His daughter was inside it screaming, 'Fr Seán, Fr Seán, my father is dying.' He was having a rigour and was shaking violently.[5]

Fr McManus is credited with persuading MacStíofáin to end his protest. Although the priest did not mention this in his memoirs, MacStíofáin recalled later how, when things calmed down, Fr McManus sat down beside him and began to talk 'in a low, earnest tone':

'Now, Seán, listen to me,' he began. 'The position is this. You are very ill. If you don't drink tonight, you will probably die tomorrow or the day after.

'You don't know what the situation is outside. There are demonstrations all over the country on your behalf, and the mood of the demonstrators is very ugly. If you go on with this and you die very soon, there will be riots. There will be a lot of bloodshed, and many people will be arrested, hurt, or even killed. Do you want that?'[6]

MacStíofáin had no such desire and ended his protest gradually after that. He began by taking fluids.

38

DON CARLOS HAUGHEY

The Godfather, released in March of 1972, was a box-office smash hit around the globe. During a vital moment in the story, a Turkish gangster called Virgil Sollozzo tells Don Corleone: 'I need a man who has powerful friends ... I need, Don Corleone, those politicians you carry in your pocket, like so many nickels and dimes.' The film swept the Oscars the following year. It reinforced the notion that corrupt politicians and gangsters could be partners in crime, at least in America.

One politician MI6 had in their cross hairs was Charles Haughey. The disdainful view of Haughey inside the service was well summarised by Anthony Verrier, a confidant of MI6's Frank Steele, thus:

> In this millionaire politician were found all those lurking sympathies for extreme action which British governments feared so much and fought so hard.[1]

In 1972 a character assassination team consisting of Hugh Mooney of the Information Research Department (IRD), Ambassador John Peck, the former head of the IRD, and others, was busily involved in a smear campaign against Charles Haughey.[2] Absurd as it might seem now, they jumped onto *The Godfather* bandwagon with a scheme to link Haughey to the American Mafia.

One of the techniques employed by MI6 and the IRD to vilify targets was to circulate their slurs by word of mouth. IRD and MI6 smearmeisters called them 'sibs', a term derived from the Latin word *sibillare* (to whisper). Diplomats from the

British embassy and MI6 officers kept profiles of Irish contacts in books at the embassy for a multiplicity of purposes. In the 1970s, they were able to identify likely gossips from their lists. Those at their disposal ranged from people who knew they were doing the bidding of British intelligence smear mongers, to those known in spy parlance as 'useful idiots'.

When it came to operations against Haughey, finding willing rumour mongers was an easy task. Most of those who were friendly with the embassy tended to look down on him as a working-class upstart, a boy educated by Christian Brothers rather than in a fee-paying school. In their world, a man entered the professional world as a graduate of a private school, not on the back of scholarships as was the case with Haughey. Haughey had made a splash in the world of accountancy before he entered politics. Worse still, he was now running the economy, a position that forced many of them to bend the knee to him.

John Betjeman of the British embassy (and later Britain's poet laureate) had trickled an assortment of 'sibs' into the Dublin gossip stream during the Second World War. They had been fed to Betjeman by Britain's Psychological Warfare department. He did so by visiting Dublin's hostelries and engaging in conversations with journalists. In the early 1970s, his successors dropped 'sibs' around Dublin in a like manner. One alleged that Haughey was friendly with Russian journalists whom he knew were, in reality, KGB spies.[3] The method was one of incremental and relentless vilification. Another yarn claimed Haughey was directing a campaign to bomb buildings in Belfast so he could purchase them at a knock-down price.[4]

These fabrications, once created, had to be guided in the right direction. They were circulated to the members of golf, rugby, yacht and bridge clubs in middle-class and upper-middle-class Ireland. Certain gentlemen's clubs in the city which were frequented by British embassy officials were hot spots for this activity too. Sibs were also circulated at garden parties at the British ambassador's residence where guests swallowed them as eagerly as the *vol-au-vents* and cucumber sandwiches offered to them on silver platters.

Overall, the anti-Haughey stories made little impact as their circulation was largely confined to the elite of Irish society who already looked down on Haughey because of what Garret FitzGerald had described to the Dáil in 1979 as his 'flawed pedigree'.

The Haughey-Mafia smear, however, had the potential to reach a wider audience due to the popularity of *The Godfather*. A slur like that could have been spread around Dublin in a night by chatting to a few garrulous taxi drivers. The groundwork was already in place. An article had appeared in an English newspaper which alleged that an international corporation with an array of subsidiaries, including a manufacturing company in Walkinstown, was controlled by the American Mafia.[5]

The FBI had drawn up a report on the organisation which found its way to MI6. An extract was passed to a private detective agency, who shall be referred to here as KSE. They handed it over to Thomas Mullen. The latter, a former C3 officer, was the man who had recruited Crinnion to spy for MI6 in the early 1960s. Mullen's task was to find some way of manufacturing a connection between Haughey and the company in Walkinstown. Mullen furnished the FBI extract to Crinnion to see what he could find out about visits by Mafia gangsters to Dublin.

Crinnion later sought to explain his interest in the probe on the basis that Mullen had 'been until recently working part-time as a Security Man and making Enquiries. One day he met me ... and showed me a letter he had received from another Private Investigator [KSE]. This letter mentioned that some MAFIA leaders had travelled to Dublin allegedly to meet Charles Haughey, TD.'[6]

If agents of the FBI had wanted to investigate suspected Mafia activity in Ireland, they would have gone to the gardaí with whom they had excellent police to police conduits. They would never have approached a firm of private detectives. The same situation applies to New Scotland Yard. Crinnion did not address a number of troubling questions which arise from this affair. Who was KSE's client? Who retained KSE if not MI6? Why did the private detective firm go to a retired C3 officer in his seventies for help, unless, of course, they had been so directed by their client? What sort of a client – other than MI6 – would have known of the existence of Thomas Mullen and that he was a suitable inquiry agent?

The notion that Haughey was breaking bread with the Mafia is comical. Crinnion, who was later described as a 'Walter Mitty' character, purported to have taken this nonsense seriously.[7] He told Malone:

At that time I was unsure of any Mafia activity in Dublin and felt the information was unfounded. When I read the FBI report from John Minnich [an FBI agent] and saw that the MAFIA had a front operation in Dublin for some years, I realised that the letter received by Tom Mullen might have some police interest.[8]

There was no evidence that linked the firm to the Mafia. None of its personnel was ever prosecuted for any crime. Crinnion was told the company manufactured 'slot machines' and claimed that:

One aspect of this which was of particular interest to me was the possibility that the components for the slot machine coming in unassembled could be used to conceal firearms in [a] knocked-down condition. As I was aware that some unknown firms in Dublin were successfully importing firearms for the Provos, it was my intention to talk to Mr Mullen and he would have told me whether his enquiries concerning the MAFIA visitors had been fruitful or not.[9]

The FBI extract presented problems for Crinnion when it was discovered in his possession later because it was a foreign intelligence document which had not been sent to the gardaí through the normal channels.

According to Crinnion, the document 'was an extract from the FBI [which] set out [a list of the] registered shareholders of the company' in Walkinstown. He sought to explain his entanglement in the saga as follows:

> Although I never found it necessary to do part-time work after the better wages came along after the Conroy Commission [into garda pay and conditions which reported in late 1969], people automatically assumed that I was still doing odd jobs. This is not correct and the only contact I had outside of the Force was with an ex-Detective Sergeant from C3, Thomas Mullen, Ramleh Villas, Milltown, Dublin.

As an aside, Crinnion had been a part-time model in the 1960s. He starred in an advertisement for a Philishave battery-operated shaver which was published in *The Sunday Independent* on 21 July 1968. The picture showed him gazing into the distance while rotating the shaver around his left cheek. A Martello tower featured in the background.

Crinnion made no reference to the fact that Thomas Mullen had recruited him to spy for MI6. Instead, he pointed out that the older man was over seventy but was still 'active and out of respect for him whenever he asked me for assistance if it was within my power to help him I would do so'.

In reality, Crinnion's value to Mullen was that he was in

a position to gain access to all sorts of information about the company, some of which might prove useful in manufacturing a smear that Haughey was a partner with the Mafia in a scheme to smuggle arms to the IRA.

The goal of linking Haughey to the manufacturing company was not as scatter-brained as it appears at first glance. Haughey had visited many factories during his political career. If any sort of a link could be found between a shareholder or employee of the company and Haughey, the IRD had the skill to transform such an encounter into an appetising treat for Dublin's army of gossips.

As Christmas of 1972 approached, Mullen and Crinnion planned to meet to discuss the operation against Haughey:

> I telephoned Mr Mullen and arranged for him to call to my home on [Saturday 16 December 1972]. He never came that afternoon and as it was just coming up to the Christmas I did not pursue the matter just then.[10]

When asked to further explain his involvement with Mullen, Crinnion claimed that:

> The slot machine factory (Mafia) intrigued me because doubtlessly a lot of mechanisms are imported either in parts or assembled. I know that from reading reports that the Mafia are active in international gun running. I could think of no better cover for importing arms illegally than this arrangement involving slot machines … Tom Mullen will have that letter, or, if not, he will recall showing it to me and asking if I had ever known of any Mafia executives visiting Ireland, to conduct business with Charles Haughey TD, until the FBI confirmed the existence of the Mafia ownership of the … factory I had never known of any Mafia activity here.

For reasons that will presently become clear, the Mafia-Haughey sib was not put into circulation. Whether it would have trundled any appreciable distance along the gossip grapevine is an imponderable. A number of matters, however, are certain: {i} the IRA did not need to deal with the American Mafia as they had long since established a watertight transatlantic arms smuggling conduit of their own, one which was not encountering any interference from the FBI; {ii} if the IRA had entered into a relationship with the Mafia, it would have risked drawing unnecessary attention to their existing and successful supply pipeline; {iii} the IRA weapons were ferried across the Atlantic in cargo ships and trafficked through Dublin Port by dockers. The IRA did not need to smuggle a trickle of weapons broken up into parts and hidden in slot machines.

Despite Crinnion's protestations that there was a legitimate garda interest in the company in Walkinstown, he had failed to put pen to paper to alert his superiors. This lapse is inexplicable if one is to believe that there was even the slimmest possibility that this was how American guns were reaching Ireland. It is difficult not to conclude that he knew full well that he was engaged in an attempt to fabricate a link between Haughey and the Mafia, as part of an MI6 black propaganda campaign. For what it is worth, his excuse for his lapse was that his investigation was a work in progress:

> I would have done my own checking before rushing into print with the report to satisfy myself that I was not going to fret away Garda effort and I am telling you this now because I would appreciate if you could arrange to interview Mr Mullen as I am unable to do so … any approach to Tom Mullen to verify my claim should be by an understanding officer who could immediately put his mind at rest and take into account his age and that he is dependent on his pension and by being frank to assist his memory and not frighten him by interrogation.[11]

39

WE HAVE A SPY IN THE CAMP, FIND HIM

It was Maurice Oldfield's job to plunge his larcenous fingers as deep as he could inside Ireland's intelligence pie. By 1972, Oldfield's appetite had become voracious. The British were able to acquire some information – legitimately – from official security meetings which had been set up by Ambassador Peck after his discussions with Jack Lynch. Peck had conducted a series of meetings with Larry Wren, the head of C3. By August 1972, Peck had been replaced by the RUC's inspector general, J.A. Peacock, at the official conferences:

> These working groups openly shared intelligence on how the IRA acquired explosive materials and information on both police force's explosive disposal practices. The gardaí even handed over samples of materials they had obtained to the RUC's forensic laboratory ...[1]

> While the British believed that Wren and his colleagues were cooperative, Peacock felt 'that full power had not been given [to the gardaí] at government level'.[2]

Happily for Oldfield, Crinnion was in a position to fill in the blank spaces as he was now editor of C3's 'monthly confidential report' (MCR). The tributaries feeding him information included all of the SDU divisional offices in the Republic, including those straddling the Border. The information flowed to him for analysis and collation. He would also visit the Garda Technical Bureau to inspect weapons seized from subversives.

Once he and Wren were happy with the MCR, it was presented to the officer in charge of C Division, an assistant commissioner. From there it went to the commissioner who, in turn, passed it to Andy Ward at the DoJ, for onward transmission to Des O'Malley and Jack Lynch.

Crinnion was at the centre of the process. When he had started at C3 the MCR was edited by the chief superintendent. After a while, it was assigned to a detective inspector, then to Det. Sgt Boyle and, in 1972, Crinnion. The latter was not only given the report to type, but to edit. He appealed to Boyle on a few occasions to continue editing it as he had been doing, as Crinnion found it impossible 'to get it typed and do the checking with [the] accuracy necessitated on many of the matters reported, because I was in a bloody impossible position to do the job satisfactorily'.

ONE CAN APPRECIATE the wealth of the information contained in the MCR from one of Crinnion's 1973 memoranda where he detailed his task thus:

Commencing approximately on Monday 11/12/72 I started to edit and type a comprehensive report. This report is addressed to the Minister of Justice and is signed by the Commissioner of the Garda Siochana [*sic*]; there is a commissioner's instruction that as far as possible this report should be ready for signature about the 20th of each month. It is such an involved summary that although it only averages 40/45 single spaced sheets of typed foolscap with introduction pages of statistics it takes a minimum of 10 working days, without any interruption to prepare it. The Garda Siochana is for administrative purposes divided into 18 areas called divisions, at the end of each month each division submits a report to C3 setting out developments under headings IRA/SF, communism, left wing, other organisations and general border incidents, arrest, arms and ammunition seized and surrendered and trade disputes, anonymous phone calls, letters, approximate strength of organisations.

> ... It was necessary to read through general C3 files because matters reported to the Dept of Justice sometimes, would be of a composite nature, a merging of information, or chain of events in several divisions or something learned about by C3 from intercepted letters, or telephone, or from one of the British Services or Dept of Defence, intelligence section ...

> As well every month, each division submitted a return under the title 'Garda action against subversive organisations' and this set out briefly the current position in every court case involving [a] member of the IRA and Saor Éire. From these I periodically prepared a comprehensive return for the Department of Justice ...

The compilation of the reports was a taxing and time-consuming job, most certainly one of the factors that led Crinnion to work for up to seventy hours a week. His commitment was such that he occasionally took papers away with him at night to complete his duties at home. While he did not have explicit permission to remove files from C3, no one ever stopped him. He would sometimes take documents away at weekends and return them on Monday with the job complete. Unless Malone, Wren and Michael Fitzgerald were asleep at the wheel, they must have been aware of this work practice. Yet, none of them ever batted an eyelid, nor interfered with him in any way.

More importantly, this practice gave him every opportunity to make the information in the documents available to Wyman.

Crinnion reminded his former boss, Patrick Malone, of the effort he put into his work in a letter to him in 1973, pointing out that in December 1972, he had been 'fully occupied during the day on the Monthly Report' but had also worked on other matters during 'the odd spare hour in the peace of my home':

> Commissioner you know well that I never gave a damn about protocol or procedure and only saw the end product. Often I approached you directly when I saw some matter that was not being

given the attention it required and I always tried to direct Garda action to the best advantage against subversives. I may never have properly expressed my thanks for your tolerance and willingness to listen to my views which although often in conflict with persons of higher rank, were the product of my keen application to the special work undertaken by C3 and maybe because I was the most experienced member of the Garda Siochana on subversive work at Headquarters level the issues I raised were rarely trivial. Now my wife [Nancy] complains that I should have just shuffled in at 9 and home at 5 like any other cog in the machine ...[3]

What Crinnion did not state in his letter to Malone was that in August of 1972, he had visited London for a week accompanied by his wife, Nancy. This was not a romantic interlude. He spent all of the time in consultation with MI6. Nancy was left on her own at the hotel into which they had booked. Crinnion did not take her out once. His time was spent being debriefed by MI6. Crinnion later boasted to one of his friends that the British spies took him and his views seriously, unlike some of his own superiors in Dublin. It is extremely likely that he spent much of this time in the company of Oldfield and Wyman. Crinnion, it would appear, gave London cause to fear that Fianna Fáil did not have the determination to tackle the IRA.

The British decided to whittle a stick with which to beat Jack Lynch into taking tougher action against the paramilitaries. The various security, military and intelligence agencies in Belfast and London pooled their information and poured it into a dossier which described the structure and activities of the IRA in the Border region with the Republic. The purpose was to slam the dossier damningly on Lynch's desk and embarrass him into acting against the Republicans on his side of the Border. Kelvin White, the former head of Irish affairs at the FCO, gave Anthony Craig, author of *Crisis of Confidence Anglo-Irish Relations in the Early Troubles,* an outline of what the British were trying to achieve with the Border Dossier when he explained that Crinnion and Wyman were responsible for 'trying to bring to the British, information on criminal activities known to the Irish government ... The Irish government would have had to explain why it had acted as an accessory before the fact to [IRA] murder.'[4]

In a secret communication dated 21 November 1972, Whitelaw informed Heath that the document showed 'exactly who, where and in what strength the IRA Border units are, and what they are doing'.[5] The Border Dossier overlapped with much of the material in the MCRs edited by Crinnion.

THE BORDER DOSSIER was passed to Ambassador John Peck in Dublin, who furnished it to the Irish government on 6 December 1972.[6] It had the opposite effect to that which London had anticipated. When Lynch read it, he picked up the phone and rang the head of the SDU, John Fleming. 'We have a spy in the camp; find him,' he ordered Fleming.

In 2007, Kelvin White commented that:

> writing a dossier that [passed back information] Crinnion had handled is absolutely news to me. If anyone had done that they deserve to be hung, drawn and quartered. If you ever use intelligence that comes from a source you should have the authority of the officer responsible for that report to quote it ... You must either not use the information, or make it so garbled that it can never be traced back.[7]

The SDU hunt for a 'spy in the camp' was added to the ever-increasing workload of the unit. It was already dealing with a series of deadly bomb attacks in Dublin city.

40

CRINNION BLAMES THE PROVISIONALS

On Sunday, 26 November 1972, a bomb exploded at 1.25 a.m., outside the rear exit door of the Film Centre Cinema, O'Connell Bridge House, on Burgh Quay in the centre of Dublin, during a late-night showing of *The Pawnbroker*. The blast hurled customers out of their seats and onto the floor. Forty of the 156 patrons were injured, some requiring hospitalisation. Patrick Crinnion was quick out of the traps to blame the Provisionals inside garda circles. Rumours to this effect were soon in circulation around the city. The organisation issued a denial. The public never came to subscribe to the notion of IRA responsibility.

No one blamed the Officials either. They had declared a ceasefire on 30 May 1972. Crinnion's views about Provisional IRA culpability did not gain traction among the gardaí investigating the atrocity. Instead, they developed an interest in a gang which included someone now known as 'Suspect C'. He had links to the Littlejohn brothers. The Littlejohns had fraternised with people associated with the Official IRA, not the Provisionals. The Littlejohns themselves had returned to England in October 1972 after the AIB Grafton Street heist.

The Burgh Quay crime was never solved.

The report by Judge Henry Barron into the Dublin bombings of 1972 and 1973 stated that on 9 August 1973, a confidential report from a garda officer:

Claimed that Suspect B was 'a very close friend' of another known republican subversive (Suspect C). The latter was known in turn to associate with the Littlejohn brothers, Kenneth and Keith.

… [The] Gardai obtained other information during 1973 which suggested that Suspect B was and remained an active republican subversive with some experience in making and handling bombs. However, no concrete evidence linking Suspect B to the Film Centre bombing was found.

In 1974, Suspect B was one of two men shot dead by British Army soldiers at a derelict farmhouse near the border. According to the British Army Press Office, the two men were observed working on beer-keg bombs, each containing 20 lbs of explosives.[1]

As late as June 1973, Crinnion was still insisting that the attack was the work of the Provisionals, rather than a group of maverick Republicans with possible links to the Littlejohns. He was critical of Wren and Fitzgerald for contemplating any scenario other than one that implicated the Provisionals. In what is one of the most bizarre passages in his correspondence with Malone, Crinnion blamed the RUC for misinforming his superiors at C3 about the cinema bombing. In 1973 Crinnion wrote to Malone stating that:

Chief Superintendent Wren, with about 14 months experience in C3 and Superintendent Fitzgerald with about 14 weeks experience in C3, were, as you should know by now, led astray by members of the Royal Ulster Constabulary about the perpetrators of the bomb explosions in Dublin although there was to hand in C3 clear proof that at least the explosion in the O'Connell Bridge Cinema was the work of members of the Provisional IRA from Drogheda. Pathetically both pursued a course which they believed was correct and neither knew any better.[2]

Crinnion did not elaborate on the nature of the alleged evidence implicating the Provisional IRA in the cinema bombing, nor did he reveal the source of that information or why the RUC would protect the Provisional IRA. What is clear is that the Provisionals had no motive for planting bombs in Dublin. Crinnion's desire to blame them, however, dovetailed neatly with Oldfield's attempts to generate hostility towards the IRA in the Republic. It also served to deflect attention from the Littlejohns. The alleged guilt of the Provisionals based in Drogheda for the bombing, which Crinnion was promoting, may have been a piece of fiction crafted by MI6.

The Burgh Quay bombing was one of four attacks on Dublin's north city centre at the end of 1972 and the beginning of 1973. There is evidence of the involvement of British intelligence operatives in a subsequent terror assault. It took place on 1 December 1972. If the December attack was perpetrated by British operatives, it supports the possibility that the Film Centre Cinema attack was their work too.

41

OFFENCES AGAINST THE STATE

A double car bombing took place in Dublin on the evening of 1 December 1972. John Wyman was seen in the city that night.

The first vehicle exploded beside Liberty Hall. Fortunately, no one died, but George Bradshaw, a CIE bus driver, and Thomas Duffy, a bus conductor, perished in a second explosion at Sackville Place. 127 were injured. No one has ever been charged with these crimes.

Despite the chaos in the city, Wyman was able to make his way to one of the bomb sites to watch the gardaí as they collected evidence and monitor the reaction of the public. John Kelly, the former Arms Trial defendant, was among the crowd at the bomb site. Kelly recalled:

> having seen Wyman assessing crowd reaction after the 1 December 1972 bombings. A 22 December [1972] *Irish Times* photograph made Wyman identifiable. From his demeanour Kelly thought initially that Wyman was Special Branch, but noted that they did not acknowledge him.[1]

Patrick Crinnion was also carrying out a clandestine probe of his own into the atrocity which shall be described in the next chapter.

At least four vehicles were involved in this act of barbarity, two were chosen to explode and a pair for the getaway. One of the vehicles was a grey Ford Zephyr which was stolen in Antrim on 11 August 1972, from an Englishman called Joseph Fleming, along with Fleming's driving licence and other documentation which his wife had left in her handbag in the boot of the vehicle. Combined, these documents comprised all that was necessary to hire a car in Northern Ireland at that time, a stroke of great luck for the carjacker. The theft was reported to the RUC in Ballymoney. The Fleming documents were later used to hire three cars in Belfast which were deployed in the attack. Fleming's Ford Zephyr was utilised as a transport vehicle during the December 1972 attack on Dublin. It was not one of the two vehicles which exploded in the city.

Fleming's licence was used three times in November 1972 by an imposter posing as him, to hire cars in Belfast. One of the vehicles was obtained on 23 November. It was not returned and was never located. The two cars that exploded in Dublin were both hired on 30 November.

An intelligence source who worked in Northern Ireland at the time has disclosed that there was a suspicion in military circles that the 'Fleming' imposter was Billy McMurray.

The Army appeared to believe that the 1972 attack was masterminded by Billy McMurray, who was a senior member of the UDA from North Belfast. At the time he also had a role in carrying out cross Border attacks from Co. Fermanagh. In his UDA role he worked closely with a former customs officer, James Campbell. Together, they and other members of the UDA were also believed to be responsible for the co-ordinated bomb attacks – all of which took place within an hour – at Belturbet, Co. Cavan, Clones, Co. Monaghan and Mulnagoad, near Pettigo, Co. Donegal, on 28 December 1972.

The fact that RUC appeared to miss many opportunities to arrest McMurray and Campbell made us think that McMurray was being protected for some reason – perhaps he was also an informant.

It was also believed that McMurray and Campbell used the identity documents of an Englishman [i.e. Fleming] to hire the cars used in the 1972 Dublin bombings. It would appear that

McMurray used a stolen driving licence as proof of identity to hire all but one of the cars on that occasion. It is inexplicable that McMurray could have been able repeatedly to use the same stolen licence to hire cars despite cars hired previously on that licence not being returned. It seems incredible that the police did not 'put two and two together' unless McMurray was some form of agent or informant.[2]

McMurray matched the description of the imposter who hired two of the cars. He was in his forties, approximately 6-foot tall and well dressed. The imposter who resembled McMurray did not acquire a third car from a rental company at which McMurray was a regular customer. A second imposter hired the third vehicle. The bombers were either extraordinarily reckless, or had good reason to believe that details of Fleming's licence had not been circulated by the RUC to car-rental companies. The man who resembled McMurray obtained a number of cars over the space of a week, a timespan which underscores his confidence about the use of the stolen licence. He did all this at a time when an epidemic of car bombings was bringing Belfast to a standstill. In addition, he left his fingerprints and handwriting on the forms he completed. He spoke with a mixture of a Belfast and English accent.

According to the source quoted above, 'a key factor in '72 bombings was that McMurray had no personal ability to make bombs. So who made them?' The answer to this question may have been provided in 1976 by *The Sunday World* newspaper in a report about a man called Albert Baker.

Albert Baker was a British agent working for the UDA. Baker, a former British soldier, became a UDA assassin and torturer.[3] He suffered from some sort of nervous breakdown in 1973 and confessed his crimes to the police in England. He was returned to Belfast where he was convicted, but his role as 'Agent Broccoli', an undercover British operative, was covered up. In 1976, Baker's brother told Frank Doherty of *The Sunday World* that Albert Baker was an associate of a senior UDA man based in Derry, who had taken part in the 1972 Dublin bombings. According to Baker's brother, the explosives and cars used in the bombings were supplied by a leading member of the UDA in Derry and this man also provided weapons and explosives for operations in Monaghan and Donegal. According to the *Sunday World* report, he 'had a close association with British Intelligence'.[4]

Baker took orders from Tommy Herron, a member of the UDA's Inner Council.[5] Baker revealed that Herron had connections to British intelligence and knew about the plot to bomb Dublin.

Where did McMurray, or whoever hijacked Fleming's car in August of 1972, hide the vehicle until it was used in the December 1972 bomb attack? If he kept it at a property he owned, it demonstrates that he had no fear of the RUC, a further signposting that he was an agent of some sort.

Alternatively, Fleming's Ford Zephyr might have been kept by the Mobile Reaction Force (MRF) at its compound at Palace barracks outside Belfast. The MRF was a British undercover organisation which was itself involved in stealing cars for unattributable uncover operations.

The MRF was a sprawling organisation established by Brigadier Frank Kitson, in 1971, to engage in agent recruitment, surveillance, drive-by shootings (deploying the type of weapons the IRA were known to carry), laundry collection (to detect the residue of explosives on clothing) and brothel management (to collect gossip and obtain blackmail material). One of its practices was to steal vehicles and use them in deniable operations, as demonstrated by the chilling case of William Black.

In *Ambush at Tully West*, Kennedy Lyndsay described how, on 18 August 1972, William Black, a forty-year-old member of the UDR, noticed a gang attempting to steal a van belonging to his neighbour, Thomas Shannon, a butcher, on Black's Road, South Belfast, at 2 a.m. Two wore anoraks with coloured stripes down the arms. The other had a dark anorak. All had long hair. They then switched their attention to a larger van, one owned by another neighbour called Seán McNamee.[6]

Black was forty and married with three sons and two daughters, who ranged in age from twelve to eighteen. He was a skilled fitter employed by Short Brothers and Harland, Limited. He was also a very brave man.

Mrs Black telephoned the RUC while her husband went out to challenge the three thieves. By the time he went outside, they were pushing McNamee's van away from where it had been parked. Black was armed with a .22 calibre sporting rifle. He stayed in the shadow of his house and ordered them to halt. One drew a pistol while the engine of a nearby large dark coloured BMC 1800 saloon started up. All three men ran towards it. Two of them managed to successfully jump into it whilst the third was dragged for a while before he fell on the road. Black fired at the tyres of the car but it sped away. He approached the individual who was on the ground and armed. He ordered him to keep his hands up or he would fire. The man obeyed but repeatedly called out in a strong English accent, 'I am security', and, 'I will show you my ID card'.

The RUC arrived with a soldier. At that moment, the escaped BMC 1800 drove past, turned at nearby Oranmore Park, returned and stopped. A policeman armed with a sterling sub-machine gun arrested the men in the vehicle. Black and the police and the prisoners proceeded to Garnock House, an army centre. Black was soon surprised by the sight of the car thieves standing around chatting to each other, rather than being detained. As he passed them, he noticed they had wigs in their hands and actually had short hair. They, in turn, recognised him and abused him crudely for his interference.

At this point, Black realised they were British army personnel. The two policemen who had made the putative arrests took Black aside and asked him to see the commanding officer, a captain. He was now informed that the thieves were undercover troops who had to do this type of thing to get into certain areas to acquire information. He was told that as a member of the UDR he was bound by the Official Secrets Act and prohibited from speaking to anyone about what had happened.[7]

This incident took place exactly one week after the theft of Fleming's vehicle in Co. Antrim.

Black did not remain silent, but rather asked questions and made his own inquiries. Shortly afterwards, he received a letter from the UDR stating that his services were no longer required by the regiment.[8] On 29 August 1972, an attempt was made to assassinate him in suspicious circumstances which may or may not have involved Republican gunmen. On 20 January 1973 the empty house opposite his was sprayed with bullets. Analysis of the cartridges demonstrated that the ammunition discharged at the house was of a type typically used by British soldiers. Black moved out of his neighbourhood.

Black was shot on 26 January 1974, at his weekend cottage, near the small town of Saintfield in Co. Down. He survived, albeit badly wounded.[9] A unit of six men had been waiting for him to turn up for three days. One was armed with a sub-machine gun fitted with a silencer. Two were SAS men.

The other four were on secondment from the Royal Engineers.

Black recalled being visited while injured by an officer who was wearing a SAS beret and badge.[10] Mr Archie Hamilton, the Armed Forces Minister, admitted, in 1990, that Black was shot by a soldier in 1974, allegedly 'while threatening the life of a soldier'. In reality, he had done nothing of the sort. He received £16,500 in compensation.[11] Ten years before Hamilton's admission, Kennedy Lindsay had described how:

> Information has come from inside the officer corps of the Special Air Service Regiment that one of their number was sent across to Ulster with the instruction to kill William Black.
>
> The assignment to assassinate an innocent, married man with five children and strong evangelical Christian beliefs caused intense indignation among certain army officers who subsequently came to learn about it from army sources. One is known to have declared that he never believed the British army could sink so low and to have considered resigning his commission. Nor was the officers' mess at the regimental depot of the SAS at Hoarwithy Road, Hereford, immune from the indignation. It is a small, elite regiment with a strong sense of regimental honour and professional integrity. It is suggested, too, that the officer given the task [of killing Black] had it emphasised to him that Black was an exceptionally dangerous subversive and that he had no opportunity during his brief special visit to Northern Ireland to check the truth of what he had been told.[12]

The Black case illustrates just how ruthless British military intelligence operations were in 1972. The MRF not only stole cars but had plenty of bases at which they could conceal them for months on end, including Garnock House and its HQ at Palace Barracks.

Returning to the Dublin bombings of 1972, it is possible that the MRF and MI6 could have had the details about Fleming's stolen car and licence erased from the RUC watch lists.

42

THE LONG FUSE THAT BLEW JACK LYNCH OUT OF OFFICE

There is a body of evidence that suggests that MI6 was behind the 1972 Dublin bombings. Maurice Oldfield was running MI6 operations in Ireland at this time. As noted earlier, Oldfield's best friend, Anthony Cavendish, who served in MI5 and MI6, wrote in 1990 that 'theft, deception, lies, mutilation and even murder are considered [by MI6] if and when necessary.'[1] MI6 had felt it 'necessary' to bomb passenger ships in 1946 and 1947 to disrupt the flow of Holocaust survivors from Mediterranean ports to Palestine deploying ex-SOE personnel at its cutting edge. It was codenamed Operation Embarrass. MI6 acknowledged the operation in 2010 by approving its inclusion in the official history of the service written by Prof. Keith Jeffery of Queens University, Belfast.[2]

THE 1 DECEMBER 1972 atrocity in Dublin took place during the final stages of the presentation to Dáil Éireann of the Offences Against the State Amendment Bill. This was the legislation which Heath and Oldfield had strived so hard to get Lynch to lay before the Dáil.

Fine Gael was in disarray with Garret FitzGerald opposed to the bill while his leader, Liam Cosgrave, was tending towards supporting it. FitzGerald later reconsidered his position about it and served in governments both as a minister and Taoiseach which not only upheld the Offences against the State Act, but expanded its provisions. His actions in 1972 were entangled with a plot he spearheaded to oust Cosgrave as leader of Fine Gael.

The Labour Party did not support the bill either.

The debate was winding up on the evening of 1 December. It faced almost certain defeat, so much so that newspapers were speculating about a snap election to be held later in December. Then, suddenly, the two bombs exploded and the attitude of the parliamentarians changed. Rumours swirled around Leinster House that the Provisional IRA was responsible for the attack in revenge for the imprisonment of MacStiofáin. The bill mustered enough votes and abstentions to struggle over the finishing line.

Had a general election taken place, the consensus was that Lynch would have come out on top. Although his party increased its share of the vote in the election that followed in February, they nonetheless lost power. This was because Fine Gael and Labour used the intervening months to hammer out a vote-transfer pact which gave them the upper hand, even with Labour's vote decreasing. There would have been no pact if an election had taken place in December 1972. The central issue would have been the anti-IRA legislation. Fine Gael and Labour had diverging views about it.

Britain's objective in securing the passage of the bill was achieved thanks to the explosions. Ambassador Peck reported to London that the two 'bombs on 1 December clinched' the passage of the controversial legislation.[3]

After the bill became law, FitzGerald persisted with his campaign against Cosgrave and tabled a motion of no confidence in him. At one party meeting, FitzGerald absentmindedly left a list of those he expected to vote against Cosgrave behind him in the Fine Gael Party room. It was found by Richie Ryan, TD, who later became minister for finance. Ryan was astonished to find FitzGerald had listed him as an opponent of Cosgrave when he was nothing of the sort.[4] FitzGerald's motion was defeated by a large majority.

Many senior gardaí and an array of Irish politicians concluded that British intelligence was behind the 1 December 1972 atrocity. Jack Lynch told a reporter from Ulster TV (UTV) that:

> Well, my suspicions naturally are more aroused now, we have no, as I said, indication who was responsible and it is now well known a lot of people in Ireland believe that many of these unexplained activities and actions could well be related to British Intelligence or other activities of that nature.[5]

If Britain was behind the bombing, it would have been organised with the knowledge, if not out-and-out involvement, of Oldfield, Rowley, Steele and Wyman. The British intelligence source quoted in the previous chapter has also stated that:

> We came to believe the [1972] Dublin attack was designed to draw attention to the legislation then in process. The bombs were extremely effective. There was a degree of efficiency in that bombing that we did not always associate with Loyalists.[6]

Curiously, Crinnion voiced his suspicion that 'the Brits' were behind the attack too. He did so during a conversation with a fellow garda officer, Éamonn Ó Fiacháin. Crinnion revealed that his brother-in-law, Seamus Lattimore, who was serving with the Royal Irish Rangers in Belfast, had told him that this was the case.[7] What better way to deflect any lurking suspicion that he was working for MI6 than to blame its agents for committing murder on the streets of Dublin?

Éamonn Ó Fiacháin wrote to the former Chief Justice of Ireland, Liam Hamilton, on 27 May 2001. Hamilton was investigating a series of bombings which took place in the

Republic in the 1970s. (These inquiries were subsequently taken over by Mr Justice Henry Barron.) In the letter Ó Fiacháin described how:

> In December 1972 a car-bomb explosion occurred in Sackville Place, which runs from Lower O'Connell Street to Marlborough Street, Dublin ... Within a few days of one or other of these explosions a Detective Garda Patrick Crinnion of C3 ... called to the Ballistic Section as was his usual practice, particularly after finds of firearms, ammunition and/or explosives had been brought to the section for examination and testing. During these visits, made during lunch hour, he sought detailed information on makes, models, calibres and serial numbers of firearms, types calibres and manufacturers' base marks on ammunition and the nature and origin of explosive substances. As this information was of legitimate interest for the purpose of Section C3 the bona fides of Patrick Crinnion were never questioned nor doubted by Detective Inspector O'Connor and myself and the information sought was supplied to him.

> On this particular occasion the subject of this latest explosion came up in the course of our conversation and I have retained a clear recollection that Patrick Crinnion stated that the British Army or 'the Brits' had been involved in causing this explosion as he had been informed of this by a brother[8] of his who was a member of the British Army.[9]

If Crinnion genuinely believed the 'Brits' were behind the attack, he nonetheless continued to work with Wyman.

The bombing became a sensitive Anglo-Irish issue, at least for a number of months. On 17 August 1972, the newly appointed British ambassador to Dublin, Sir Arthur Galsworthy, met with Garret FitzGerald, who was now Minister for Foreign Affairs. Galsworthy made the following note of their conversation:

> Dr FitzGerald then said that he knew one of the Irish newspapers was conducting its own investigations into the Dublin bombings of last December and January, and that shortly they would be

coming out with fresh allegations that British agents had after all been responsible. None of this would be evidence, but there would be a lot of pseudo-circumstantial surmise ... Not for one moment did he think that the British Government could conceivably have authorised such acts of violence. But was it not possible that some disreputable characters in our employ or in some way associated with us might have acted on their own authority? If this should prove to be the case, and it came to light, the effect would be total disaster [for London].

FitzGerald was referring to an article that would appear in the *Evening Herald* on 21 August 1973 entitled *Shock New Evidence on Dublin Bombings: Government Told of British Army Link* by Jim Cantwell, who was known to have had garda sources. With the benefit of hindsight, it is clear that Cantwell's sources were gardaí who had picked up some details about the investigation which was being led by Chief Superintendent John Joy. However, it is also plain Cantwell's sources were relying on speculation and were hardly members of the core investigation team. Joy's team did not find evidence of a link to the British army.

The Joy inquiry faced censure from Mr Justice Barron who was critical of the gardaí for their failure to make more use of photographic tools to assist the inquiry.

Although the photofit impressions of the man who hired the cars were not published in newspapers, they were circulated amongst members of the security forces on both inquiries at places where such a man might have been seen – hotels, guest houses, air and rail termini, ports and the like. The suggestion of C/Supt [Larry] Wren that the photofits be shown to members of the Defence Forces who had attended courses in Britain indicated a willingness to pursue any possible lead in this matter.

However, unlike the Dublin and Monaghan bombings of eighteen months later, it seems that no effort was made to obtain photographs of any known subversives.

In addition to those who saw the man who hired the cars, a garda officer obtained a very good view of someone who was a passenger in a car believed to be that stolen from Joseph Fleming, as well as of the same person in a different car some days later. In each case this man appeared to the officer to be acting suspiciously. This officer was obviously somebody to whom photographs of possible suspects could have been shown, had they been obtained.

In addition to the garda officer, another witness claimed to have seen Fleming's car in Dublin, this time on 4 December. Yet despite these sightings, it appears from the documents available to the Inquiry that no effort was made to make this information public, in the hope that others might come forward to corroborate this evidence.

If other sightings of these cars could have been confirmed, there was the possibility that further descriptions of those using such cars might have been obtained. This in turn might have resulted in a decision to obtain and show photographs of possible suspects to those witnesses.[10]

Jack Lynch and others – including gardaí – suspected British involvement in the Dublin bombings. If they were wrong and, instead, Loyalist paramilitaries carried out the attack *entirely on their own*, all of the following facts have to align:

- ❖ A Loyalist stole Fleming's car, in August 1972, and hid it until December 1972, and;

- ❖ Loyalists drove the Ford Zephyr across the Border with its original registration plates on display despite the fact they knew it had been stolen, and;

- ❖ The RUC neglected to circulate Fleming's name to car rental companies with the result that the bombers were able to hire the other vehicles used in the attack with Fleming's driving licence without hindrance from the police;

- ❖ The men who hired the vehicles gave little or no thought to the possibility that they might be arrested for using Fleming's stolen licence by the RUC;

❖ They were not concerned that details about Fleming's car were supplied – as they should have been in normal circumstances – to the gardaí who mounted check points along the Border;

❖ The bombers also knew that the cars they were hiring would not be returned to the car rental company. Instead, they would be used in a terror attack which the RUC would investigate. Despite this, they showed their faces to various employees of the car rental companies, and at least one of them left his fingerprints on documents;

❖ Albert Baker, Tommy Herron and any other British agent with foreknowledge of the attack chose not to warn their British contacts about it;

❖ Jim Hanna and Billy Mitchell (members of the UVF whose actions are described in the next chapter), and the family of Albert Baker, invented lies about British collusion with the Loyalist paramilitaries involved in the 1 December attack for no apparent reason;

❖ John Wyman was in the centre of Dublin city on 1 December by coincidence.

43

DEFLECTION

Jim Hanna of the UVF was a British agent. He claimed responsibility for the December 1972 bombing of Dublin.

His intention may have been to deflect attention from the culpability of the UDA at the suggestion of his controllers. He certainly fitted the bill as a believable bomber. According to the British intelligence source quoted in the preceding chapters:

> There is no doubt that [Jim] Hanna worked very, very closely with Army intelligence. He lived in Lisburn and some of my colleagues were very close to him socially and they took him out and visited him at Lisburn.[1]

Hanna was involved in multiple UVF bombings. In 1973, he and some of his colleagues held a series of meetings with Cathal Goulding, and other Officials, to discuss matters of mutual interest. The meetings took place in Dublin and Belfast. Goulding hoped to make peace with the Loyalists whom he did not see as his enemy, rather British imperialism. He wanted to talk about housing and unemployment. As events transpired, it became apparent that one of the reasons Hanna was present was to further the aims of his contacts in British intelligence. At a session at the West County Hotel, in August 1973, Hanna alleged that he had been involved in the 1 December bombings and that he was working with British military intelligence. Goulding later told Joe Tiernan:[2]

> [Hanna] asked me if we, the Official IRA, would be willing to carry out bank robberies here in the South, and they, the UVF, would claim them. Then, if we wished, they would carry out

similar robberies in the North and we could claim them. He said [British] Army Intelligence officers he was in contact with in the North had asked him to put the proposition to us as they were anxious to bring about a situation in the South where the Dublin government would be forced to introduce internment.

Goulding was not interested in the proposal whereupon Hanna tried to assure him that the British state would not cause them a 'problem', i.e., the Officials would not be harassed or prosecuted for the bank raids the UVF would carry out in Northern Ireland while masquerading as the Official IRA. Hanna boasted of his close relationship with British intelligence:

> When I refused to accept his proposition, as we were already on ceasefire, he put his hand on my shoulder and said, 'Look there's no problem. You see the car bombs in Dublin over the last year, well we planted those bombs and the [British] Army provided us with the cars. There's no problem'. When I asked him how the bombings were carried out, he said the 1972 bombs were placed in false petrol tanks in both cars. He said they travelled down the main road from Belfast to Dublin and were stopped at a Garda checkpoint at Swords [North County Dublin] but because the cars were not reported stolen and the Gardaí found nothing suspicious in them they were allowed to proceed.

On the face of it, it seems exceedingly odd that Hanna would have made such an incriminating admission to someone like Goulding. What was his objective? One explanation is that he was trying to deflect attention away from the UDA for the Dublin bombing, onto the UVF at the request of his handlers.

Hanna's intelligence controllers may also have hoped that Goulding would welcome an opportunity to raise funds and, second, embrace an opportunity to have the Provisional IRA swept up by the gardaí in internment swoops. Since the Officials were on a ceasefire, it was unlikely that any of them would have been taken out of circulation by the gardaí unless, of course, they were caught red-handed during a bank robbery, or betrayed by an informer.

There is further evidence of Hanna's links to undercover British soldiers. Journalist Kevin Myers played a key part in arranging the talks between the UVF and the Officials. Myers had become acquainted with Hanna while he was working in Belfast. He knew him as an extraordinarily indiscreet heavy-drinking individual. Hanna told Myers about his relationship with a number of British military intelligence personnel. He revealed that he had even gone on hunting trips with a few of them.[3] There was evidence of his contact with the soldiers: Hanna had posed with them in a number of photographs. After Hanna was assassinated, in April 1974, the British army confiscated the photo collection from his widow, but overlooked one taken by Hanna which featured Lieut Alan Homer and Lieut Timothy Golden. Mrs Hanna gave it to Myers. Myers published it in *Hibernia* magazine.[4] The article described how:

> By 1973, Hanna had become the senior military commander for the UVF in Northern Ireland. He had also become a close friend of Captain Anthony Ling and Anthony Box and Lieutenant Alan Homer, all of 39th Brigade Intelligence at Lisburn, and a Timothy Golden, who is not listed as a member of Intelligence Corps but was possibly an S.A.S. man attached to Intelligence. They were frequent visitors to Hanna's home near Lisburn, and group photographs of Hanna, Homer and Golden were taken away by police after Hanna was murdered last year.

The remarkable thing is that Hanna remained on good terms with these intelligence officers while he was masterminding a bombing offensive for the UVF:

> Hanna told me that the officers had often spoken to him of his involvement in the U.V.F. The U.V.F. magazine 'Combat' was to claim after Hanna's death that Golden and Homer (who studied

at Queens University, while still in the army, in 1971) were responsible for the interrogation in depth of detainees. Presumably this claim is based on what Hanna told the U.V.F. of his talks with his Army friends (with whom he frequently went out hunting), but there is no substantial evidence for this.

But still, a remarkable relationship was struck up between four leading Intelligence officers and the effective military commander of the U.V.F. It is possible that Hanna was being milked for all he was worth by his graduate chums from Sandhurst. However, they did not hinder his military activity …

Joe Tiernan made another important discovery: he spoke to Billy Mitchell, a UVF member, in the 1990s, who told him that Hanna was 'run as an agent' by four officers from Army Intelligence based at Lisburn, naming them as two captains, one lieutenant and an SAS officer.[5]

Hanna's British army contacts, named in this chapter, were active in Northern Ireland. There is no suggestion they were involved in MI6 operations in the south, let alone the bombing of Dublin. They are merely named to illustrate the extent of Hanna's known links to British intelligence. The man in overall charge of all intelligence operations was Allan Rowley, an MI6 officer. He worked with Frank Steele and others in MI6. The finger of suspicion with regard to the Dublin attacks points at MI6, not the soldiers listed above.

There was one intriguing allegation in what Hanna said about the Dublin bomb attacks. He claimed that alterations had been made to the petrol tanks of the cars used in bomb attacks. If this was true, it begs the question: who was capable of such an alteration?

The MRF had access to skilled engineers who had the ability to instal secret compartments in vehicles. They built a concealed observation post in a laundry van used by the MRF to visit Nationalist estates. The MRF vehicle masqueraded as part of a front company known as the 'Four Square Laundry'. The unit used the van to observe and photograph people in Nationalist estates. On 2 October 1972, the IRA attacked it after it had driven into the Twinbrook estate. Sapper Ted Stuart, who was hidden in the observation post, was killed. His colleague Lance Corp. Sara Jane Warke managed to escape with her life.

Thus, there is no doubt that the MRF had access to engineers with the skill to instal a false compartment disguised as a petrol tank in the type of vehicles which exploded in Dublin. In the extremely unlikely event of a future inquiry into the Dublin bombings of 1972, the records of the MRF and or British army engineers who adapted the 'Four Square Laundry' vehicle should be examined to see if they worked on vehicles similar to those that exploded in Dublin on 1 December 1972.

Hanna did not live long after his discussions with Goulding. An MI5 agent may have prompted his killing, an event that took place on 1 April 1974. According to the British intelligence source quoted above:

Laurence Imrie of MI5 worked with RUC Special Branch Inspector Harry McCrumm. McCrumm had close links to [William] 'Frenchie' Marchant of the UVF. Marchant was a thug, a nasty piece of work. Our belief was that [Jim] Hanna was fingered by Marchant. We believe [Jim] Hanna was killed by his own side. Marchant allegedly brought in a guy from Sandy Row, also an RUC Special Branch informant, to do the killing.

Hence, if Hanna had circulated the story that the UVF had perpetrated the Dublin bombing to distract from the role of McMurray, Baker and others in the UDA, he took that secret with him to the grave.

44

THE THIRD MAN

An Englishman calling himself 'Alex Forsey' came to live in Dublin in the early 1970s, managing a shop in Ballyfermot. He gave his neighbours the impression that he was a member, possibly treasurer, of a local Sinn Féin cumann, in either Ballyfermot or Inchicore. He displayed photographs of dead IRA Volunteers on the walls of the flat he rented. The owner of the property, an Irish Air Corps captain, felt that Forsey 'might not be all he claimed to be'. He spotted a Morse code transmitter, which Forsey explained away by claiming to be an amateur radio ham.[1]

At this time, a large number of Sinn Féin offices spread right across the county were under surveillance by the SDU. On one occasion detectives noticed a man acting suspiciously around the location of one of them in Dublin. He possessed keys to a flat next door to a Sinn Féin office.[2] They picked him up. During his interrogation, he protested that he was doing nothing more than they were, namely, gathering intelligence about the IRA.

The man in detention was Alex Forsey. According to a note taken by Jack Lynch, after receipt of a phone call from C3, Forsey 'had come under notice recently – believed to be sympathetic to the IRA'.[3]

Forsey was in fact a member of Wyman's MI6 network in the Republic. The gardaí raided Forsey's flat on Decies Road, Ballyfermot, on 15 December 1972. They found 700 rounds of .22 and .303 ammunition, a smoke bomb, half a stone of a white powdery substance and two walkie-talkies. The fact he had two walkie-talkies implies that he had an accomplice who was not arrested.

Forsey appeared in court on 15 December 1972, to answer charges in respect of these materials.

An investigation by Margaret Urwin and Niall Meehan, published in *History Ireland* magazine entitled 'The "third man" in the case of British agent John Wyman and Garda Sergeant Patrick Crinnion', revealed that:[4]

> The third man was 31-year-old Englishman Alexander Forsey (reported as 'Fursey'). Gardaí initially thought him 'sympathetic to the IRA' ... Forsey's connection to the Wyman–Crinnion saga is revealed officially in a handwritten instruction within a Military Archives file in Cathal Brugha Barracks. Beside a newspaper report of Forsey's first court appearance is written, 'Associate with Patrick Crinnion case'.[5]

Urwin and Meehan also revealed:

> In Dublin in April 1972 Forsey had obtained an advertised post as manager of a grocery/hardware store in Decies Road, Ballyfermot. He claimed that he had been living in Derry and was married to a Derry woman, and reported having two children. In 2008 Margaret Urwin interviewed the shop's owner (now deceased). He occasionally visited the Forseys, who lived over the premises, but could not recall seeing any children.

In custody, Forsey informed the SDU that he had an appointment to meet a contact who was due to fly into Dublin Airport on Sunday, 17 December 1972. A rendezvous with Forsey was set for the following day at West County Hotel, Chapelizod. The contact arrived at the Burlington Hotel, in Dublin, on 17 December, where he furnished the receptionist with an address at Swan Walk, Chelsea. On 18 December, he drove a car bearing the registration number 3104 ZC to Chapelizod. An SDU unit consisting of DI Patrick Doocey, DS Patrick Culhane, and Detective Garda Michael Hughes followed him to the West County Hotel, Chapelizod. He strolled inside but did not locate Forsey. He returned to his car and settled in, presumably to keep a look out to see if Forsey might yet turn up.

At 5 p.m. Culhane approached the man, identified himself as a garda and asked him for his name. The reply he received was 'John Wyman of Swan Walk, London'. Wyman claimed he could verify this with his driving licence. He was arrested under section 30 of the Offences Against the State Act, 1939, and conveyed to the Bridewell station for questioning. At first, he told his interrogators he was an executive in the firm of Bateman Investigations, of 43 Marlboro' Crescent, Long Handeborough, Oxfordshire. He said he had flown in from England that day and was staying at the Burlington Hotel. The SDU officers examined some papers found on him, including a page from a loose-leaf notebook. Culhane ascertained that Wyman was indeed staying at Room 411 at the Burlington. It later transpired he had booked two rooms at the hotel.

Inquiries about Number 3 Swan Walk later revealed it was occupied by two sisters, Daphne and Primrose Nowesome. They told news reporters that they 'knew John [Wyman] was an inquiry agent, but knew nothing about his work'. One of their cousins was to add that Wyman's family were friends of the Nowesomes. Later again, the Nowesomes contended: 'We were friendly with his parents ... They are living abroad and we have not seen them for a very long time. We've no idea what he did for a living.'

The SDU now focused its attention on Room 411 of the Burlington Hotel.

45

THE SPY LEFT OUT IN THE COLD

Garda Culhane drove out to the Burlington Hotel at 7 p.m., on 18 December, where he and the hotel's chief of security, Capt. McGannon, searched Room 411. He found a briefcase under the telephone table and some shaving equipment in the bathroom. Aside from that, there was no other property and he slipped away quietly. No one was left behind to keep an eye on the hotel.

Crinnion arrived later, borrowed a pencil from one of the staff and left a note for Wyman in room 411. He may have come back once or twice to see if Wyman had returned. He was waiting outside the room when Patricia Thomson, a cleaner, saw him waiting in the corridor. He explained he was waiting for the occupant to return. She told him there was no one inside and he replied 'that he seemed to be missing him all day'.[1]

Culhane returned at 9.20 p.m., ascertained that Wyman was not at the hotel and went to his room to find Crinnion's note on the dressing table which read: 'John, will call again at 9:05 p.m. Okay.' Culhane took the note.

The following evening, Culhane and Hughes installed themselves inside Room 411. At 9:15 p.m. Crinnion came along the corridor. He knocked on the door of room 411. When Culhane opened it, Crinnion asked him: 'Is John in?' Culhane responded: 'John who?' and was told, 'John Wyman'.

Crinnion stated later that Hughes and Culhane were strangers to him. They agreed they did not know him either. Hughes and Culhane were based at Dublin Castle. While the lack of familiarity may seem surprising, Crinnion had left Dublin Castle for the Phoenix Park at the end of 1960.

'Don't get excited, I'm a policeman myself,' Crinnion told them before barging past Culhane into the room. Crinnion feared they were IRA men and was concerned for Wyman, who would have been in mortal danger if he was right. Once inside, it became clear Wyman was not present. Crinnion's pluck now proved his undoing. His account of what happened is as follows:

> I knocked on the door and when it was opened I saw two men in the hall. I enquired if John Wyman was there and was told, we are police officers, will you please come inside, I followed them in through the hall into the room and asked, 'Where is John, has something happened to him, has he had an accident'. I got no reply. I asked again was he injured, had he an accident. The taller of the two, who I now know as Sergeant Culhane, asked who I was and I told him, taking out my identity card and holding it to him to examine. I asked them again had something happened to John and again got no reply. I then said I wanted to see their identity cards while both produced Polaroid cards similar to mine neither permitted me to handle them. I asked for my card back and was refused, Sergeant Culhane asked me where I was stationed and who my boss was and I told him. I asked them where they were stationed and he said don't you know (I had never seen either of these two men in my life). I asked again where they were stationed. Culhane said we will go over to the Bridewell and sort this out. Both he and his partner searched me, removing my wallet and a piece of white paper fell out of my breast pocket with the name ... and a phone number and the name of the model railway on it then some keys as they searched me, I half turned and my right jacket pocket was untouched.[2] It contained my service pistol loaded with seven rounds and a spare magazine with another seven rounds. In common with other members of the detective branch engaged on subversive work, I was authorized to carry my pistol at all times (even on holidays) without restriction within the state.

Culhane's recollection was that he suggested to Crinnion that the latter was indeed a police officer he would not mind going to the Bridewell. Crinnion agreed but he was playing for time, waiting for an opportunity to escape from the pair he suspected – or alleged he suspected – might be IRA men. Crinnion elaborated on his fears thus:

> Due to my work and [the] fact that a member of the garda from headquarters was charged in connection with conspiracy to produce explosives for the Provisional IRA, I knew that my address and identity was known and I had a feeling that [the IRA] were not beyond kidnapping me …
>
> For this reason I had the pistol with the safety off and a round in the chamber, the weapon was quite safe having an external hammer but, was ready to fire on one firm squeeze of the trigger. On my last firing practice on the range I achieved 92 with this pistol. These two men who refused to tell me whether Wyman was injured or even dead or even refused to let me handle their ID cards, refused to return my ID card and refused to tell where they were stationed and the fact that I never seen them before created an impression in my mind that they were not garda at all. When they finished searching me they returned my property with the exception of the papers I had in my wallet.

The SDU men asked Crinnion if he had been in the hotel the previous night and had left a note for Wyman:

> I confirmed that I had, they then said we will go over to the Bridewell. We walked out of the room, turned left down the hall and called the lift, we were the only passengers, we descended down to the ground floor and walked across the lobby and out the main door (D/Inspc Doocey said in the book of evidence that [garda identity] cards were easily obtained). Coming down in the lift the fact that they had used the term 'police' and 'policemen' suddenly struck me, never once referring to Garda or Garda Siochana [sic]. The Polaroid ID cards were used widely in N/Ireland by all the state and large organisations. During the time it took to cross from the lift to the door I realised that these were two phonies. Outside the door they hesitated not knowing seemingly which way to go, there was no garda and no garda car in sight. I decided to get clear of them and turned and ran to the left of the building after about ten paces my left shoe lace broke and my shoe flew off,

I stumbled and was held by Sarg Culhane, who held my left arm back up between my shoulder blades and his companion held my other arm. I did not fight or struggle, they called to the elderly doorman who arrived on the scene to call 999. I realised then that they must be genuine garda and asked for my missing shoe.

Culhane's recollection was that Crinnion kicked him and 'called us a pair of bastards'.[3] In one of his 1973 memoranda, Crinnion stated:

If I called anyone a bastard I apologise, but was the bastard label not applied to me by them and not the other way around.

Crinnion, who still had his gun, was taken to the Bridewell for interrogation.

CRINNION CUT A lonely figure at the Bridewell garda station. His career was in serious peril unless, as he hoped, someone came to his rescue. He waited in vain for one of his superiors to arrive and secure his release. There was no sign of Larry Wren nor Michael Fitzgerald. At a later stage, he asked to see John Fleming, the head of the SDU. The request was relayed but 'he never came and as I saw clearly with the blind hysteria which smothered any effort to sort things out, that my explanations were simply futile'.[4]

Crinnion had boasted to those around him that he was a friend of John A. Costello, the former Fine Gael taoiseach. In reality, Crinnion's only connection to the politician, who was born in 1891, was that he had acted as a guard outside his house for a year during the Border Campaign. Costello's son, Declan, was now attorney-general. Crinnion made 'frantic efforts to enlist the help of Mr [John A.] Costello and Mr Liam Cosgrave without success'.[5]

Instead of rescue, SDU officers came to trouble him with questions:

When left in the small room I was sitting down beside a table and Culhane handed me my missing shoe, before he left the room leaving me alone with Hughes. I took the lace out of my right shoe and broke it in half and then put on both shoes, each tied with half a lace. I examined my wrist watch and the glass was shattered. I then said to Hughes this seems to be official all right. Now I don't want you to be alarmed and taking out the spare pistol magazine from my right jacket pocket I put it on the table. I said 'now I'm going to take my pistol out of my pocket and unload it'. Unfortunately he became alarmed and insisted on putting his [hand] on top of mine as I withdrew the pistol. This was dangerously awkward because my right side was close into the wall and he was bending across in front of me. I told him to be careful, that if he preferred I would hand him the pistol as I withdrew it from my pocket. He did this and as he did not know how the pistol worked I stood to his right and behind him and instructed him how to remove the magazine and then extract the round in the chamber. He left the room with the gun and the magazine and when he returned he asked me to empty my pockets, which I did.

Crinnion was allowed to make a call to let his family know what was happening. He reached a friend, a man who lived in Dundrum, not far from his own house in Kilmacud. This resulted in the dispatch of an unmarked garda car to watch the house of his friend. It parked outside on the pavement much to the distress of the family inside. The friend went to the Bridewell where a garda called Murphy allowed him inside the complex to visit Crinnion and give him some clothes and toiletries.

Culhane returned after this and asked Crinnion 'where my car was and I described its location and identified the different keys on my ring for him. He returned my wallet containing money, a bank card and some stamps, he also returned my comb and pen'.

At 12.45 p.m., Culhane took Crinnion's car keys and

returned to the hotel where he found the vehicle. It was locked. Culhane had the vehicle brought to Dublin Castle.

After Culhane parked the car and departed, one of two things happened: the car was left untouched, or, at some stage that night someone with access to CS files swooped on the vehicle, opened it and placed incriminating files inside it.

The car was later searched, and ten documents, or groups of documents, were found behind the passenger seat on the floor under the carpet.

Later that morning, Culhane gave them to DI Doocey, who returned them to him on 22 December. On that date, he gave the package to DS O'Dea, who returned it to him later.

46

'I ONLY KNEW WYMAN FOR A SHORT TIME'

Bracing himself as he faced into these headwinds, Crinnion tried to downplay his association with Wyman, alleging he had only met him six times, then revised this figure downwards to three.[1] Yet, by reference to the 1973 memoranda and other documents, it is clear six was the absolute minimum number of meetings that took place between the men. The first encounter took place, according to Crinnion, when Wyman had masqueraded as a Scotland Yard officer. There was a second occasion, in the early 1960s, when he realised that Wyman was actually a spy, something he had not grasped before, allegedly due to 'immaturity'. They met twice in relation to the Rita O'Hare phone tap. A fifth meeting took place to discuss the closure of the Sinn Féin HQ at Kevin Street and a sixth when he was told MacStíofáin had access to phone scramblers. He surely met Wyman during the week he spent with MI6 in London, in August of 1972. There were other get-togethers concerning Jock Haughey, the Knockvicar convention and the Arms Crisis, not to mention the occasions on which he was given information about attempts by the IRA to import arms. Recall his words: 'I cannot give even an approximate tally but the number of weapons lost on abortive smuggling attempts must be somewhere in the 2,000 region.'[2]

When he wrote to Patrick Malone in 1973, he added another element to the mix, namely that he 'only knew Wyman for a short time'.[3]

This statement is extremely problematic. How could Crinnion describe Wyman, someone he first met in the early 1960s, and was still in contact with as late as December 1972, as someone he only knew 'for a short time'?

Another spin tendered by Crinnion was that Wyman 'gave me information on a number of matters relating to [the] activities of the IRA which I used by incorporating it in work or in other ways to the benefit of Garda counter I.R.A. measures. All these matters appear on files in C3 and I can detail them if necessary. None of the matters he mentioned to me ever proved to be misleading, false or time-wasting, all were solid useful items of information.'[4]

Crinnion would stand trial for possession of the files allegedly found in his car. He would be charged with the intention of passing them to Wyman. By way of defence, he would insist that the documents produced at his trial had never been in his possession. In a letter to Patrick Malone, Crinnion admitted that he had other files in the vehicle but that:

> … any documents I may have carried from my desk at C3, even though by an oversight, were not in the position that the Prosecution misled the Court to believe.[5]

Other searches were carried out. Super. Fitzgerald accompanied a group of his colleagues to Crinnion's house in Kilmacud where additional documents were found.

Detective Garda Michael O'Driscoll, a close ally of Wren, participated in the search of the house. He testified later that he found a document made up of fifteen sheets clipped together in a drawer of a desk upstairs which he had seen in C3.

Another searcher, Insp. Michael Gormley, found a document in the pocket of a jacket, the extract from the FBI report about the slot machine manufacturing company in Walkinstown. He also discovered an envelope containing £90 made up of nine English £10 notes.[6]

The search party conducted their inspection in a sloppy manner. There was far more incriminating material at the house which they failed to discover.

Meanwhile, John Wyman of MI6 was facing his own round of questioning.

47

WYMAN THE SPYMAN

John Wyman was trying to find a way off the plank along which he was stumbling. His first gambit was to stick to his cover story. He told DI Patrick Doocey that he was a private detective with Bateman Investigations. The head of his firm, he said, was Brian Bateman, an ex-chief superintendent of the Oxford City police. He had been tasked, he claimed, with vetting an individual for a client but refused to disclose his identity as it was confidential. He added he had no interest in politics.

In the morning Doocey interviewed Wyman along with Ned O'Dea. They told him they were satisfied that he was in the Republic to acquire information about the IRA. Bowing to the inevitable, Wyman revealed he worked for a British ministry and conceded he had been in the Republic on a number of occasions, where he met contacts in hotels and elsewhere. By way of background, he said he had been born in 1937 in Bulu, Cameroon, and had once served with the Royal Marines. This was far from a full disclosure. He did not tell them that he was the head of an Irish network which he had set up, expanded and maintained for over a decade.

When he was shown a loose-leaf sheet from his notebook, Wyman explained that it contained details relating to events which his superiors had instructed him to investigate while in Ireland. The reference to 'R.L.'s' meant 'rocket launchers' which had been used in Northern Ireland and were capable of going through steel, he explained. A reference to 'Car bombs' was to the explosions in Dublin on 1 December, about which he claimed: 'We are as interested in finding out who did this as you are'.

Asked about an entry concerning 'arrest policy' Wyman made no comment. This was probably a reference to the Offences Against the State (Amendment) Act which had been passed after the bombs in Dublin on 1 December 1972. That was the legislation that would have been defeated but for the explosion of those bombs. Wyman did not volunteer that he had been in Dublin on the night of the bombings, nor that he had visited one of the explosion sites to monitor what was going on.

Inevitably, Wyman was asked about his relationship with Crinnion. According to O'Dea:

> When asked about the information he got from this man [Crinnion] he stated that it was mostly in the past tense about the activities of the IRA, and that he gave [Crinnion] information about the closing of [the Sinn Féin HQ] at Kevin Street and about Seán MacStíofáin ... He also stated that the information he wanted most from this man was information about the future policy and activities of the IRA and in particular any information about the smuggling of arms from the Continent and the USA here ... Wyman was asked if Crinnion did any other type of enquiry for him, outside of getting information about the IRA, and he said 'No.' At this stage Wyman refused to answer any further questions.[1]

One of the reasons Wyman needed to keep quiet was because had he answered the question about 'other' enquiries, he would have had to lie or admit that he was looking for information about Charles Haughey with the help of Crinnion and Thomas Mullen. It does not appear Wyman was asked for whom he had booked the second room at the hotel.

Jack Lynch was kept informed about developments. Amongst his private papers he preserved a note which indicated that 'Wyman has asked to meet the Deputy Commissioner'.[2] There were two people in the force with that rank at the time.

Wyman's request to meet the deputy commissioner came at a sensitive moment for the garda top brass. Garda Commissioner Michael Wymes was due to retire in January. It had already been officially announced that Patrick Malone, one of his two deputies, was going to succeed him. Malone's appointment could yet be withdrawn by Lynch and his ministers. A meeting with a British spy at this juncture would hardly have commended him to them.

Malone had met New Scotland Yard officers such as Ferguson Smith during his time as commander of C3. Wyman might have been given Malone's name by Maurice Oldfield, Ferguson Smith or Crinnion, as someone likely to ensure nothing untoward would happen to him if he was caught by the gardaí. There is no suggestion that Malone was a British agent. In fact, all the signs point in precisely the opposite direction. A number of years later, Fred Holroyd, a military intelligence officer who doubled as an MI6 operative, visited Dublin where he collected approximately 150 confidential garda intelligence files on the INLA from Assistant Garda Commissioner Ned Garvey. Garvey told Holroyd he wanted to conceal their relationship from his superiors. Garvey's superior at the time was Malone. Hence, it is unlikely Malone was part of a pro-British intelligence clique in Dublin.

The other deputy commissioner in 1972 was Cornelius 'Con' Donovan, who had overseen C Division which included C3 since the late 1960s, and was still in place, but only just. He had announced his retirement on 19 December 1972. There is an equally good chance that he was the individual to whom Wyman wanted to speak. When Patrick Malone was head of C3, he had once asked Donovan if it was appropriate for him – Malone – to meet two men from the UK who were on their way to the Phoenix Park to have an informal chat with him. Donovan not only approved of the meeting, but had already known about the visit and the names of the individuals who were on their way. Again, Wyman might have been supplied with his name as an officer who would most likely ensure nothing untoward would happen to him if he was arrested by the gardaí. There is no suggestion that Donovan was a British agent of any class.

Neither Malone nor Donovan went to see Wyman. However, Wyman did receive a visit from Fleming at a later stage while in custody. According to Crinnion:

> Indeed even after his arrest on 18/12/72 John Wyman continued to assist the Garda Siochana and he gave certain information to Chief Supt. John Fleming which will be of assistance to him in his work. As I regard this matter as secret I cannot give details at this time.[3]

Colin Wallace, who worked as a psychological operations officer at Lisburn with the British army, recalled what happened after Wyman's arrest:

> News spread around Lisburn that an MI6 officer was in custody in Dublin. We [in the army] considered what might be the potential exposure for us; what the fall out might be. We realised quickly it didn't directly affect us. The impact would be in Dublin and London. There would be quite a serious fall out, but not in Belfast. The army was sympathetic towards his plight but – professionally – unfazed. We knew we were not going to look bad. I never saw Wyman myself in Lisburn. I had no dealings with him but could easily have passed him on the corridor.[4]

Across the Irish Sea, an army of Britain's most senior officials were becoming increasingly alarmed at the mess unfolding in Dublin. Wyman was in Mountjoy, a place where IRA prisoners were incarcerated. If given the chance, they would seize and torture him for information about his activities, contacts and sources. There was a lot to hide. For a start, Wyman was the handler of the Littlejohn brothers. They had attacked garda stations and were involved in discussions about the assassination of Seán MacStíofáin, Seán Garland and Séamus Costello. Wyman was undoubtedly in contact with Thomas Mullen and knew about the smear campaign against Charles Haughey. Wyman had also fed Crinnion lies about Fianna Fáil, Saor Éire and Knockvicar. If MI6 had been involved in the bombing of Dublin on 1 December 1972, John Wyman would have known all about it. He might also have known who sent the letter bomb to MacStíofáin's home.

Maurice Oldfield too must have been beside himself with concern. At this point, the most powerful man in the UK became directly involved in Wyman's plight.

48

PANIC INSIDE 10 DOWNING STREET

On the morning of 21 December 1972, Lynch and his ministers met to discuss the startling espionage drama unfolding on their doorstep. The consensus reached on the available information was that Crinnion had been suborned by Wyman, either on his own or with others who were working for 'the British Department of Defence'. Patrick Hillery, the minister with responsibility for relations with the UK, was instructed to 'protest to the [British] Ambassador about that activity'. Taoiseach Jack Lynch asked Hillery to convey his 'personal disappointment in so far as this activity betrays a lack of confidence in the relations that should exist between two friendly governments'.[1]

Wyman and Crinnion sought, and were refused, bail in the Special Criminal Court that same day. Their cases were remanded to 12 January.

Hillery summoned Ambassador Peck for a formal rebuke. Hugh McCann, Secretary of the Department of External Affairs, sat in at the encounter during which Peck, a practised purveyor of lies 'expressed surprise and denied any knowledge of the activity'.[2] Peck kicked the ball to touch claiming he only knew about the affair from the media, and that like Lynch, he too would be concerned if Wyman turned out to be a British agent. He agreed to let London know of the disquiet in Dublin.[3]

Hillery then remarked that the information in the Border Dossier demonstrated that Britain had gained access to greatly improved information. The implication was that Wyman had secured the information from Crinnion about subversion in Ireland:

Peck commented that that in itself was not proof of the allegation made. While agreeing that it was not proof in itself, Hillery said that the fact that it had improved following the activity complained of was significant. The Ambassador then withdrew in order to report the matter immediately to his government.[4]

Wyman's arrest was a calamity for MI6. Soon, a sizeable part of Wyman's Irish network, one that he had spent a decade constructing, was in disarray. The gardaí announced they were 'still looking for another man' who was not a garda. This was a reference to Andrew Johnstone, a thirty-nine-year-old first secretary at the British embassy. Not wishing to place his head on the chopping block, he fled Dublin in a hurry. Peck does not refer to his departure in his memoirs, nor to what the pair discussed before he hightailed it out of Dublin. He and Wyman had liaised at MI6 safe houses in Dublin and at Johnstone's flat in Wellington Road, near the Burlington Hotel, and a second flat in Castlecomer, Co. Kilkenny; as well as at the home of another member of the network, a former colonel with the Royal Marines, named Simpson, who lived in Sandyford, Co. Dublin. Johnstone was also linked to the Littlejohn brothers.[5] Completing the circle, the Littlejohns were handled by Wyman. Johnstone's name was erased from the Diplomatic Service List in 1973. If Johnstone was not 'Oliver', the second man to handle the Littlejohn brothers, he undoubtedly knew who was. Thomas Mullen was also in danger. Alex Forsey was in custody and his 'wife' had disappeared. The IRA men who dropped reports in milk churns for Wyman and MI6 must have been shivering in their boots. In England, Wyman's alleged employer Brian Bateman likewise must have been discommoded as were the Nowesome sisters, whose address Wyman would give as his own. At the top of the intelligence and diplomatic tree Oldfield, Rowley, Steele and Peck must have been feeling uncomfortable.

The man who was probably the MI6 head of Station in the Dublin embassy, John Williams, left Dublin at around this time, though perhaps before Wyman was arrested. He next surfaced at the NIO.

Wyman and Crinnion were charged with offences of a very serious nature. The prospect of lengthy prison sentences loomed. Yet, while Dublin made its protests to the British, the Irish ambassador to London, Dr Dónal O'Sullivan, held a meeting with Edward Heath. He then flew to Dublin where he met Lynch before returning to London where he was received by Heath's private secretary, Robert Armstrong on 23 December 1972. O'Sullivan gave Armstrong an assurance that Wyman was unlikely to serve a prison sentence. Armstrong prepared a memorandum along with a separate note for Heath's eyes only. The private note for Heath explained that:

1) For public relations reasons [the Irish] government would have to oppose bail: but the strength with which they would do so was another matter.

2) You had expressed concern about the effects of a long sentence. [The Irish ambassador] had the impression that this was unlikely: indeed he said that there might be no sentences at all.[6]

The memorandum, which had a wider circulation in London also revealed that the:

Wyman incident presented the Irish Government with a difficult problem, particularly in public relations terms. Wyman had suborned a police official who was in a delicate position of trust. Information of a critical nature had passed, not all of it related to the IRA. The fact that Wyman was found operating in this field had to be taken very serious note of. There was no doubt that this would be used by the IRA as evidence of collusion between the British and Irish security forces, to the embarrassment of both governments. The allegations that British agents may have been involved in the recent [December 1972] bomb outrage in Dublin, however ill-founded, would also be put to good use by the IRA.[7]

Robert Armstrong's note reveals something else of interest: someone in Dublin was bad-mouthing Crinnion. Armstrong wrote that Crinnion:

> had volunteered to give information [to MI6], because of his belief that the IRA was the common enemy. It had occurred to us as a possibility that [the Irish] Government was aware of and was countenancing his activities. *The [Irish] Ambassador said that it was not clear that the motives of the official concerned were as high-minded as this suggested [my emphasis].*[8]

Crinnion's detractors in Dublin were alleging that he had been about to pass information to Wyman that was not related to subversion. Armstrong's memorandum noted that London had been told by Dublin that:

> the papers found in Crinnion's car at the time of his arrest suggested that *he was preparing to pass other information, unrelated to the IRA,* some of which had not been submitted to the Minister for Justice *[my emphasis].*[9]

The reference to 'other information' may have related to the attempts to link Charles Haughey to the American Mafia, albeit that this information – the FBI document – had been found in a jacket pocket at Crinnion's home, not in Crinnion's car.

The Armstrong memorandum reveals that Lynch was now trying to make amends to London for the arrest of Wyman. London was keen to accept the olive branch:

> The [Irish] Ambassador asked me to report what he had said directly to the [British] Prime Minister, in case the [British] Prime Minister might wish him to go to Chequers to report to him

personally. I therefore reported to the [British] Prime Minister, in the presence of the [Irish] Ambassador. The Prime Minister asked me to thank Dr O'Sullivan for all that he had done. It was evident to him from my report that Dr O'Sullivan's visit to Dublin had cleared the air, and had been extremely useful. He was most grateful to the [Irish] Ambassador, and did not think that he needs further interfere with his holiday plans by asking him to come to Chequers to report personally. I so informed the [Irish] Ambassador.[10]

In his memorandum, Armstrong also explained that:

So far as the personal safety of Wyman was concerned, the points made by the [British] Prime Minister were much in the Irish Government's mind, and they would exercise every precaution.

The [Irish] Ambassador said that he been asked to say that his Government would not interfere with the legal processes, or anticipate the decisions of the Court. Wyman would come up on remand on Wednesday, 27 December. The question of bail would then arise. The Government would be bound, for public relations reasons, to oppose the granting of bail. Nonetheless it was not beyond the bounds of possibility that [bail] would be granted. Mr Lynch had indicated that there was a good prospect that the case would be disposed before the end of [December].[11]

While Wyman enjoyed the support of Edward Heath, the FCO, the JIC and MI6, Crinnion had no champion at his side, only detractors.

49

THE MANUSCRIPT IN THE GOVERNOR'S SAFE

Larry Wren must have known, or, at the very least, suspected that Crinnion had a source in MI6 long before Crinnion's arrest. Yet, he never interfered with the arrangement. Bearing this in mind, the least he owed Crinnion was a visit to hear his side of the story. Instead, Wren hung Crinnion out on the bleachers.

Crinnion's time in prison was miserable. Republican prisoners inside Mountjoy subjected both him and Wyman to incessant chanting. Crinnion's life was threatened.[1] His wife and two young sons had to leave their house in Kilmacud. It was subsequently attacked by vigilantes who broke some of the windows of the property.

He received a visit from the archbishop of Dublin which gave him some comfort. In a letter addressed to 'His Holiness, The Pope, Cardinal Conway, Armagh' and 'Archbishop of Dublin, Most Rev. Dr Ryan' dated 19 June 1973, he stated:

> At this point I have written only to a very limited number of people all of whom are named on the enclosed copies of correspondence and accordingly I trust you to treat this letter in confidence. I wish to thank My Lord, the Archbishop of Dublin, Most Rev. Dr Ryan for his advice and aid while I was in Prison.[2]

Garda Commissioner Wymes asked Joe Ainsworth to serve Crinnion with a notice of suspension of his service as a garda while he was in Mountjoy.[3] The man Ainsworth encountered was a thoroughly subdued individual. He was wearing civilian clothing, a high-necked grey jumper. Crinnion did not ask him any questions about what was happening in the outside world, nor attempt to engage him in conversation. This was the very opposite of what had happened during Ainsworth's visits to C3 to work on his 'secret' operations file. On those occasions, Crinnion had been chatty and friendly.

For technical reasons Crinnion had to be served with his suspension notice twice. On both occasions the task was performed by Ainsworth, rather than someone from C3. When Ainsworth saw him the second time, Crinnion had about ten to fifteen days' worth of stubble and his hair was going grey. Once again, he had no questions, nor made any attempt to converse.

When the case came before the Special Criminal Court on 12 January 1973 for mention, the three judges were told that the trial was likely to take two days and that further charges might be preferred against the defendants. Mr Justice Andreas O'Keeffe, president of the High Court, stated that the court had 22 January in mind for a hearing, but because further charges might be preferred, the court would not fix a date for the hearing until the following Monday when the case would come up for mention again. The judge asked Crinnion if he wished to proceed on an application for legal aid and Crinnion said he did not wish to do so at that juncture.[4]

On Monday, 15 January 1973, the court was told that additional charges were being preferred against both defendants but that they were still being typed up. The following day 16 new charges were introduced to the proceedings and the trial date was set for 1 February.[5] Crinnion and Wyman's lawyers told the court that their clients wished for the hearing to take place in public where it was legally possible.[6] The judges decided that some of the charges would be heard *in camera* because the information to which they related was highly sensitive due to considerations of national security.

While he was in Mountjoy, Crinnion drew up a detailed account about what had happened to him. It was locked in the governor's safe. Later, Crinnion wrote to the attorney-general, Declan Costello, about the manuscript:

> While I am anxious not to make your examination of the case more complex it might assist you to know that after my arrest and while in the Bridewell I commenced a statement which I completed in Mountjoy Prison. I handed the statement in the form of a letter to the Prison Governor for dispatch to the Taoiseach. It was acknowledged by intensified spiteful measures at the Prison. I gave a copy of the report to the Governor addressed to William Cosgrave, T.D., Leader of the Opposition, under a covering letter addressed to you. The Governor said he could not send this letter out either to you or Mr Cosgrave or permit it to be taken by my wife's hand or even the hand of the Archbishop of Dublin.
>
> After my release from Prison due to the fact that I was being sought by the IRA for execution I went into hiding and at the first opportunity wrote to the Governor of Mountjoy Prison requesting him to retain the letter or statement carefully until such time as I was in a position to collect it or have it collected. He replied that being aware of my difficulties after my release he had destroyed the letter. It had until then been held in the Prison safe.
>
> However the original comments I made on the Book of Evidence for my counsel, Mr Robert Barr, on Mountjoy Prison headed and dated writing paper still exist and they contain in substance the same data as my statement. I have no copying facilities nor the means to arrange any but am willing to attend at the nearest Irish Embassy so that copies of the 100 or more pages can be made [available] if you feel they would be material in getting this awful blunder rectified.[7]

It is far more likely that the manuscript prepared at Mountjoy was handed over to a senior garda, or an official at the DoJ. This is the first indication of a policy by officials lurking in the background to destroy all of the paper trails linked to Crinnion. Crinnion referred to the true role of MacStiofáin as a *faux* informer, and that he had precipitated the Arms Crisis, in his 1973 correspondence with Malone and others. It is likely these revelations were also contained in the manuscript that went missing from Mountjoy prison. These were embarrassing secrets which senior gardaí desperately wanted to keep hidden from Jack Lynch and the public.

There was no internal inquiry to ascertain if Crinnion was part of a wider conspiracy. This was a cause of astonishment to many senior officers who were not serving with C3 or the SDU, particularly Ainsworth. He found the silence emanating from inside C3 'deafening'.

When Wren sent his investigation file to the chief state solicitor, he highlighted Crinnion's escape attempt at the Burlington to substantiate Crinnion's guilt. The letter that accompanied the file stated:

> It is clear that [Crinnion] was in search of John Wyman, whom he actually named, and admitted that he was the man who had borrowed the pencil and left the note for Wyman on the previous evening. He agreed to accompany the other members to the Bridewell Garda station as he said, 'there is obviously some explanation for this.' However, his determined effort to escape on reaching the ground floor would appear to indicate that the explanation was not obvious.[8]

Prosecuting counsel, Donal Barrington SC, made use of this information at Crinnion's trial the following February suggesting it was 'highly significant' because it indicated Crinnion had some guilty knowledge of matters about which he did not want the police to learn.

Thomas Mullen, the C3 officer who recruited Crinnion to work for MI6, and admitted his role as an MI6 agent to Mick Hughes of the SDU, was left to enjoy his retirement and garda pension. This book represents the first occasion on which the public has been told of his collaboration with MI6.

The trial of Crinnion and Wyman was scheduled for February 1973. In the meantime, the pair were held in solitary confinement for their protection while Wyman's solicitor and barrister went to London, where they met some peculiar characters who portrayed themselves as lawyers.

50

SPIES IN THE DOCK

John Wyman was represented by Michael Gilbert, a solicitor from London. Gilbert held himself out as someone retained by Bateman Investigations, Wyman's alleged employer.[1] Wyman's solicitor in Dublin was Ronnie Ringrose.

Wyman's barristers in Dublin, Ernest M. Woods, SC, and Frank Martin, BL, visited London where they were brought to a meeting up a rickety staircase on the fifth floor of a building on the Mall. There they met someone who presented himself as a solicitor. It did not take long for the Irishmen to think he was lying to them and that he was not a lawyer, rather some sort of a British secret agent.[2]

Robert Barr, SC, later a high court judge, appeared for Crinnion.

Two trials took place. The first, which commenced on 1 February 1973, at the Special Criminal Court, was the more serious of the two. It dealt with the indictable charges laid against Crinnion and Wyman.

An application was made by the FCO just before the trial commenced. The FCO wanted permission for one of its consular officials to attend the proceedings. This would have allowed the official to hear the evidence presented to the judges *in camera*.[3] The application was made under the Diplomatic Relations and Immunities Act. The presiding judge, Mr Justice O'Keeffe, said it was a pity the application had not been made at an earlier stage. The barrister making it, Anthony Hederman, SC, replied that he had not had an opportunity to mention it. 'I only got this specific instruction late last night,' he explained.[4]

When the case resumed, the judges stated that the indictable charges would be heard *in camera* and that they would decide if the summary charges would proceed in open court after the indictable charges had been dealt with.

The application by the FCO to attend the trial was subtly dismissed. When the case started at 2:10 p.m., the judge stated that only the lawyers, court officials and garda witnesses would be allowed to remain for the hearing. The garda witnesses, he added, would only be present while giving their evidence. Although no express remarks were made about the British consul, his presence was excluded by his non-inclusion on the list of those entitled to attend.

There was a heavy presence of gardaí inside and outside the court building. Wyman and Crinnion were brought to the court under heavy escort. Wyman wore sunglasses and had a newly grown beard. Crinnion wore a grey suit. They were escorted to the dock in handcuffs by prison warders.[5]

The defendants faced charges under the Official Secrets Act, 1963. Joe Neville, one of the gardaí assigned to security duties, paid close attention to the case as it was being opened to the three judges.[6] He became perplexed at how the prosecution proposed to prove it without revealing some very sensitive information. His bewilderment was to be short lived.[7] The prosecution announced that it wanted to describe the documents without producing them. Wyman's barrister objected to this. Having considered the matter, the judges ruled that the documents would have to be produced in court and that secondary evidence relating to what the documents concerned would not be acceptable. The judges were told by the prosecution that some of the C3 files were so sensitive they could not be disclosed, even at an *in camera* hearing.

Des O'Malley issued the order to withhold the papers. He revealed in his memoirs that he was protecting potentially identifiable garda sources. That was not something that had bothered him when he had permitted John Fleming to appear at the Public Accounts Committee, in 1971, to talk about the 'confidential sources' who had told the SDU about the alleged payment of large sums of money by Capt. Kelly to Cathal Goulding.

In the absence of the files, the defendants managed to have the six more serious indictable offences thrown out with relative ease at the conclusion of the case for the prosecution. Now, only the summary charges remained. The trial on foot of those charges was set for later in the month.

While the first trial of Wyman and Crinnion was heard *in camera*, it nonetheless attracted a lot of media attention. The same cannot be said for the prosecution of Alexander Forsey, who went into the dock in Dublin for possession of an explosive safety fuse, 710 rounds of .22 and eight rounds of .303 ammunition, on 7 February 1973. He was convicted and received a three-year suspended sentence. His counsel, Patrick MacEntee,[8] hinted at his role as a spy by describing the case as 'a strange and special case with no possibility of a recurrence'.[9]

Forsey's connection to Wyman did not emerge at the hearing.

Forsey fled to England. His wife informed the Irish Air Corps captain who owned the grocery/hardware store and living accommodation above it, where she and her husband had worked and lived, that Forsey had felt his life was in danger.[10] By now, MI6 had surely realised that Forsey had cracked under the pressure of interrogation and had given up Wyman, the more important of the spies. Forsey appears to have been an 'agent' as opposed to an 'officer' of MI6. The distinction is that an officer is a full-time trained employee of the service, whereas an agent is someone who is recruited from among the public for a specific purpose, e.g., to report on a neighbour.

'Mrs Forsey' may or may not have been Forsey's wife. There is every chance she was part of the spy network and masqueraded as his spouse. She too disappeared.[11]

The Forsey affair did not grab the attention of the public despite the fact *The Irish Press* had reported at the outset that two British suspects and a garda 'employed in a clerical capacity at Garda Headquarters' had been rounded up. Media interest in Forsey had faded after this report.

The second Wyman-Crinnion trial, the one allotted to deal with the lesser charges, began, in public, on the morning of 26 February 1973. The same judges sat on the bench. On this occasion Crinnion was charged that on 19 December, at the Burlington Hotel, Dublin, he had in his possession, or under his control, official documents without authority and had attempted to communicate the official information to John Wyman. Crinnion was found guilty of the unauthorised possession of official documents while Wyman was found guilty of attempting to obtain the information from Crinnion, a public official.

In his letter to Commissioner Malone, Crinnion complained that:[12]

> Perhaps I would not feel so aggrieved if all the documents produced [at the trial] had in fact been in my car – well, not alone was there no ulterior reason behind my oversight [in leaving the documents in the vehicle] but some of those documents were never at any time in my car. I feel sure that there was no criminal intent by witnesses but there was confusion and grave error, understandably when you realise the pressures in the case.

All told, it was alleged that Crinnion had attempted to pass ten documents or groups of documents along with the papers found in his jacket pocket. Wren testified he had been shown them by Culhane after Crinnion's arrest.

Crinnion had an explanation for the presence of certain other files in his car. On the day before his arrest John Murphy, a film director, had called to see him at his office. Murphy was working for an Italian film company. Several props which resembled guns had been confiscated at Dublin Airport. Crinnion, who had worked as a security guard at Ardmore Studios, in Bray, to earn extra cash when he was not on duty, was probably favourably disposed towards someone like Murphy, a man in the film industry. However, since Wren did not tolerate the presence of civilians at C3, Crinnion rushed Murphy out of his office while grasping certain papers he had intended to file away. Once he had ushered Murphy outside, he dropped the papers in his car so he could talk to Murphy. The documents were for record and statistical purposes, some of which were notes written in his handwriting. They were not, he claimed, the ones which were later alleged to have been in the vehicle.

Murphy gave evidence at the trial. He testified that he had travelled to Dublin to organise the production of a film about the Mafia in which gun props were going to be used. He was staying at the Burlington Hotel when he received a phone call from Crinnion about the impounding of the items at Dublin Airport. He was subsequently introduced to Crinnion at Garda HQ and had asked for the return of the props, albeit without success. Having tried several contacts in the DoJ and elsewhere, he failed to recover them, and being 'fed up of the whole situation' he went to see Crinnion again.

Crinnion brought him to see his colleague at C3, Michael

Fitzgerald, but to no avail. Murphy and Crinnion left C3's offices and went over to Murphy's car to look at an official document from Italy confirming the props were intended for the film. Murphy testified that he had been preoccupied while at Garda HQ with retrieving his props. He had no memory of Crinnion having taken any documents with him, nor had he gone near Crinnion's car.

Murphy was a stranger to Crinnion. He owed him no favour. If anything, he might have been irritated by the treatment he had received from the gardaí.

In his letter of 9 May 1973 to Patrick Malone, Crinnion claimed that:

> In my own fashion I am illustrating the absurd logic behind the prosecution's case against me. Certainly I had some documents in my car through an oversight and the papers in my house were about explosives, the sort I studied to keep abreast of current IRA innovations and so be in a position to discharge my responsibilities without shortcomings. (I had been ordered by D/Inspector Gormley to draft a paper for a proposed F.B.I. Publication concerning Explosive Devices used by Terrorists and was actually engaged on this task but as I was fully occupied during the day on the Monthly Report this task was one for the odd spare hour in the peace of my home).

He was also angry about the way his personal inquiries into the factory in Walkinstown had been portrayed at the trial:

> Just as my possession of this piece of paper [i.e. the extract from the FBI report about the Mafia] was magnified and distorted out of all proportion to reality so also were the contemptible allegations of the prosecution completely irrational but fundamentally pursued. I am not making a claim to have been the victim of some deliberate malice but the person who laid the foundations of the case in November was in a position to realise the outcome even then and I do not know his mind.

It is a matter of deep concern that only those opposed to the existence of the State [i.e. the IRA] benefited from the confusion and doubt raised by the court proceedings.[13]

Unfortunately, Crinnion did not identify the 'person who laid the foundations of the case in November'. Clearly, it was not Malone, the recipient of the letter.

The reference to the month of 'November' is significant. Crinnion was not arrested until December. This indicates that Crinnion believed he was framed because of something that had happened as early as November 1972. This is surely a reference to the Border Dossier which was compiled in November in the UK and presented to Dublin on 6 December 1972. This was the document that had prompted Jack Lynch to order John Fleming to find the 'spy in the camp'. Was Crinnion hinting that someone else was involved in supplying information to the British government?

Of all the mysteries that still cling to the Crinnion case, none is more perplexing than the evidence his superiors gave at the trial about the function he performed at C3, and his length of service at the unit.

51

THE CRINNION MISNOMER

Larry Wren, head of C3, played down the extent of Crinnion's espionage with the media. The narrative concocted for the press was that:

> Crinnion's work as a British spy was dated by the gardai as having occurred between August 1 and December 10, 1972. It would appear from an examination of his movements that the Special Branch place importance on a visit Crinnion made to London around, August 1972.
>
> The trip – of a week's duration – was important for Crinnion spent all of the time in consultation with his spymasters. His wife, who accompanied him on the London visit, was left to sit out the week's holiday in a hotel. He did not even take her out once during the period.[1]

While the August trip did take place, it was not the dawn of Crinnion's relationship with MI6. The correspondence between Crinnion and Malone make it perfectly clear that Crinnion was in contact with Wyman long before August 1972, e.g., Wyman had relayed information to him about the December 1969 IRA convention at Knockvicar House. The gardaí knew perfectly well that Crinnion had been spying for MI6 since the early 1960s. Thomas Mullen confessed when he retired from the force in or about 1961 that he had recruited Crinnion.

During Crinnion's trial, a garda from the records section told the court that Crinnion had joined the force on 10 May 1955, had been appointed to the SDU on 20 June 1961, and assigned to the Phoenix Park, i.e., C3, in February 1965.[2]

Someone went to considerable trouble to alter Crinnion's

records. The 10 May 1955 graduation date was correct, but the other two were false. Crinnion joined the SDU at the end of the 1950s, not in 1961. He went to C3 in December 1960, not in 1965. The misleading picture meant that the media, the public and elected politicians did not have to concern themselves with the full extent of Crinnion's espionage for London.

In addition, the ruse threw a potentially suspicious garda off the scent of Thomas Mullen. Mullen was long gone by 1965, and so the implication was that there had been no overlap of service featuring the pair while they were at C3. Larry Wren, who was present in court during this evidence, did not see fit to correct the error. Mullen was never charged with any sort of offence, despite admitting to the SDU that he had spied for MI6 and had recruited Crinnion.

When Michael Fitzgerald, one of Crinnion's superiors at C3, testified, he said that he knew Crinnion, with whom he had worked at C3. Crinnion, he alleged, was a detective garda working as a clerk. That was far from the 'whole' truth that Fitzgerald had sworn to tell. Clerks did not trace the whereabouts of the chief-of-staff of the Provisional IRA, thwart international gunrunning by paramilitaries, edit MCRs, carry guns, hunt Saor Éire members on the streets of Dublin, nor dress as a doctor while on an operation with the SDU in a disguised ambulance, or enjoy a stature that gave him access to the head of the SDU, John Fleming, without appointment.

Fitzgerald was asked if he had seen a particular document at C3 which had allegedly been found in Crinnion's car. He replied that he had, and added that Crinnion had not been authorised to remove it from C3.

Wren testified after Fitzgerald. Wren, an outwardly deeply religious man, climbed into the witness box, placed his hand on a bible and swore to tell the truth, the whole truth and nothing but the truth, and then proceeded to sing from the same duplicitous hymn sheet as Fitzgerald. He too described Crinnion as a clerk.

Wren had been plotting against Crinnion for months. He had pointed out to the prosecution team – in a private letter – that Crinnion had made a dash for freedom at the Burlington Hotel.[3] Wren argued this indicated that Crinnion had something to hide. In the witness box, Wren's evidence dovetailed with that of Fitzgerald: Crinnion was a detective garda performing clerical work, one who did not have any authority to remove documents from the section, nor to disclose information received in the course of his duty.

Wren knew perfectly well that Crinnion was responsible for the compilation of monthly confidential C3 reports, hardly the work of a clerk, rather that of a top-level intelligence analyst. Wren must have known as well that Crinnion routinely took files home to work on them into the night.

In a letter of 26 June 1973 to Malone, Crinnion argued that:

> A false and misleading picture was put before the Court when it laid great stress on my duties as being solely that of a Garda Clerk. Although some of the staff in C3 are qualified clerks and are employed on routine clerical functions I was not so qualified and was not so employed. I was a Special Branch Detective employed on Special Branch duties and those mainly concerned the Provisional IRA. My work was to utilise my special knowledge of these matters for the benefit of the State.
>
> ... As a Detective in C3 I certainly used a desk and typewriter but still did not qualify for the misleading title of Clerk. At the time of my wrongful arrest, at my Desk in C3, I was editing the Monthly Confidential Report from the reports sent in by each [of the force's eighteen divisions]. I was typing the report then, addressed to the Minister for Justice to be sent under your signature ... You know from your personal knowledge of me that I was the man who scanned IRA documents and kept track of the various types

of explosive devices utilised by the IRA so that I was in a position to spot new variations or mechanisms so that I could alert the Force and Military to fresh dangers.

The evidence that Fitzgerald and Wren presented during the second trial, which was held in public, was widely reported in the media.

The statements made by the C3 and SDU witnesses had been typed up on an old-fashioned typewriter. Pieces of carbon paper were placed underneath to duplicate the statements. Some of the witnesses had access to these copies. After each witness completed his testimony, Wren instructed them to hand over the copy. No one left the court in possession of his duplicate statement.

When Joe Ainsworth began to probe into the Wyman-Crinnion affair in 1979, on the orders of Garda Commissioner Patrick McLaughlin, his first port of call was Michael Fitzgerald, whom he circled cautiously asking a few subtle questions about what had happened. Fitzgerald was unhelpful and evasive. Ainsworth discovered the absence of a paper trail. All of the witness statements Wren had collected were missing.

Clearly, Wren did not want any hint to emerge that he knew, or ought to have known, that Crinnion had been involved with MI6.

A lot of questions should have been asked of Wren, who passed away in 2016. They never were. Who did he believe was the source of Crinnion's knowledge regarding the multiple arms importation attempts which the gardaí had thwarted? Whom did he think was Crinnion's mysterious 'Informant', if not a British spy? Had Crinnion told him about Wyman? What did he and other senior officers know about Crinnion's involvement in the Arms Crisis? Why did he not correct the error about the timing of Crinnion's assignment to C3? What was so imperative that Wren – a religious dogmatist – was driven to lie under oath directly after placing his hand on the bible by describing Crinnion as a clerk?

On 27 February 1973, Crinnion and Wyman were found guilty on the lesser charges and sentenced to three months' imprisonment but released on account of time served. As the sentences were being handed down, Crinnion glanced over at Wyman. Their eyes locked for a moment. Seán Boyne, who attended the trial, felt the message they communicated to each other was: 'We are all right now.'[4]

The country was now in the grip of spy fever. There was enormous pressure on newspaper photographers to snatch a clear picture of Wyman. At one of the early court appearances, a reasonably good shot of him had been captured by a photographer. This was the one that enabled John Kelly to recall having seen him at the bomb site on 1 December 1972. After that Wyman had taken to disguising himself. He turned up on a subsequent occasion with a blanket drawn over his head, as did Crinnion. On the final day of the trial, at least one determined photographer climbed to the top of a block of nearby flats which overlooked the court house and took some shots from above of the English spy. On this occasion Wyman was protecting his identity with his new beard and a pair of dark glasses instead of a blanket.

Crinnion's wife and children were still in hiding due to threats which had been made against them. Crinnion now made arrangements to join them. He claimed later that the IRA placed a bounty of £10,000 on his head which made him fearful as he stepped back into the outside world.

52

HUNG OUT ON THE BLEACHERS

After Crinnion's trial ended on 27 February 1973, some of the lawyers and gardaí involved in the case repaired to the Chinaman Pub, a favourite haunt of the SDU, to let off steam. A lot of alcohol was consumed and, by the night's end, a little ditty on the affair was composed. It was called 'Wyman The Spyman'. A few lines have survived: 'I am Wyman the Spyman I am; I came to Ireland and got in a jam.'

After his trial, a dishevelled Crinnion arranged for a friend to collect him from Mountjoy Prison and ferry him, and his family, to his brother-in-law, Seamus Lattimore, in Belfast. The latter was serving with the Royal Irish Rangers at the time. Crinnion, however, had departed by the time his friend arrived, having grabbed a lift with Wyman in a red Daimler driven by the latter's barrister, Frank Martin. This enabled Crinnion to get away before the media or anyone with hostile intentions descended upon Mountjoy. Martin drove the pair towards Dublin Airport followed closely by a SDU escort. During the trip, Wyman asked Crinnion if he and his family wanted to join him on the jet the British government was sending over to Dublin to collect him. Crinnion accepted the offer and jumped out at the traffic lights, at the crossroads at Whitehall, to make an arrangement to rendezvous with his family and get to the airport.

Wyman proceeded towards the airport. Crinnion was shadowed by a number of SDU officers to a barber shop where he had a shave and a haircut. He was then traced by the television crew to O'Connell Street, but gave them the slip in a taxi.[1]

When Wyman reached Dublin Airport, Frank Martin entered the terminal with him. Normal passenger formalities were waived and Wyman was ushered through a side entrance where he was met by British officials and whisked to safety.

Crinnion and his family made it to the airport in time to catch the flight. The plane took Wyman to Birmingham at approximately 6 o'clock. According to Kenneth Littlejohn, Wyman lived in Kettering, Northamptonshire, which is a little over fifty miles from Birmingham.

Having dropped Wyman to the airport, Frank Martin was invited by the SDU officers to join them at the Chinaman pub. He accepted the offer and was amused to watch a procession of undercover SDU men, including one who was posing as a hunchback, arrive to join the merriment. Part of the fun was watching the evolution of 'Wyman the Spyman', line by line. Each of the officers involved was offered an opportunity to contribute a line to the mock ballad.[2]

Crinnion was bitter about his plight. In a letter he wrote the following year, he bemoaned, how:

> For carrying out my sworn duty, faithfully, loyally, impartially and effectively, I was arrested by my own brother police officers, held in isolation in Prison, in solitary confinement, for three months awaiting trial and then when set free from the court, although it was public knowledge, having been openly stated and accepted during the court hearing, that my life was forfeited to the illegal I.R.A. (Irish Republican Army) I was left on the streets without any protection or means of defence despite the indisputable efficiency of the IRA as killers of those who oppose them.[3]

In his March 1973 letter to Commissioner Malone, he pointed out that:

> in the eyes of the IRA and their supporters I am regarded as fair

game. Although I know the Gardai may have matters to attend to and cannot always afford citizens the attention they may need, nonetheless in my situation, to be turned loose onto the streets without any means of defence or protection and with nothing but my instinct for self-preservation between me and a fast car trip for a hooded death on a Border roadside, after 3 months less almost 10 days in solitary confinement, it was a nerve shattering experience to have to evade not only Provo and TV people but potential executioners as well.

After 18 years service in the Gardai, some 14 of which I spent on counter-IRA work, I have no illusions about my fate if I am unlucky enough to fall into the hands of the IRA. But to be treated as an enemy by my former colleagues is the most saddening aspect and I am genuinely puzzled to know what terrible crimes I am thought to have committed.[4]

When he wrote to Cardinal Conway, he displayed a more suspicious line, raising the far-fetched spectre that someone in officialdom wanted him dead:

Whether I was turned loose without any means of defence and an easy victim for IRA justice by genuine police oversight *or otherwise* [my emphasis] is something I cannot answer and because of this I have remained in hiding since.[5]

He added that:

When the IRA failed to find me as easily as they had expected they put a price of £10,000 on my head. You will appreciate the awful position I am in, not merely a refugee but one who must try and cloak his identity to avoid mindless murder, hampered also by being unable to get a proper job without revealing my identity and supplying references. I had to move my wife and two children to avoid reprisals and their position is the same as my own.[6]

Crinnion's arrest and conviction brought an end to the mole hunt that Jack Lynch had ordered when he told Fleming that there was 'a spy in the camp'. The investigation had turned up a second culprit, Thomas Mullen. Yet, there is no indication that Lynch was told anything about Mullen. He was never prosecuted despite admitting that he had spied for MI6 and had recruited Crinnion. His explanation to the SDU officer to whom he admitted his guilt was that someone was required 'to pass on the information' to London.[7]

On 10 January 1973, Jack Lynch assigned Ned Garvey, then an assistant commissioner, to oversee C division, which included C3. Larry Wren, who had commanded C3 since September 1971, remained in place. In what must rank as one of the more notable U-turns in the history of An Garda Síochána, Garvey and Wren would hold six to eight meetings with Capt. Fred Holroyd, a British special military intelligence unit (SMIU) officer who worked for MI6 during the period 1973–76.

In 1975, Holroyd travelled to Dublin to visit Garvey and Wren at the Phoenix Park in the company of Frank Murray of the RUC. In later years, Garvey purported not to recall the encounter. Judge Barron, however, determined in his report on the 1974 Dublin Bombings that:

> The visit by Holroyd to Garda Headquarters unquestionably did take place, notwithstanding former Commissioner Garvey's inability to recall it ... On the Northern side, there is conflicting evidence as to how, why and by whom the visit was arranged. Regrettably, Garda investigations have failed to uncover any documentary evidence of the visit, or to identify any of the officers involved in arranging it from the Southern side.[8]

A garda with close connections to MI6, dubbed 'The Badger' by Holroyd, organised the meeting. He and one of his garda colleagues, Colm Browne, drove Holroyd and Murray to Dublin. At the meeting, Garvey passed approximately 150 photographs and details of INLA suspects to the Englishman.

The provision of these files clarifies a comment made by Maurice Oldfield's friend and hagiographer Richard Deacon, in his biography of Oldfield. Deacon, who relied upon Oldfield and his friend Anthony Cavendish, among other sources, wrote in the book about MI6's closeness to the gardaí and the 'comprehensiveness of certain of [MI6's] intelligence reports'.[9]

The perceived wisdom for decades has been that Crinnion – and he alone – supplied the confidential data in the Border Dossier to Britain. Crinnion denied that he was responsible for the classified files allegedly found in his car. If we give Crinnion the benefit of the doubt on this, it raises the ugly prospect that Oldfield had other horses in the race and that Crinnion was trampled underfoot to protect them.

The information in the Border Dossier, based on C3's MCRs, that had spurred Lynch to order Fleming to find the 'spy in the camp', had passed through many hands at the Phoenix Park HQ, and thence to the DoJ, and, finally, onwards to O'Malley and Lynch. All told, dozens of people had access to the data as it meandered through the distribution pipeline. A leak could have sprung anywhere along the route.

Did someone at Garda HQ place the files in Crinnion's car to ensure that he – and he alone – went down in flames? If so, it was an unnecessary step for there were other files – and guns – in Crinnion's attic in Kilmacud that could have been used to incriminate him, but they had not been disturbed during the search of his house.

53

THE CACHE IN THE ATTIC

The gardaí conceded at Crinnion's trial that he had been entitled to carry the Walther pistol he had surrendered during his interrogation at the Bridewell garda station. Some emphasis was placed on the fact it was apparently customary to carry it in a shoulder holster, not in the pocket where Crinnion had placed it.

In a letter to Patrick Malone, Crinnion emphasised that as 'a member of Detective Branch engaged on Special Branch duties I was issued with an official firearm and authorised to retain it in my possession at all times and to carry it even on holidays anywhere in the State'.[1] Little did the SDU know that Crinnion had other weapons at his disposal for which he had no licence.

On 24 March 1974, *The Sunday Independent* carried a front-page report by Joe MacAnthony, based on information from a variety of sources, including a man who had helped Crinnion during his time in Mountjoy Prison. He shall be called the 'Contact' in these pages.[2] The Contact was exposed to great danger by helping Crinnion.

By 1974, the prevailing wisdom was that Crinnion had gone to Australia but the Contact knew otherwise. He was aware that Crinnion was living in London under an assumed name and had been provided with work by MI6. He also knew that Crinnion had returned to Dublin at least twice, including in early March 1974.

Joe MacAnthony reported that Crinnion had returned to Dublin at 'considerable risk to himself' due in part to 'an extraordinary Special Branch blunder on the night of his arrest.

It was a blunder of which even the head of the special branch, Superintendent Fleming, is still unaware ...'

The SDU had failed to find a number of 'papers' which Crinnion had stored in the attic at his home in Kilmacud. There were also at least two handguns, one of them a German-made Luger, hidden there.

While in custody, Crinnion had realised that the SDU had not searched his attic when the officers who questioned him at the Bridewell failed to make any reference to the cache in the attic. When Crinnion realised this, he passed out a message, on toilet paper, to the Contact asking him to remove them from the house as soon as possible, without raising suspicion.

As MacAnthony highlighted in his article, Crinnion was 'seriously worried because the documents involved were apparently so sensitive that they could have led to an even heavier sentence than what he expected'. Crinnion was determined to preserve what was left of his own skin. This meant placing the Contact in the path of great danger. Had the Contact been caught with the cache, he would probably have been charged with an array of criminal offences.

Crinnion wanted the guns to 'be dumped and that the documents be destroyed. Within a week of his request, the items involved were removed from the house' by the Contact.

MacAnthony also reported that:

> The possibility which now arises is that the documents, after being taken from [Crinnion's house at] Rathmore Avenue [Kilmacud], may have been re-hidden elsewhere and that Crinnion volunteered to return and collect them. This could explain his first return to Ireland in September, 1973, five months after his release for he was positively identified at that time although he had tried to change his appearance by growing his hair long.

Crinnion may have returned to Ireland again in November [1973] as he left his family at that time in London to 'go away on a trip':

> He certainly returned to Ireland again this month [March 1974] for he was seen by a close friend in Harcourt Street on March 9 ... He was wearing a suit and dark glasses but he was instantly recognisable.

MacAnthony also reported that:

> During all that time [in Mountjoy prison] he was able to send out messages regularly and also made it clear that he found the warders in the prison especially nice at all times.

The article proceeded to reveal a cover story Crinnion had employed to disguise his covert activities:

> When he had regular meetings with Wyman at the Burlington he used to hint around that his work involved acting as a bodyguard to a diamond merchant and that he was seriously thinking of taking up a job as a diamond courier in South Africa.

The article also stated that Crinnion:

> used to boast of his long connections with the family of the present Attorney General, Declan Costello, although the only link was in acting as a guard on the house of the former Taoiseach, John A Costello. Indeed, after his arrest he made frantic efforts to enlist the help of Mr Costello and Mr Liam Cosgrave without success.

Crinnion might have felt that Cosgrave was indebted to him because he had delivered the 'GARDA' note to his house in May of 1970, the event that sparked the Arms Crisis.

MacAnthony's source was the Contact himself. The latter spoke to MacAnthony to deter Crinnion from coming back to Dublin to beg for further favours.

54

MI6 IGNORES AN OPPORTUNITY FOR BLACK PROPAGANDA

After a run of sixteen years in power, Fianna Fáil lost the February 1973 general election, but Jack Lynch retained his leadership of the party.

MacStíofáin was released from prison the following April. The day after MacStíofáin's release, a NIO official mentioned a rumour that MacStíofáin had provided the gardaí with a memo containing information about Dáithí Ó Conaill. It stated that:

> Seán MacStíofáin was released from prison yesterday and we need to consider what likely impact, if any, that will have on the current PIRA campaign. There is clearly a growing rift between the PIRA membership in the North and the organisation's Dublin leadership. During a recent conversation between [redacted] and [redacted] from the Markets area of Belfast [redacted] described MacStíofáin as a 'music hall Republican who was born a Protestant'.

> There is growing evidence that Rory and Seán O'Brady, plus David O'Connell [i.e., Ruairí Ó Brádaigh, Seán Ó Brádaigh plus Dáithí Ó Conaill] are also at odds with Seán MacStíofáin and may not welcome him with open arms. It is even being seriously suggested in Republican circles that MacStíofáin may have informed the Irish Authorities of O'Connell's planned arms smuggling trip to Holland [with Maria Maguire] at the time of internment. There is little doubt that MacStíofáin has attempted to ingratiate himself with the Dublin authorities but his alleged role in compromising David O'Connell is probably false. It is more likely that the allegation is a symptom of his apparent loss of credibility with Republicans in general – especially after his theatrical hunger strike in prison where he allegedly drank his shaving water.

Rory O'Brady and Dave O'Connell are generally being given credit for the creation of the Eire Nua strategy which emerged about two years ago but MacStíofáin's attitude to that political initiative was believed to be negative. What is particularly significant is Cathal Goulding's increasingly hostile attitude to MacStíofáin. The full reasons for that are unknown but there is little doubt that MacStíofáin played a significant part in [the] split within the IRA in 1969. The current divisive nature of MacStíofáin's presence at the top of the PIRA should be seen as particularly helpful to the security situation but it is believed that his days in the PIRA Army Council are probably numbered.[1]

MI6, of course, knew about MacStíofáin's masquerade as an informer from information supplied to them by Crinnion. In turn, C3 and the SDU must have concluded that London was now aware of MacStiofáin's machinations.

MI6 had deployed David Astor, the owner of *The Observer* newspaper, to undermine MacStiofáin's reputation during the Maria Maguire affair, a year earlier. They had also asked the Littlejohns to kill him.

The rumour that MacStíofáin had betrayed Ó Conaill was psychological dynamite. In normal circumstances, British propagandists would have exploited the claim to destabilise the IRA, but the rules of the game had altered since Crinnion's arrest. If Whitehall used the information, it now had the potential to seriously embarrass the SDU and C3.

The Observer operation had been directed from London. The black propagandists in Northern Ireland had not been a party to it. Colin Wallace, a senior psychological operations officer in Lisburn at this time, has stated that:

A key function of the Army Psy Ops unit in Lisburn was to target, primarily, the leaders of those organisations which were causing death and destruction, but it is also important to stress that we did not engage in such activities against leaders when their organisations were observing a ceasefire. I cannot recall any Psy Ops activity being directed by the Army specifically at Seán MacStíofáin at any time, nor am I aware of any such activity directed at him by another Government agency.[2]

The Information Research Department (IRD) of the Foreign Office acted as Britain's black propaganda machine during the early 1970s. Hugh Mooney, a Trinity College Dublin graduate and ex-*Irish Times* employee, pumped out lie after lie on its behalf. Mooney and the IRD tried to link a variety of targets – including the British Labour Party – to the Soviet Union and the IRA. Bank statements were forged to smear John Hume and Edward Short, the deputy leader of the British Labour Party.[3] Another rumour Mooney and the IRD put into circulation was that IRA leaders were embezzling funds.[4]

Mooney could have used the MacStíofáin situation to undermine the morale of the Provisionals, e.g., by pretending MacStíofáin had been feeding genuine information about an array of Provisionals – not merely Ó Conaill – and their activities to the gardaí all along. The impact of this would have been shattering for the Provisionals. Yet, nothing was done to exploit the MacStíofáin scenario.

Suffice it to say, MI6 had no desire to provoke the wrath of the key players in garda intelligence. Richard Deacon, Oldfield's friend and biographer, pointed out in 1984 that Oldfield prized his garda contacts.[5]

MacStíofáin believed he was going to resume his leadership role within the IRA. To his surprise, he was sidelined.

55

OLD HABITS DIE HARD

A month after MacStíofáin's release, a group of Saor Éire prisoners in Portlaoise prison, including Martin Casey, issued a statement proclaiming that the movement had 'ceased to play a progressive role' and that during the previous two years 'undesirable elements [had] been able to operate around its fringes and carry out actions'.[1] Saor Éire did not quite disappear. In June 1975, one of their number, Larry White, was shot dead by two Official IRA men who pumped fourteen bullets into him with machine guns. The remaining members of Saor Éire wound up the organisation in 1975. All told, approximately sixty members had participated in its activities.

In the mid-1970s, MacStíofáin attempted to set up his own paramilitary organisation but without success.

In 1975, Jack Lynch, still leader of Fianna Fáil, brought Charles Haughey back onto his opposition front bench, a development that sent a shiver down the spine of the SDU. It was a 'humiliating event for [the DoJ and SDU]. Haughey had been acquitted in 1970 and was now destined to return to power [as a minister] if Fianna Fáil won the next election', Joe Ainsworth said.[2]

Also in 1975, MacStíofáin published his memoirs. The book, while informative in many respects, did not reveal how he had led the SDU a merry dance for eleven or more years. Hugh McNeilis of the SDU, who remained in contact with him, revealed that MacStíofáin furnished a copy of the book to the gardaí before it was published.[3]

McNeilis told Liam Clarke and Barry Penrose that he and three other gardaí had maintained contact with MacStíofáin.

An uneasy relationship was maintained during the mid-1970s. To be specific, MacStíofáin continued to provide information which the force was prepared to accept from him even though he had concealed important intelligence from them in the past. At this juncture, MacStíofáin was probably supplying details about his opponents inside the Provisional IRA, the people who had blocked his return to a leadership role within the organisation, such as Gerry Adams and Martin McGuinness.

McNeilis also revealed that RUC officers had been aware that MacStíofáin had acted as an informer.

Fianna Fáil swept back to power in 1977 with a large majority. Many of the new TDs were Haughey supporters. The stage was set for a succession battle between Haughey and George Colley. The latter was Lynch's anointed successor.

Meanwhile, MacStíofáin had not abandoned hope of a return to paramilitary activity. A group of discontented Officials, led by Séamus Costello, had set up the Irish National Liberation Army (INLA) and the IRSP, its political wing, at the end of 1974. A feud developed between the Officials and the INLA. Costello was assassinated by Jim Flynn, an Official IRA gunman, while he sat in his car on Northbrook Avenue, off the North Strand Road in Dublin on 5 October 1977. Shortly after the shooting, Flynn rang Seán Garland, head of the Officials, and told him he had taken care of the 'job'. The call was intercepted by the SDU, whose officers recognised Flynn's voice.[4] Disingenuously, the Officials denied responsibility and Sinn Féin The Workers' Party, the political wing of the Official IRA, issued a statement condemning the killing. The INLA suffered a bout of internal feuding after Costello's demise. Some in the INLA thought that MacStíofáin was the man to steady the ship and made contact with him. They considered appointing him as chief-of-staff.

MacStíofáin confirmed he was interested. A series of meetings took place in 1978 and 1979, some of them in a restaurant on the main street in Dalkey, Co. Dublin. Ironically, the spot was close to a pub frequented by the gardaí. Some of the INLA negotiators were being watched by the SDU. When the SDU teams followed the INLA men to Dalkey, they were told to withdraw by their superiors who already knew precisely what was afoot. MacStíofáin, it transpired, was keeping McNeilis informed about the discussions.[5]

It eventually became clear to the INLA that MacStíofáin wanted total control of their organisation. The negotiators were not prepared to meet his terms and the parties went their separate ways.[6]

McNeilis believed the SDU had a hold over MacStíofáin which was linked to the death of a member of Saor Éire, presumably Peter Graham, who was shot dead in 1971.

Jack Lynch resigned at the end of 1979 and Haughey triumphed over George Colley for the leadership of Fianna Fáil. Haughey retained Colley and Des O'Malley as full ministers in his first administration. It lasted from 1979 to 1981. Haughey's victory gave the SDU a strong and abiding motive to conceal MacStíofáin's role in the Arms Crisis. In office, Haughey set about crushing the IRA in a way Lynch had failed to do, even to the extent of winning plaudits from the RUC.

In March 1983, MacStíofáin appealed to the IRA to declare a ceasefire.

ONE OF MACSTÍOFÁIN's passions was the promotion of the Irish language. He lived in the Meath Gaeltacht and remained active in the revival and use of the language through his involvement in Conradh na Gaeilge. When its centenary celebration was held in Dublin on O'Connell Street in 1993, he was invited onto the platform as a guest of honour. He remained a member of Conradh's standing committee (Coiste Gnó) until his death.

One Irish speaker who became acquainted a little with MacStíofáin from Irish language circles was surprised when he told him about certain of his interactions with the SDU. One evening, without prompting, at a wedding in Malahide, MacStíofáin told him a similar story to the one he had relayed to the journalist Kevin O'Connor in the early 1970s, namely that he was being tailed by the SDU and occasionally engaged in chat with them. On this occasion he added that they were on first-name terms with him. He may have continued to believe that if he was spotted by someone from the IRA talking to Hugh McNeilis, he could explain that he was merely chatting about irrelevant matters.[7]

MacStíofáin must have enjoyed the political feuding that engulfed Fianna Fáil in the 1980s, much of it sparked by the toxic legacy of Arms Crisis. Colley and O'Malley never accepted the outcome of the Fianna Fáil leadership vote in 1979, and became involved in a series of plots to topple Haughey. O'Malley became the spearhead of anti-Haughey dissent in the party after Colley died from a heart attack in 1983. O'Malley was expelled in 1985 and set up the Progressive Democrats. He then executed one of the sharpest handbrake turns in recent Irish political history by coalescing with Haughey, after the 1989 general election, to elect him as Taoiseach. O'Malley went on to maintain Haughey in power until 1992.

Hence, there was a strong continuing motive for the gardaí to suppress the fact MacStíofáin had told McMahon about the arms flight to Dublin Airport which sparked the Arms Crisis.

They maintained the secret into the 1990s as Haughey's successor, Albert Reynolds, had taken a keen interest in the

Arms Trials and would have been less than impressed by the negligence surrounding the fiasco.

In 1993, aged sixty-five, MacStíofáin suffered a stroke. On 18 May 2001, he died at Our Lady's Hospital, Navan, after a long illness. He was seventy-three. He is buried in St Mary's Cemetery, Navan.

Ruairí Ó Brádaigh, who attended the funeral, said he had been an 'outstanding IRA leader during a crucial period in Irish history' and was the 'man for the job' as first Provisional IRA chief-of-staff. Gerry Adams and Martin McGuinness, two of the key figures in thwarting his return to the IRA after his release from prison in April 1983, also attended his funeral.

In the wake of the publication of my book, *Deception and Lies*, in 2020, in which the role of MacStíofáin was described in some detail, another retired garda with knowledge of the MacStíofáin case confirmed that MacStíofáin was indeed considered an 'informer' by the gardaí.

On 22 September 2020, Helen McEntee, the Minister for Justice, confirmed the existence of unreleased 'sensitive' garda files concerning the Arms Crisis but failed to make any commitment for their release. She did not, however, rule out releasing them in 'appropriate' circumstances. Her comments were made in response to a question put by Seán Haughey, TD, of Fianna Fáil, who asked her to confirm that MacStíofáin had been a garda informer but – crucially – one who had misled the SDU for his own devious ends, and had sparked the Arms Crisis. Seán Haughey is the son of Charles Haughey.

Seán MacStíofáin passed away without knowing that John Wyman of MI6 was responsible for providing Rita O'Hare's phone number to Patrick Crinnion, the event that triggered the end of his career in the IRA.

56

CRINNION'S VEILED THREATS

Patrick Crinnion corresponded with Garda Commissioner Patrick Malone in the months after his trial. Malone responded to Crinnion on 28 March and 26 April 1973. Crinnion was dissatisfied with the replies. On 26 June 1973, he wrote to Malone stating that:

> it is with despair that I see from the tone of your communications that you have ignored, failed to read or decided not to bother verifying the accuracy of my statements. I was relying on your impartiality to assert itself so that this charade might be seen for the blunder it is. I was never so naive as to think that right automatically triumphed over wrong but that the harm that has been done to me should be condoned and upheld when even if you have been confused by the allegations of the prosecution, with your experience you must realise that it contained false and misleading statements which were necessary to support wrongly conceived basic allegations.[1]

There is a subtle menace in Crinnion's correspondence with Malone, exemplified elsewhere by his reference to the Rathdrum bank robbery incident, i.e., the occasion on which he had placed a document in the files of the SDU at Dublin Castle to cover up the fact no one at C3 had circulated a report stating that Frank Keane of Saor Éire was wanted for the raid.

In the correspondence to Malone, Crinnion also made an uncomfortable reference to MacStíofáin's 'brilliant use of subterfuge to mislead and thwart Garda intelligence' something that could 'best be demonstrated by referring to MacSTIOPHAIN's twelve year masquerade as an Informant'.[2]

Crinnion's subtle intimidation is also evident in the letter which mentioned Thomas Mullen of C3 and the alleged links between Charles Haughey and the Mafia. The menace was the fact that the gardaí had covered up Mullen's activities, another MI6 agent in the gardaí. Also, Mullen had been trying to fabricate a link between Haughey and an international crime syndicate, something else the SDU had covered up.

If the wider correspondence is read on the assumption that Malone knew Crinnion had been in touch with a British source, the letters take on a more overtly threatening quality. Crinnion reminded Malone that:

> Along the Border every Detective with an interest in his job has discreet contact with his opposite number in the Royal Ulster Constabulary and this personal conduct is not discouraged by Garda HQ although it is not specifically authorised. I at my level was in touch with roughly my opposite number and you know of some of the aid he gave the State through me. If you cannot see the truth in this I am afraid, genuinely afraid of the awful decision I must make.[3]

Just what was Malone meant to understand from the words: 'If you cannot see the truth in this I am afraid, genuinely afraid of the awful decision I must make'?

Was he threatening to tell the public that Malone and other gardaí knew, or must have known, that he had been in contact with a British undercover operative?

Was he threatening to tell the public about the role Mac-Stíofáin had played while masquerading as an informer?

The 9 May 1973 letter to Malone was copied to Liam Cosgrave, who had taken over from Jack Lynch as Taoiseach. There was a mysterious reference therein to 'deaths' having 'been caused because of the way a file was dealt with in C3'. The use of the plural 'deaths' – as opposed to a single 'death' – indicates he was not merely alluding to the Garda Fallon tragedy.[4]

Why the veiled intimidation? In May 1973, he still believed he could retrieve his old life. In his letter to Malone, he requested his suspension pay, and stated that:

> Since my release from prison and up to this moment I have not received any suspension pay. To some extent this could be because of the precautions I have taken and post only reaches me in a roundabout fashion and only one relative knows my whereabouts. I have been living on money raised from the sale of my car and household furniture that is now running out. Can I have my suspension pay, please? I have placed my home in the hands of a solicitor and asked him to start the preliminaries towards selling it. However before taking this final step I must ask you what course the State intends to pursue towards me?[5]

The question about the 'course the State' intended to take could only have concerned his future employment as a garda. He next expressed shock that his suspension might result in his dismissal:

> The text of communication, 2.2/44/72 dated 23/3/73 astounds me. Seemingly despite the verdict of the Courts my dismissal is under consideration. I cannot believe that this letter [was] issued with your approval. Surely the one charge on which I was convicted should at most, if a saner atmosphere [had] prevailed ... been a matter for the internal disciplinary machinery, if indeed at all.[6]

He also highlighted to Malone that a judicial inquiry into his activities might generate a lot of turmoil for the force:

> Apart from the fact that I am almost destitute and cannot afford to get legal representation it is my feeling that any public inquiry that may be contemplated would not alone divert personnel from their duties, where diligent performance at this time can so often result in the saving of human lives, but that the disclosures would have a demoralising effect on the force and simply ensure more harm than good. However I await your decision without any preconceived conditions.[7]

He then alluded to the possibility that incriminating files found in his car had been planted there:

Perhaps I would not feel so aggrieved if all the documents produced had in fact been in my car – well, not alone was there no ulterior reason behind my oversight but some of those documents were never at any time in my car. I feel sure that there was no criminal intent by witnesses but there was confusion and grave error, understandably when you realise the pressures in the case.[8]

As a weathered garda officer, one who viewed life through a prism of intrigue, treachery and betrayal, Crinnion hardly felt that files could have found their way out of the C3 complex and into his car due to mere 'confusion'. He could not have expected Malone to have believed so either. The reference to 'confusion' was perhaps a veiled warning of what he might raise at a judicial inquiry. He wanted Malone to take a position:

At this time I am anxious to get some indication of your intentions in this matter and I would thank you for some form of reply as soon as possible.[9]

An inquiry was not set up.

By July 1973, Crinnion had abandoned his hope of reinstatement or support from Dublin. He appealed to the Secretary-General of the UN hoping he might take up his case:

Due to the continued interest of the Press I cannot use my correct name or proper documents to get work to feed and house my family. If the press locate me they would cause me no direct harm but as the IRA has offered £10,000 reward for my whereabouts and has notified its members in Ireland and abroad so I must constantly conceal my true identity and whereabouts.

Without producing genuine documents and references I can only work in temporary jobs within the common travel area of Ireland and Britain and even in these unskilled posts my obvious unfamiliarity with the work, my manner and appearance immediately made me a subject of curiosity and interest so that I am obliged to move because of the hazard of recognition and its fatal consequences.[10]

Apart from the physical, mentally I feel so exhausted now that if my wife and children could be provided for, I would welcome the peace that my murderers will bring.[11]

... I cannot earn a livelihood without deceiving employers and workmates. My wife must be constantly on guard to lie about our identity and supervise the children nearly all day, every day, to prevent their chatter leading to tragedy. Despite our vigilance we have come close to disaster and recognise only too well that we cannot go on like this much longer.[12]

He asked the secretary-general, if he might provide him with help in light of how he had been mistreated:

I am not alleging that the Irish Government deliberately employs imbeciles and villains but the motivation of officials about the larger issues involved in my case leaves me shocked and bewildered. They have systematically deprived me of the means of survival and reduced my alternatives where unless I can obtain sanctuary and employment within an organisation such as the UN I will be forced to come to terms with a Publisher. As I had some preliminary talks with a Publisher I recognise his requirements must be met so that a marketable book would result. In order to produce this book it would be necessary to cover recent events in clear and accurate detail. I have no illusions but that the facts so disclosed would result in greatly aggravating the bloodshed in Ireland. I would also be turning my back on all I have believed in and worked for all my adult life. But now I am going to have to sacrifice my wife and children in favour of the lives of nameless citizens of Ireland if I continue to adhere to my principles and after being vilified put at the mercy of the I.R.A. by the public or official representatives of these same citizens you surely would vindicate me if I had already taken this step and published the saleable of story of the I.R.A campaign as known to me.[13]

He was also angry at how he had been portrayed to the public.

... I became a victim of the war myself when despite the contradictions of illogical allegations, inexperienced police and government officials concluded that I was an enemy of the state and then,

> despite the Acquittal of all serious charges by the three Judges of the Special Criminal Court the State continue to act against me in such a fashion that it is clear that it is not going to abide by the Court's findings. Is it any wonder that during my imprisonment that my hair, normally brown colour, turned completely white.[14]

Crinnion was not as destitute as he maintained. Oldfield had put him, his wife and two boys up in a small flat in Hackney, London. They were later relocated to a three-bedroom house.

Overall, the picture that emerges is one of Crinnion hoping to find a way back to his old life while accepting hospitality from MI6, a fact he conceals in his correspondence. Oldfield, a legendary agent handler, was content to leave the disorientated Irishman troubling deaf heaven with his bootless cries until he realised his only salvation lay with MI6.

In September 1973, Crinnion returned to Dublin, lightly disguised with longer hair, to retrieve the documents and guns the 'Contact' had removed from the attic at his house in Kilmacud.

57

C3 HOODWINKS THE PRESS

Mick Hughes of the SDU ascertained from Thomas Mullen of C3 that MI6 had enjoyed access to C3's secrets since the Second World War. In 1973 and 1974 briefings from an anonymous source attempted to conceal this severe embarrassment from the media and the public. The deception was successful. This became possible because the public had little or no knowledge of the internal structures of the gardaí at the time.

Behind the scenes, Crinnion's conviction and Mullen's admission had led to a collapse of confidence on the part of the SDU in C3. John Fleming of the SDU, and Larry Wren of C3 were soon locking horns. The public was presented with a glimpse of what was happening in 1974. In November of that year, *The Sunday Independent* reported:

> THE DISPUTE between the head of the Special Branch, Chief Supr. John F. Fleming, and the top brass of the security service, the men of C.3 at Garda Headquarters, has worsened since the confrontation between the officers last Tuesday. Chief Supt. Fleming … [is] insistent that his reports should no longer be channelled through C3.[1]

C3 was part of C Division. Such was Fleming's distrust of C3 that he wanted to leapfrog Wren's head and deal directly with the assistant commissioner who oversaw C Division, Ned Garvey, or the Minister for Justice, Mr Cooney. *The Sunday Independent* reported that:

> The reason is that Mr Fleming no longer has trust in security at Headquarters. There have been allegations that there is not sufficient

screening of junior personnel in C3. This view is supported by [the] Army ...[2]

The Sunday Independent newspaper report is accurate to this point. Someone, however, stepped in to distort the article with a volley of lies. One of these was that C3 could not have been responsible for Crinnion as it had not been in existence in 1972. The report continued to state that:

> C3, as a unit was not in existence at that time. It was formed shortly after the Crinion (*sic*) case.[3]

Crinnion was arrested in December 1972, and convicted in February 1973. According to the timeframe of the person who was deceiving the newspaper, C3 must not have come into existence until sometime in 1973. Yet, Crinnion had worked at C3 since the end of 1960. According to a source who misled the paper, Crinnion had been transferred from Donnybrook to work as a clerk in some unspecified part of the Phoenix Park.

> ... The allegation has been made that Crinion (*sic*), who was a detective-clerk in Donnybrook station and a good typist and 'secretary type', was recruited to headquarters simply for that reason without any check on his background or possible political affiliations. 'If it happened in Crinion's case it could happen again' is what is being said.[4]

Another brazen untruth in the piece was that Larry Wren, Michael Fitzgerald and others at HQ were responsible for catching Crinnion, not the SDU team comprised of Hughes, Doocey and Culhane:

> The other side of the argument is that neither Crinion nor Wyman would ever have been caught if it had not been for the activities of the personnel who now comprise C3. *It has seen said by them [my emphasis]* that Crinion, when caught and confronted with his

guilt, was persuaded to co-operate and that this led to the arrest of Wyman. [5]

This quote – particularly the phrase 'It has been said by them' – indicates that the source of these lies was someone or group working at C3 in November 1974. This marked the commencement of a practice which lasted for decades and involved senior gardaí feeding misleading information to a selection of journalists. A lot of the disinformation concerned Charles Haughey and those around him, but that is a story for another day.

58

HIGH FLYER

The spying endeavours of John Wyman, Seán MacStíofáin and Patrick Crinnion were intimately interlaced. They all walked into a world of danger, deceit and subterfuge in the early 1960s. After a decade of playing the game well, they all came crashing to earth with a loud thud. Short prison sentences were meted out to all three. Only Wyman was able to pick up the threads of his life and return to the business of intrigue.

Crinnion had been preparing for Christmas when his world imploded. Instead of enjoying the festivities of the season with his family, he was incarcerated in Mountjoy, where he was subjected to incessant taunts. In the outside world, the windows of his house were shattered. His sons were torn from their friends, relatives and school, and shunted to a flat in Hackney, London, to begin a new life. One son was five, the other eleven. A slip of the tongue could – quite literally – have brought chaos, disruption and perhaps even death to the family.

The wider family was endangered too. Crinnion's friend and brother-in-law, Seamus Lattimore, had become a captain in the Irish Rangers. After the Troubles had begun to take root, the soldiers of that regiment were assured they would not be rostered for tours of duty in Northern Ireland, but they were. That created difficulties for the soldier from Donnybrook, especially on home leave. The threat to Lattimore's life increased tenfold after the Crinnion–Wyman scandal erupted. In March 1974, Joe MacAnthony, linked Wyman to Lattimore in his article in *The Sunday Independent*. MacAnthony revealed that 'Capt. Séamus (Jimmy) Lattimore of the Royal Irish Rangers' had been stationed at Waring Street, Belfast, in 1972 and that he had served in the Ulster Defence Regiment (UDR). The article stated he had operated in plain clothes, something that suggested he worked in intelligence.[1] Lattimore later became a teacher at Sandhurst. He shunned Crinnion for the rest of his life, except on infrequent family occasions.

After Crinnion's arrest, there was little prospect Lattimore could return home, even temporarily, without having to look over his shoulder at every turn. Into the bargain, he became the inevitable target of speculation that he had been entangled with Crinnion. There is no doubt that he became involved with the affair after Crinnion's arrest. In one of the notes Crinnion smuggled out of Mountjoy prison, he made a reference to 'the man in the North [who] has arranged everything'.[2] This was presumably a reference to Crinnion's plan to cross the Border when he gained his freedom and meet up with Lattimore in Northern Ireland. Another of the Lattimores, who had joined the British army, had to maintain a low profile. He rose to become a sergeant major before he retired. Other members of the family suffered fallout from the scandal, not the least of which was attention from the SDU and, later, the stress of being associated with a British spy.

Seán MacStíofáin's household faced travails of its own. The man of the house spent over six years behind bars. A parcel bomb was sent to the family home in Meath in 1972. The low point for the MacStíofáins must have been watching a husband and father waste away to the point of near death during his hunger and thirst strike in 1972. MacStíofáin undoubtedly had leadership qualities which he could have put to good use elsewhere and enjoyed a peaceful and thus prosperous life.

The disruption Crinnion and MacStíofáin inflicted on their

loved ones was reflected in the chaos they generated for the Irish public. Jointly, they derailed the trajectory of Irish history. MacStíofáin became one of the principal midwives at the birth of the Provisional IRA. Together, Crinnion and MacStíofáin – in their different ways – lobbed a political grenade into the Irish body politic by precipitating the Arms Crisis which split Fianna Fáil. The crisis severely undermined the defence committees in Northern Ireland, something that was a factor in the rise of the Provisional IRA.

Oldfield, Rowley, Steele and Wyman diverted the course of Irish history too. If they were responsible for the December 1972 Dublin bombing, it means that MI6 pushed the Offences Against the State (Amendment) Act of 1972 across the finishing line. Its provisions allowed a court to convict a person accused of membership of a proscribed organisation if a garda of the rank of chief superintendent or above gave evidence of his opinion that the accused was so affiliated. The gardaí went on to arrest and imprison hundreds of IRA members with the benefit of the 1972 legislation.

MI6 complicity in the 1972 bomb attacks would also mean that MI6 contributed to Lynch remaining in office for another three months. In turn, that period of time gave Fine Gael a breathing space within which to recover from its internal difficulties and conclude a vote-transfer pact with the Labour Party. The agreement with Labour enabled them to win the February 1973 general election. Had a snap poll taken place in December 1972, Lynch would have led his party to victory. Cosgrave would probably have been ousted as leader and perhaps replaced by his deputy leader, Tom O'Higgins, a man who was perceived as a bridge between the conservative and liberal wings of the party. Suffice it to say, easing Fine Gael into power under Cosgrave was not the motive for the attack, rather an unintended consequence thereof. Nonetheless, whoever planted the December bombs was the *sine qua non* factor in placing Fine Gael and Labour in office.

The explanation for Wyman's involvement in criminality is clear: *he was a member of MI6.* MacStíofáin's motives are reasonably transparent. But what drove Crinnion?

Crinnion was always concerned about his finances. He accepted as much overtime as he could get; he worked on the side as a model and undertook security work at Ardmore studios in Bray during the making of films.[3] He kept lodgers in his house and had the audacity to sue the garda commissioner for the cash he had stumbled across while on duty as a young garda.

It is unlikely that MI6 failed to put Crinnion on a retainer in 1961 when he became its agent. It can hardly be a coincidence that while his colleagues were still on their bicycles, he was driving about Dublin in a car.

When his house was searched after his arrest in December 1972, a garda inspector found £90 sterling, made up of nine ten-pound notes, in a briefcase in a room upstairs in his house.[4] Fumbling in the greasy till, however, hardly explains Crinnion's decision to serve MI6.

Crinnion came from a family beholden to the Powerscourts, one of the oldest Anglo-Irish families in Ireland. His parents resided in the humble cottage their employers provided. The Powerscourts were good employers. They did not suffer the fate of other Anglo-Irish families who were burned out of their mansions. The family looked after Crinnion's mother long after her service to them had ended. Did Crinnion look up to them, perhaps with a little too much deference? Did a respect for the Anglo-Irish Ascendancy render him susceptible to recruitment by Her Majesty's secret service, particularly when he joined an organisation, the SDU, which shared a common goal in defeating the IRA? Thomas Mullen told his interrogator that 'someone has to pass the information along' to the British. Did Crinnion, who became Mullen's mentee, adopt this view too?

The character that emerges from his correspondence and memoranda is that of an ambitious individual with an inflated opinion of himself. Had he remained in the gardaí, he would surely have ascended to a high rank, especially after Wren became commissioner; probably Head of C3, if not an assistant or deputy commissioner. Who is to say he might not have reached the very top rung of the Phoenix Park ladder?

During the nadir of 1972 and 1973, while he was pleading for his suspension pay from Patrick Malone, he could hardly have envisaged the positive fortune that lay in store for him.

Curiously, no effort had been made by the gardaí to probe him about MI6 while he was in custody. They passed on an opportunity to learn the methods MI6 officers had used to suborn him. It also indicates they were prepared to let other potential spies slip the net. In one of his letters to Malone, he stated that:

As at no time throughout the affair was I permitted or even asked to explain to the proper authorities my knowledge of John Wyman ...[5]

Oldfield provided Crinnion with a new identity and passport to start life afresh. Meanwhile, back in Ireland, Crinnion's name became a dirty word. During a criminal prosecution in the early 1970s, before Judge Robert Ó hUadhaigh, a defendant hurled the following insult at the prosecuting garda: 'You are just a Crinnion.' Everyone knew what he meant, including the judge, who admonished the accused.[6]

Crinnion did not sell his house in Kilmacud until the end

of October 1976, an indication that he was not under financial pressure at all.[7]

He secured a job working as a security guard for rich Middle Eastern dignitaries. Some of this work involved accompanying Arab wives on shopping trips. He was amused by the fact that they were not allowed to carry cash and purchase goods. Instead, he would step forward with the cash to complete sales in an array of high-end establishments in London. He soon became financially secure and was able to afford to send his sons to a private British boarding school.

His technical expertise stood him in good stead. He re-invented himself as an international salesman for a Swedish aeroplane-parts manufacturer, some of whose products had military components which were sold to air forces.

He eventually purchased a four-bedroom house, on 6 Tangier Road, in affluent Guildford, Surrey. This was the centre of Conservative-voting England. One of the MPs who represented him was Nicholas St Aubyn, a man educated at Eton and Trinity College, Oxford. The latter became parliamentary secretary to Michael Portillo. As the years progressed, Crinnion, the boy from a humble cottage in Bray began to wear a cravat and adopt airs and graces. He once made a condescending remark about being served a meal in a kitchen. He had no compunction in giving unsolicited advice, such as that it was not acceptable to allow a dog in the kitchen, at any time.

A curiosity of the back garden on Tangier Road was the presence of a Second World War bunker where he kept his tools. He resisted all attempts to demolish it. Perhaps it symbolised a safe haven for him.

There were visits from family members to see him and Nancy in London. The most frequent guests were Nancy's sister and his mother. Peter Crinnion, his younger brother, never made the journey.

For a decade after Crinnion's disappearance, there was speculation in garda circles about what had become of him. Assistant Commissioner Joe Ainsworth began a belated investigation into the nagging prospect that he had not acted alone. That probe began in late 1979, after Ainsworth took over C3. A cabal of serving and former C3 officers resisted Ainsworth. The inquiry threatened to reveal the gardaí who had worked with Fred Holroyd. In early 1983, the probe was shut down by the new government led by Garret FitzGerald.

Until the mid-1980s, Crinnion was occasionally recognised by former colleagues passing through far-flung airports. He was spotted at a hotel in Kenya. A reliable eyewitness caught a glimpse of him in New Zealand, giving rise to speculation that he had settled there. Others suggested he was living in Australia or South Africa. He often took trips to Sarasota, Florida, a place to which he gave serious consideration as a new home. The international sightings of Crinnion proved useful to him for no one guessed he was living in England. The people who saw him in Africa and other far-flung posts, where he was usually spotted at airports and hotels, were not mistaken. It was Crinnion they saw all right, but he was visiting these locations as a sales rep on behalf of his Swedish employer, or as a tourist.

His wife Nancy enjoyed living in London and developed a taste for luxury department stores such as Harrods and Debenhams. She took to international travel too, often with her sister, but as a tourist. The ladies enjoyed painting as a hobby, and went on weekend courses to improve their skills. She and her husband purchased other properties in England which they let to tenants.

The Crinnions returned to Ireland, fleetingly, for funerals and other family events. The SDU, sometimes aware of a connection to Crinnion, anticipated his return and kept a watchful eye lest an incident occur. Nothing ever did.

Time was on Crinnion's side. Memories faded as did the youthfulness of his complexion. With each passing day, the chance of anyone recognising him receded that little bit more. By the late 1980s, he had become a distant memory, even at the Phoenix Park. At his sentencing in 1973, Crinnion's barrister had sought sympathy for him by telling the court that:[8]

> Crinnion knows he can never again live in peace with his family in this country. He will have to flee his own country and live somewhere abroad, where he can get work and provide for his family. He was a police officer with an unblemished record. His life and his career have gone, as has his family home, and everything he held dear has been lost to him as a result of what he has done.
>
> He has been grievously punished for what he has done and will continue to be so punished to the end of his days, and his wife must bear this punishment too, which will add considerably to his suffering.[9]

By the turn of the millennium, Crinnion was no longer recognisable. In 2002, he sold his house on Tangier Road and returned to Ireland, where he built a house in a remote rural area with few neighbours, on the east coast. The property was within striking distance of a sea port, with a regular ferry bound for Pembroke, a factor that enabled him to travel back and forth to Britain without having to venture through Dublin. When he flew out of Ireland, he availed of Cork Airport. His normal practice, however, was to travel by ferry. It was always possible to buy a ticket at the last minute when travelling by sea.

During his time with the gardaí, Crinnion had been teetotal but in later life he developed a taste for hot toddies.

If anyone in the SDU ever learned of his return from exile, they kept it a secret.

He was not popular with his neighbours due to a condescending tone he adopted when dealing with them. While he was an intelligent man, he had 'no cop on'.[10]

Seamus Lattimore, who had shunned him in England, ignored him while on visits to Ireland after the latter's return to live on the east coast in 2002. Once, when Lattimore went to visit a retired army colleague, a man who lived close to where Crinnion and Nancy were residing, he did not take the opportunity to make a detour to see them.

To all outward appearances, Crinnion appeared a relaxed man who never became agitated nor excited, but there was an ever-present underlying fear. He kept a special breed of Alsatian dog which he trained to obey his every command. He taught a line of them, including one called Ted, to bark when anyone raised their voice in his presence. His dogs seemed to specialise in growling ferociously. Despite all this, his house was burgled twice, and on one occasion, expensive jewellery was taken.[11]

He was reconciled with his brother Peter who attended the celebration for the sixtieth anniversary of his marriage to Nancy in 2019.

His health gave way in the end. He was diagnosed with Parkinson's disease and, despite the best medical care, began to waste away.

59

THE FORGOTTEN MAN

British intelligence sources told the late Paddy Hayes, author of a book about Dame Daphne Park of MI6,[1] that John Wyman was still alive during the first decade of the new millennium.[2] Wyman may have passed away since. In any event, he maintained a silence about the crime spree he oversaw in Ireland. Not everyone has been so reticent.

In 1973, the Littlejohns revealed that MI6 had mandated them to attack garda stations and engage in assassination operations. As the years passed, further allegations about MI6 misconduct in Ireland began to emerge. These and other revelations must certainly have given Patrick Crinnion cause to reflect on his decision to serve MI6.

In 1972, Crinnion had expressed his alleged concern to his garda colleague, Éamonn Ó Fiacháin, that the 'Brits' had been involved in the bombing of Dublin in December of that year. If he truly believed this, it did not deter him from attempting to meet Wyman at the Burlington hotel less than three weeks after the attack. The note he left in the Englishman's empty room was a friendly one addressed to 'John'. When he approached Wyman's room, he was aware of the progress the Ballistics Section of the gardaí had made into the attacks. At that time, the section was located at the Phoenix Park. Crinnion had visited it during one of his lunch breaks to speak with Ó Fiacháin.

A series of official reports by the likes of John Stevens, later chief constable of the Metropolitan police, and Northern Ireland Police Ombudsman, Nuala O'Loan, raised serious issues about collusion between Loyalist paramilitaries and Crinnion's former masters in British intelligence. Unless Crinnion was living in a cocoon devoid of television, radio or newspapers, he must have read accounts about these shocking events and discoveries.

What did he make of revelations about the UVF and the Dublin bombings of 1972 by Kevin Myers and Joe Tiernan? What of the 1974 Dublin and Monaghan atrocity that stole 34 lives? The latter attack was perpetrated by British agents in the UVF such as Billy Hanna and Robin Jackson.[3]

What of the rape of children at Kincora Boys' Home in Belfast by a gang of Loyalist and Unionist paedophiles, protected by their handlers in British intelligence, especially Oldfield who played a central role in that scandal?

Closer to the bone, he must have been aghast at the revelations of Fred Holroyd which exposed clandestine British intelligence co-operation with the gardaí in the period from 1973 to 1975. Holroyd dealt with a string of gardaí including Ned Garvey, the 'Badger', Colm Browne and Vincent Heavin, none of whom was put through the same meat grinder as he – Crinnion – had been.[4]

As noted earlier, Judge Barron found in his report on the 1974 Dublin bombings that the 'visit by Holroyd to Garda Headquarters unquestionably did take place'.[5] During this visit, Garvey gave Holroyd files about the INLA. Garvey emerged unscathed by the controversy surrounding his contact with MI6.

The Badger helped the British for decades. In the early 1980s, the RUC's E4A unit followed suspects in the Republic, with the assistance of the Badger. Two were shot dead in a 'shoot-to-kill' action in Northern Ireland after they crossed the Border under the watchful eye of the this garda officer. The E4A killings were investigated by the deputy chief constable of Manchester, John

Stalker, who was vilified when he determined to pursue the truth. Much of this intrigue became public knowledge. Holroyd and Stalker published books, as did others. The issues were widely discussed in the press. There were two substantial reports on RTÉ presented by Michael Heney, one on Holroyd, the second on Stalker. *The Stalker Affair* became an epic tale in Britain.

Larry Wren, as garda commissioner, 1983 to 1987, protected Garvey, 'the Badger', Browne and Heavin. This was the self-same Wren who had thrown Crinnion to the wolves, had described him as a 'clerk' at his trial, and forced him into exile.

Crinnion clearly gleaned that he had been a cog, albeit a vital one, in a large machine constructed by Oldfield to crush the IRA. Oldfield's tradecraft involved murder, bombings and bank robberies. MI6 and other branches of British intelligence let Saor Éire roam freely; they sent over the Littlejohns, and steered Loyalists such as Jim Hanna, Billy Hanna and Robin Jackson. While Oldfield's monstrous construct carried out its dirty work in the Republic, it was matched in its ferocity by the actions of Brigadier Kitson and his ilk in Northern Ireland. The latter unleashed his brutal tactics – fine tuned in the colonies – on the Nationalist communities of Northern Ireland. Kitson's paratroopers perpetrated the Ballymurphy massacre and the Bloody Sunday atrocity. In addition, British spies sparked feuding between the various factions of the IRA while ignoring Loyalist serial killers.

Did Crinnion believe that the benefits of his relationship with MI6 in the 1970s outweighed the crimes that had been committed by them? In 1973 he identified some of the positive entries on his ledger thus:

> To the best of my knowledge I believe that without [MI5's] training (given freely) to several hundred Garda the service given to the public would fall short of the present standard. All the

technical bureau key men, all the junior men, the drug squad and last but not least their assistance to the Special Branch is a debt we could never pass off lightly.

In addition, Crinnion was proud of the fact MI6 had given the gardaí access to the inner workings of the Provisional IRA's GHQ *via* the O'Hare phone tap; had helped catch Mac-Stíofáin; and had thwarted arms importations.

When he weighed up all these pros and cons, what was his conclusion?

We don't have Crinnion's words to describe how he felt. We must therefore look at his actions. Crinnion chose to become a forgotten man. He never tried to defend the choices he made as a garda. Unlike spies such as Kim Philby, the man who betrayed MI6 to Russia, Crinnion never published a book, nor granted a single interview to anyone from the press. He simply disappeared. If he ever wrote his memoirs, as he had once threatened when he claimed he needed cash, he made no effort to see them published after he righted his finances. He chose to fade from memory. This was not the behaviour of a man proud of what he had done.

Unless he left a manuscript or something similar behind, which his family has yet to produce, it seems Crinnion concluded that what he did was not defensible.

He died in June 2021, under his false name.[7] His funeral ceremony was sparsely attended. His remains were cremated and, in accordance with his final wish, released at the top of the Sugarloaf mountain, Co. Wicklow, by a small contingent of mourners, including his brother Peter. The Sugarloaf looks down over Bray where Crinnion grew up. After the ashes blew away, there was no earthly trace of Patrick Joseph Crinnion.

ENDNOTES

Fog of Deceit
1. Interview with MacStíofáin published in *On Our Knees* by Rosita Sweetman (Pan Special, London, 1972), pp. 159.
2. Patrick Bishop and Eamon Mallie, *The Provisional IRA* (William Heineman Limited, London, 1987), pp. 50 and 84.
3. Seán MacStíofáin, *Memoirs of a Revolutionary* (Gordon Cremonisi, London, 1975), p. 62.
4. Sweetman (1972)., p. 159.
5. *Ibid.*, p. 159.

1. The Man from Mensa
1. Peter Crinnion became a champion cyclist. He represented Ireland at the 1960 Olympic games in Rome.
2. The Wingfields were among the most influential families of the Protestant Ascendancy in Ireland. They occupied an exalted position in the social pecking order. Mervyn Wingfield, the 8th Viscount of Powerscourt was appointed Lord Lieutenant of Wicklow, on 15 February 1910, and was created a Knight of the Order of St Patrick on 18 April 1916. Mervyn was married to Sybil Pleydell-Bouverie. Mervyn was the great-grandfather of Sarah, Duchess of York, be-cause his granddaughter, Susan Barrantes, was Sarah's mother. In the 1920s there were approximately 300 estate workers in the employ of the Wingfields. The Wingfields remained at Powerscourt until 1961 when it was sold to the Slazenger family.
3. Penny Perrick, *Something to Hide, The Life of Sheila Wingfield, Viscountess Powerscourt* (Lilliput Press, Dublin, 2007), p. 123.
4. *Ibid.*, p. 121.
5. Nancy Lattimore was born Anne Lattimore.
6. Daniel Costigan served as garda commissioner, July 1952-February 1965.
7. A letter in my possession from Patrick Crinnion to Attorney-General Declan Costello, dated 27 June 1973.
8. Letter in my possession from Patrick Crinnion to Patrick Malone, 9 May 1973.
9. *Ibid.*
10. *Ibid.*, p. 3.
11. Letter in my possession from Patrick Crinnion to Patrick Malone, 26 May 1973.

2. The De Valera Bomb Plot
1. Statement of Gerry Madden available on the Cedar Lounge website.

https://cedarlounge.wordpress.com/?s=Swanton&searchbutton=go%21

2. Ó Lionachain, 'A Rebel Spirit' – the Life and Times of Seamus Ó Lionachain - 1963 reproduced by 'The Cedar Lounge Revolution at https://irishrepublicanmarxisthistoryproject.wordpress.com/2015/01/05/seamus-o-lionachain-on-the-night-before-republican-desmond-swanton-was-killed/

3. *Ibid.*

4. Gerry Madden can be seen at 4:34 on a video of a commemoration held for Des Swanton on the first anniversary of the latter's death: https://irishrepublicanmarxisthistoryproject.wordpress.com/2013/08/26/desmond-swanton-commemoration-1964/

5. In 1964, Charles Haughey as Minister for Justice, began the process of abolishing the death penalty by removing it for 'ordinary murders'.

4. Serving Her Majesty

1. Private interview.

2. There was a musical strain in the Lattimore family. Small amounts of money were put aside for one of the children, a boy, to purchase a guitar, but those paltry sums were then assigned to Nancy who needed them for dancing lessons.

3. MI6 recruited an asset of enormous power and influence in the Republic in the 1970s, the 'Businessman'.

5. The Visitors from London

1. *The Irish Times*, 3 February 2001.

2. Sir John Hermon, *Holding the Line* (Gill and Macmillan, Dublin, 1997), p. 37.

3. Hermon (1997), p. 37.

4. Private information.

5. Peter Berry was born on 7 June 1909, in Killarney Co. Kerry. His family moved to Charleville, Co. Cork where he grew up. He joined the DoJ in January 1927.

6. *Magill* (June) 1980, p. 76.

7. *Ibid*, p. 76.

8. *Ibid*, p. 75.

9. A letter from Patrick Crinnion to various religious dignitaries in my possession, dated 19 June 1973.

6. IRA prince, IRA pauper

1. Sweetman (1972), p. 153.

2. Bishop and Mallie (1987), pp. 50 and 84.

3. MacStíofáin (1975), p. 17.

4. *Ibid.*, p. 39.

5. *Ibid.*, p. 45.

6. *Ibid.*, p. 47.
7. *Ibid.*, p. 42.
8. *Ibid.*, p. 44.
9. *Ibid.*
10. Sean Boyne, *Gunrunners* (O'Brien Press, Dublin, 2006), p. 58.
11. Bishop and Mallie (1987), p. 86.
12. Joe Cahill as quoted in *A Life in the IRA*, Brendan Anderson (O'Brien Press, Dublin, 2002), p. 155.
13. MacStiofain (1975), p. 77.

7. Climbing the Republican Ladder
1. MacStíofáin (1975), p. 80.
2. *Ibid.*, pp. 83-4.
3. *Ibid.*, p. 85.
4. *Ibid.*, p. 89.
5. *Ibid.*, p. 89.

8. A Cuckoo in the Garda Nest
1. MacStíofáin (1975), pp. 89-90.
2. A letter in my possession from P. Crinnion to Garret FitzGerald and Conor Cruise O'Brien, dated 12 June 1973.
3. Crinnion to Malone, 21 March 1973.
4. MacStíofáin (1975), p. 90.
5. *Ibid.*
6. Multiple interviews with Joe Ainsworth.
7. *Ibid.*
8. *Ibid.*
9. *Ibid.*
10. Private information.

9. Sailing Close to Danger
1. Brian Hanley and Scott Millar, *The Lost Revolution, The Story of the Official IRA and the Workers Party* (Penguin Ireland, Dublin (2009), p. 44.
2. *Ibid.*, pp. 44-45.
3. Hansard, UK House of Commons debate 30 November, Volume 703, cc24-5.
4. Roy Johnston, *A Century of Endeavour* (Lilliput, Dublin, 2003), p. 170; Hanley and Millar (Dublin, 2009), p. 40.
5. The 'Battle of Dungooly' took place on the Louth-Armagh border on Thursday, 27 January 1972. Approximately 1,000 shots were exchanged between the British army and a unit of the IRA, during a four-hour clash. The following day the gardaí arrested seven IRA men in a dawn swoop in the Dundalk area and brought them before a special sitting of Dundalk Court. The IRA unit was led by Martin Meehan, a Belfast

Republican who had escaped from the Maze (Long Kesh) prison the year before. For a more detailed account, see *The Irish Independent*, 1 February 2012. See also: https://www.independent.ie/ regionals/louth/ lifestyle/the-battle-of-dungooly-lasted-for-four-hours/26960265

6. Hanley and Millar (2009), p. 46.
7. NAI Taoiseach 98/6/495 1965-09-30.
8. *Manchester Guardian*, 21 September 1965.
9. NAI Taoiseach 98/6/495 1965-09-30.
10. Private discussion, 6 November 2023.
11. NAI Taoiseach 98/6/495 1965-09-30.
12. *Ibid.*
13. *Ibid.*

10. The Director of IRA Intelligence

1. MacStíofáin (1975), p. 100.
2. Bishop and Mallie (1987), p. 86.
3. *Ibid.*
4. Private Interview with Roy Johnston, Dublin, 28 September 2012.
5. Stormont Premier Terence O'Neill had warned the Home Office in London in December 1965 that the IRA was training volunteers for hostile action in Northern Ireland in time for the 1966 Easter Rising celebrations. Stormont Minister for Home Affairs Brian McConnell shared these views, 1964-66.
6. Billy McKee as quoted in Peter Taylor, *Provos, The IRA and Sinn Fein* (Bloomsbury, London, 1997), p. 28.

by Peter Taylor, at p 28.
7. Eunan O'Halpin, *The British Joint Intelligence Committee and Ireland, 1965–1972*, Centre for Contemporary Irish History, Trinity College Dublin, March 2007.
8. Interview with a member of Col Hefferon's family.

11. Northern Ireland, A Garda Blind Spot

1. McKeague and McGrath were disturbed individuals. Both were paedophiles. McGrath was imprisoned for sexual abuse at Kincora Boys' Home in Belfast in December 1981. McKeague was interviewed about child rape by the RUC in early 1972. After he threatened to reveal what he knew about British intelligence involvement in the Kincora scandal, he was killed in February 1982. Paisley knew that McGrath was a paedophile, yet never reported him to the RUC.
2. Paddy Devlin, *Straight Left* (Blackstaff Press, Belfast, 1993), p. 105.
3. Cabinet minutes, 'Situation in the Six Counties', 14 August 1969, TAO, 2000/6/657, NAI.
4. *Irish Independent*, 1 August 2012. See also: https://www.independent.

ie/regionals/louth/dundalk-news/former-garda-corrigan-sent-to-falls-road-as-an-observer/26965637.html

5. David Burke, *An Enemy of the State* (Mercier Press, Cork, 2022), p. 25.
6. Boyne (2006), p. 56.

12. MI6 in the Republic of Ireland

1. The Foreign, Commonwealth and Development Office (FDCO), formerly the Foreign and Commonwealth Office (FCO).
2. 'C' is the code name within Whitehall for the chief of MI6.
3. Ian Cobain, *Cruel Britannia: A Secret History of Torture* (Portobello Books Ltd, London, 2013), p. 9.
4. Tom Bower, *The Perfect English Spy* (Heineman, London, 1990), p. 231
5. Anthony Verrier, *Through the Looking Glass British Foreign Policy in an Age of Illusion* (W. W. Norton & Co., New York, London, 1983), p. 301.
6. *Ibid*.
7. *Ibid*., p. 302.
8. Private interview with MI6 operative.
9. A more in-depth profile of Oldfield is contained in my book, *An Enemy of the Crown*. In 1972 Rennie and the D-G of MI5, Michael Hanley, established the Irish Joint Section (IJS) to co-ordinate their respective activities. Stella Rimmington described Hanley in her memoirs as 'a large, gruff, red-faced man, who had a reputation for being abrupt and having a fierce temper'. Stella Rimmington, *Open Secret: The Autobiography of the Former Director-General of MI5* (Hutchinson London, 2002), p. 116.
10. Anthony Cavendish, *Inside Intelligence* (Collins, London, 1990), p. 3.
11. *Ibid*.
12. Burke (2022), pp. 60–4 for a profile of Gilchrist and his links to the intelligence world.
13. *Ibid*.
14. Tony Craig, *Crisis of Confidence* (Irish Academic Press, Dublin, 2010, p. 58.
15. FCO 33/764/1; also Clifford (2009), p. 657.
16. Roger Faligot, *The Kitson Experiment* (Brandon Book Publishers Limited, Kerry, 1983), p. 102.

13. MacStíofáin's Friends in Saor Éire

1. https://www.youtube.com/watch?v=mCj_TzFGZm8&t=2520s
2. Boyne (2006), p. 37.
3. *Saor Éire, The Unfinished Revolution, The Struggle for a Socialist Republic - 1967–3* (An Irish Republican & Marxists Project publication, Dublin 2021), p. 7, column 2.

14. Playing Catch Up

1. Crinnion to Patrick Malone, 9 May 1973.

2. A letter in my possession from P. Crinnion to Declan Costello, 17 May 1973.
3. Crinnion to Malone, dated 9 May 1973.
4. MacStíofáin (1975), p. 129.
5. Doherty (2001), p. 125.
6. *Ibid.*
7. *Ibid.*, p. 126.
8. *Ibid.*
9. *Ibid.*
10. James Callaghan, *A House Divided* (Collins, London, 1973), pp. 190-91, which reproduces 'The Downing Street Communique and Declaration;' in full at Appendix I.
11. Discussion at The Foreign and Commonwealth Office, London, 15 August 1969, concerning Northern Ireland NA, 2001/6/658. The document is reproduced in its entirety in Angela Clifford's *Ireland's Only Appeal to The United Nations* (A Belfast Magazine, March 2006)
12. *Ibid.*
13. *Ibid.*
14. Anderson (2002), p. 176.
15. The RUC was led by Sir Arthur Young, an Englishman, who had been appointed to the post by James Callaghan.

15. Ministers in Dublin Hatch a Plan

1. Boyne (2006), p. 54.
2. Burke (2022), passim.
3. On 11 August 1970, the Provisional IRA killed two RUC officers, Samuel Donaldson and Robert Millar in a booby trap car bomb. At the time the Provisional IRA did not issue a statement claiming responsibility.
4. Callaghan (1973), pp. 47-48.
5. *Ibid.*

16. A Man Called Jock

1. Interview with Caoimhe Haughey, December 2023.
2. Crinnion to Malone, 9 May 1973.
3. Interview with Roy Johnston, Dublin, 28 September 2012.
4. Boland, Kevin, *Up Dev* (self-published, 1977), p. 45.
5. John Kelly was not involved in the operation. He discovered what had happened by speaking to Jock Haughey about it later.
6. Hanley and Millar (2009), p. 138.
7. *Ibid.*
8. Anderson (2002), p. 196.

17. SDU Tunnel Vision

1. McKeague and two co-accused were placed on trial in February 1970.

On 18 February, a bomb exploded outside the court. The UVF claimed responsibility for it. This, many observers believe, had a salutary effect on the jury who were frightened into acquitting McKeague and his co-defendants. They returned their verdict on 4 March 1970. Two days later McKeague was acquitted on other UVF bombing charges. McKeague later boasted to members of the Red Hand Commando, a paramilitary assassination gang he established in 1972, that he was the mastermind of the UVF bomb campaign that had toppled Northern Ireland's prime minister, Terence O'Neill in April 1969. See Ed Moloney and Andy Pollak, *Paisley* (Poolbeg Press Ltd, Dublin, 1986), p. 186.

2. Boyne (2006), pp. 97–9.
3. *Ibid.*, p. 99. Ó Conaill was also involved in the creation of the Irish Northern Aid Committee (Noraid), a US-based fund-raising body that financed the purchase of weapons for the Provisionals.
4. Desmond O'Malley, *Conduct Unbecoming* (Gill and Macmillan, Dublin, 2014), pp. 60–1.
5. MacStíofáin, p. 129.
6. *Ibid.*
7. *Ibid.*

18. The Parker-Hale Connection
1. Crinnion to Malone, 9 May 1973.
2. *Ibid.*
3. In November 1971, Casey was jailed for four years for possession of firearms in connection with the bomb blast.
4. Liz Walsh, *The Final Beat, Gardaí Killed in the Line of Duty* (Gill & Macmillan, Dublin, 2001), pp. 2–3.

19. MI6 and the Eltham Factory Sting
1. Crinnion to Malone, 9 May 1973.
2. Dick Walsh, 'Abortive London arms deal', *The Irish Times*, 10 February 1971.
3. Boyne (2006), p. 56; also Burke (2020), pp. 47–50.
4. Walsh, *The Irish Times*, 10 February 1971.
5. *Ibid.*

20. Crinnion Loses the Plot
1. Crinnion to Malone, 9 May 1973.
2. *Ibid.*
3. James Kelly, *The Thimble Riggers* (Self-published 1999), p. 24–5.
4. Burke (2022), p. 93.
5. *Ibid.*, p. 95.
6. A more detailed account of Markham-Randall's visit to Dublin can be found in Burke (2022), pp. 90–96 and 130–143.

7.   Kelly (1999), p. 24–5.
8.   *Ibid.*

21. The Truth about Knockvicar

1.   I had many pleasant discussions with Gerry Callanan in the 1980s and 1990s while I lived not far from his shop. I was oblivious to the events described in this chapter which only came to my attention in 2023.

2.   Kelly's election required, and duly received, the votes of Fine Gael councillors to secure his seat in the Seanad. This became a cause of embarrassment to Fine Gael after Saor Uladh carried out a raid on Rosslea Barracks, Co. Fermanagh, on 26 November 1955, during which one of their volunteers, Connie Green, was killed. The other members of Costello's administration were Labour and Clann na Talmhan (Family of the land).

3.   The 'gyration' remark was made at a time when an array of new dances were becoming popular in Ireland. A student at the time, Hugh O'Flaherty, later a judge of the Supreme Court, recalls that when MacBride visited the Literary and Historical Society (L&H), the main debating society in UCD, a student made fun of the remark, as if MacBride was the choreographer of a new dance. MacBride, a man with a sense of humour, enjoyed the 'heckle'.

4.   The initial purpose of the group was to monitor the show trials that were taking place in the wake of the Hungarian uprising of 1951. JUSTICE transformed into the UK section of the International Commission of Jurists (ICJ). MacBride served as ICJ secretary general, 1963-1971.

5.   In 1968, he was elected chair and, in 1975, president, of the International Peace Bureau in Geneva, a position he retained until 1985. He was also involved in the International Prisoners of Conscience Fund and was appointed to a number of senior UN postings as well.

6.   Anna Barron was a leading member of the 1916–1921 Club which had masses said for MacBride after his death. She lived on Mount Eden Road, Donnybrook and was a lecturer at the Dublin Institute of Technology, Cathal Brugha Street. She died in 2017.

7.   Interview with a member of the Callanan family, Dublin, December 2023.

8.   Crinnion to Malone, 9 May 1973.

9.   *Ibid.*

10.   MacStíofáin (1975), p. 133.

11.   Robert W. White, *Ruairí Ó Brádaigh, The Life and Politics of an Irish Revolutionary* (Indiana University Press, Indiana, 2006), p. 149.

12.   Ruairí Ó Bradaigh told his biographer, Robert A. White, that he believed Seamus Costello was responsible for the expulsion of Daithí Ó Conaill.

13.   MacStíofáin (1975), p. 134.

14. *Ibid.*, p. 134.
15. *Ibid.*, p. 137.
16. *Ibid.*, p. 136–7.
17. White (2006), p. 151.
18. Crinnion to Malone, dated 9 May 1973.
19. Gerry Furlong Callanan became involved in a tiff with Private Eye magazine in 1980. See *Private Eye* editions 472 and 475. Callanan wrote a letter to the magazine in which he attacked it for referring to Haughey's private life. See the chapter *Private Spy* Magazine in Burke (2020), pp. 242–247, for further details about the use of *Private Eye* by Maurice Oldfield to smear Haughey in the 1970s.

22. The Rise of the Provisionals

1. Tim Pat Coogan, *The I.R.A.* (Harper Collins Publisher, London, 2000), p. 341.
2. White (2006), pp. 134 and 162; Clarke died aged 94 in 1976.
3. *Saor Éire* (2021), p. 8, column 1.
4. *Ibid.*
5. Crinnion to FitzGerald and others, 12 June 1973.
6. *Ibid.*
7. Bishop and Mallie (1987), p. 170.
8. Boyne (2006), p. 36.
9. *Ibid.*, p. 37.

23. MI6's Debt to Saor Éire

1. Burke (2022), p. 130.
2. Walsh (2001), pp. 10-11.
3. Verrier (1983), p. 302.
4. Crinnion to Malone, 9 May 1973.
5. Kelly (1999), p. 22.
6. Private information.
7. *Saor Éire* (2021), p. 6, column 2.
8. Private information.
9. Walsh (2001), p. 10.
10. *Magill*, June 1980, pp. 72-73.
11. *Ibid.*
12. O'Malley (2014), pp. 80-81.
13. Crinnion to Malone, 9 May 1973.

24. One of Crinnion's Darkest Secrets

1. Fingerprint evidence was also adduced at the trial of Joe Dillon and Sean Morrisey of Saor Eire at a later stage. Sean McBride represented them. A jury acquitted both men.

25. The Cat Jumps Out of the Bag

1. Boyne (2006), pp. 97–98.
2. La Main Rouge was a French terrorist organisation controlled and directed by the French foreign intelligence agency, Service de Documentation Exterieure et de Contre-Espionnage (SDECE), in the 1950s. Its mission was to eliminate supporters of Algerian independence during the Algerian War.
3. Boyne (2006), pp. 70–71.
4. *Magill*, May 1980, p. 46
5. Justin O'Brien, *The Arms Trial* (Gill and Macmillan, Dublin, 2000), p. 94.
6. See Michael Mills, *Hurler on the Ditch* (Currach Press, Dublin, 2006), p. 69; Boyne (2009), p. 449.
7. Mills (2006); Boyne (2009), p. 449.
8. Private information. It is reasonable to assume that John Kelly informed MacStíofáin about the arms that were scheduled to fly into Dublin airport in April 1970.
9. Michael Heney, *The Arms Crisis of 1970, The Plot That Never Was* (Head of Zeus London, 2020); Burke (2020).
10. 'IO' denotes 'intelligence officer'.
11. The 'X' here is short for 'ex-'. Col Hefferon had retired as director of G2 the previous April having reached the age of retirement.
12. The Jones brothers were innocent of any wrongdoing. Jerry Jones became a victim of MI6-IRD smears; see Burke (2022), pp. 147–8 and pp. 227–9.
13. Cosgrave had served in the Irish Army during 'The Emergency'. He followed his father into politics and was elected to the Dail in 1947.
14. Conor Brady, *The Guarding of Ireland* (Gill and Macmillan, Dublin 2014), p. 40.
15. Stephen Collins, *The Power Game* (O'Brien Press, Dublin, 2001), p. 75.
16. Collins (2001), p. 75.
17. Garret FitzGerald, *All In A Life* (Gill and Macmillan, Dublin, 1991), p. 93.
18. For an account of the role played by Paudge Brennan see: https://villagemagazine.ie/paudge-brennan-the-forgotten-man-of-the-arms-crisis/#disqus_thread

26. The Midnight Postman

1. *Magill*, June 1980, p. 63.
2. Liam Cosgrave attended the funeral of Col Hefferon after his death in 1985.
3. His assignment on protection duties at the British embassy offered an opportunity to Crinnion to liaise with the MI6 Station inside the building at the expense of the Irish taxpayer.
4. Letter in my possession, dated 12 June 1973.
5. The series appeared in the May, June and July 1980 editions of the magazine.

6. Clifford (2009), p. 672.

7. Crinnion to Malone, 9 May 1973.

8. *Ibid.*

9. Dick Walsh, *The Party, Inside Fianna Fail* (Gill and Macmillan, Dublin, 1986), p. 118

10. Letter in my possession from Patrick Crinnion to the Secretary-General of the United Nations, dated 10 July 1973.

27. MI6 Links Fianna Fáil to Saor Éire

1. Letter in my possession from Crinnion to Declan Costello, dated 17 May 1973.

2. Crinnion to Malone, 9 May 1973.

3. *Ibid.*

4. Paul Williams, *Badfellas* (Penguin Ireland, Dublin, 2011), pp. 22–3.

5. See Burke (2022) *passim.*

28. The Door Swings Open for the Provisionals

1. Kevin Boland, *We Won't Stand (Idly) By* (Kelly Kane Limited, Dublin, 1972), p. 84.

2. Paddy Doherty, *Paddy Bogside* (Mercier Press, Cork, 2001), p. 227.

3. Brady (1971), pp. 154–5.

4. *Hot Press*, 11 June 1990.

5. Andrew (2009), p. 618.

6. Burke (2021), p. 50.

7. *Ibid.*; Kitson had been due to remain in Northern Ireland until at least September 1972.

8. Paddy Devlin, *The Fall of the Northern Ireland Executive* (Self-published, Belfast 1975), p. 119.

29. The State Betrays its 'Confidential Sources'

1. *Magill*, July 1980, p. 23.

2. Kelly (1999), pp. 279–80.

3. *Ibid.*

4. *Ibid.*

5. Private interview with Peter Sutherland after I explained the role of MacStíofáin in the machinations that revolved around the Arms Crisis.

6. Kelly (1999), pp. 279–80.

7. *Magill*, May 1980, p. 35.

8. *Ibid.*, p. 36.

30. Her Majesty's Loyal Correspondents

1. A more detailed account of this incident is contained in Burke (2022), pp. 150–58.

2. *Ibid.*

3. 'Haughey and the UVF Made a Killing', Burke (2022), pp. 224-30.
4. Burke (2022), pp. 171-2.
5. Wright p. 369; King's role as an MI5 agent was disclosed by Peter Wright of MI5 in his book *Spycatcher*. In this context, an 'officer' serves an intelligence organisation as one of its employees whereas an 'agent' assists it from the outside. Wright revealed: 'Feelings had run high inside MI5 during 1968. There had been an effort to try to stir up trouble for [PM Harold] Wilson then, largely because the *Daily Mirror* tycoon, Cecil King, who was a long-time agent of ours, made it clear that he would publish anything MI5 might care to leak in his direction. It was all part of Cecil King's "coup", which he was convinced would bring down the Labour Government and replace it with a coalition led by Lord Mountbatten.'
6. Cecil King, *The Cecil King Diary 1970–1974* (Jonathan Cape London 1975), pp. 171–72.
7. John Martin, *The Irish Times: Past and Present* (Belfast Historical & Educational Society Belfast 2008), p. 102.
8. Burke (2022), pp. 180–82.
9. MacStíofáin, p. 307.
10. *Ibid*.
11. *Ibid*.
12. Daphne Park, BBC *Panorama*, 1993.
13. Maria Maguire disappeared from public view for decades. In later life she became a public representative in London under an assumed name.
14. Maria Maguire, *To Take Arms, A Year in the Provisional IRA* (Macmillan, London, 1973), pp. 130–31.
15. *Ibid.*; Maguire was in error on this point. Two young women were killed in the Abercorn restaurant, five other young women and men were horrifically injured. All told approximately 130 people were injured.

31. High-Priced Chaps

1. The first permanent undersecretary (PUS) of the NIO was Sir William Nield. He was transferred from the cabinet office. From the start, Neild pushed for a high-powered espionage contingent at the NIO. He deemed the collection of intelligence a priority for the new administration as well as the co-ordination of the various spy agencies in the territory.
2. William Whitelaw, *The Whitelaw Memoirs* (London, Aurum Press, 1989), p. 85.
3. Trevelyan had certain links to the intelligence community. His connection can be gauged from his retirement which included partici¬pation in the Oxford College Intelligence Group. He sat on its steering committee which invited guests such as former JIC chairmen to attend to talk about intelligence matters.
4. Peter Taylor, *Brits* (Bloomsbury, London, 2001), p. 114.

5.   *Ibid.*
6.   Denis Payne was a ruthless individual. As DCI he oversaw all MI5 and MI6 operations in Northern Ireland including the egregious Kincora scandal and Operation Clockwork Orange. See https ://coverthistory. ie/2023/02/23/the-first-installment-of-covert-ireland-historys-new-30000-word-digital-pamphlet/
7.   Andrew (2009), p. 621.
8.   Richard Deacon, *'C' A Biography of Sir Maurice Oldfield, Head of MI6* (MacDonald, London, 1984), p. 169.
9.   My 60,000 online ebook which describes the Kincora scandal can be found on the Covert History Ireland and the UK website at: https://coverthistory.ie/2023/02/23/the-first-installment-of-covert-ireland-historys-new-30000-word-digital-pamphlet/
10. Patrick Mulroe, *Bombs, Bullets and the Border* (Irish Academic Press, Kildare, 2017), p. 85.
11. Mulroe (2017), p. 85; See Margaret Urwin, *Fermanagh: From Plantation to Peace Process* (Wordwell Books, Dublin, 2021), pp. 210-11.
12. Mulroe (2017), p. 85.
13. Peter Berry died on 14 December 1978 from a heart attack.
14. Maguire (1973), p. 121.

32. The House on the Thames

1.   Jack Lynch's personal papers as quoted in Dermot Keogh's book, *Jack Lynch: A Biography* (Gill and Macmillan, Dublin, 2008), p. 345.
2.   Keogh (2008), p. 345.
3.   Taylor (2001), p. 80.
4.   Verrier (1983), p. 302
5.   Robin Ramsey, *Ringside Seat* (Irish Academic Press, Dublin, 2009), pp. 85–6.
6.   Taylor (2001), pp. 116–117.
7.   Verrier (1983), p. 307–8.
8.   *Ibid.*, p. 309.
9.   *Ibid.*
10. Woodfield later became PUS at the NIO.
11. Gerry Adams, *Before the Dawn, An Autobiography* (Brandon Press, Kerry, 1996), p. 203.
12. Verrier (1983), p. 309.
13. *Ibid.*, p. 311.
14. *Ibid.*
15. *Ibid.*, p. 312.
16. Adams (1996), p. 205.
17. Verrier (1983), p. 312.
18. *Ibid.*
19. *Ibid.*

20. *Ibid.*
21. *Ibid.*
22. *Ibid.*
23. *Ibid.*
24. Gerry Adams disputes this and maintains that the soldiers were detained in Derry by the IRA by coincidence and were lucky that a ceasefire was taking place. See Adams (1996), p. 203.
25. Verrier (1983), p. 313.
26. *Ibid.*
27. Peter Taylor, *Operation Chiffon* (Bloomsbury, London, 2023), p. 37.
28. Taylor (2001) p. 123.
29. Frank Steele enjoyed his own sojourn in 'cloud-cuckoo-land'. Shortly before he returned to London in May 1973, he told Whitelaw that relations between the Army and the Catholic Bogside were 'so good that one feels they cannot be true ...' There is gratitude and admiration for the work and restraint of the Army in very difficult conditions ... the Provisionals were now regarded as a nuisance and a hindrance to the much-wanted return to normal life.' See William Beattie Smith, *The British State and the Northern Ireland Crisis, 1969–70. From Violence to Power Sharing* (United States Institute of Peace Press, Washington, 2011), p. 282. Steele retired in 1975 and went to work in the oil industry. In 1981 he became Chairman of Network Television, a post he held until 1987.

33. Colonel Lee of MI5 lectures the Garda

1. MacStíofáin (1975), pp. 102-3.
2. Celina Bledowska (Editor), *War and Order* (Junction Books, London, 1983). See contribution by Frank Doherty, pp. 117–21.
3. *Ibid.*
4. *Ibid.*
5. *Ibid.*
6. *Ibid.*
7. MacStíofáin (1975), p. 54.
8. James Kelly (1999), p. 25.
9. Private interview with an official who worked with Jack Lynch and Charles Haughey.
10. Peter Wright, *Spycatcher* (Viking Penguin Inc., New York, 1987), p. 358.

34. Oldfield's Gloves Come Off

1. Private interview with Sean Garland.
2. Faligot (1983), p. 104; Raymond Murray, *The SAS in Ireland* (Mercier, Cork, 1990), p. 77; Martin Dillon, *The Dirty War* (Arrow; New edition, London, 1991), p. 104.
3. Faligot (1983), p. 104; Murray (1990), p. 76.

4. Wyman also used the pseudonym, Michael Teviott. See Faligot (1983) p. 100.
5. Faligot (1983), pp. 103–4.
6. Hanley and Millar (2009), p. 185.
7. Faligot (1983), p. 107.
8. *Daily Express*, 19 September 1981. See also Jonathan Bloch and Patrick Fitzgerald, *British Intelligence & Covert Action*, Brandon Press, Kerry, 1983), p. 219.
9. MacStíofáin (1975), p. 240.
10. *Ibid.*
11. *Time Out* magazine, 10–16 August, 1973.
12. *The Telegraph* newspaper had connections to a number of former MI6 spies and others with links to the intelligence community. They included Ian Colvin, an ex-Foreign Office official. Colvin was the paper's Africa correspondent, 1955–75. He had served in a variety of intelligence roles earlier in his career, including SOE and the Political Warfare executive. His wife, Mary, was a former MI6 secretary. Another was Sir Colin Coote, deputy editor of the paper 1945–50, and managing editor, 1950–64. He worked with MI6, in the Home Office and at the Ministry for Information. David Floyd, the paper's specialist on Soviet Union disseminated the IRD propaganda while at the paper in the 1950 through to the 1970s.
13. MacStíofáin (1975), pp. 322-3.
14. *Time Out* magazine, 10-16 August, 1973.
15. White (2006), p. 171
16. *Ibid.*
17. *Ibid.*
18. Dillon (1991), p. 104.
19. Murray (1990), pp. 78-9.
20. *Ibid.*, p. 85.
21. Interview with Fred Holroyd.
22. Murray (1990), pp. 85–6.
23. Dillon (1991), p. 104.
24. Craig (2010), pp 141.

35. The Rita O'Hare Windfall

1. Crinnion added: 'I immediately made a report to this effect and it is on file 30/207/49.' The source of this record number is a letter in my possession dated 21 March 1973, from Patrick Crinnion to Patrick Malone.
2. *Ibid.*
3. *Ibid.*
4. *Ibid.*
5. *Ibid.*

6. *Ibid.*
7. *Ibid.*

36. The Straw that Broke the Camel's Back

1. Letter in my possession, dated 19 June 1973.
2. Both SDU officers and Provisional IRA members are still puzzled by this. While brigades were responsible for monitoring their membership, there was no centralised list. The secrecy levels intensified later with the advent of cell structures whereby the names of members became even more restricted.
3. Letter in my possession, dated 12 June 1973, from Crinnion to FitzGerald and O'Brien.
4. *Ibid.*
5. Crinnion to Malone, 21 March 1973.
6. *Ibid.*
7. *Sunday Independent*, 27 September 2020, p. 4.

37. Crinnion's Bedside Manner

1. Fr Sean McManus, originally from Kinawley, Co Fermanagh, is now the director of the Irish National Caucus in Washington and chief judge of the World Peace Prize awarding council.
2. Interview with Fr Sean McManus, October 2023.
3. Fr Sean McManus, *My Struggle for Justice in Northern Ireland* (Collins Press, Cork, 2011), p. 69.
4. MacStíofáin, p. 349.
5. Interview with Fr Sean McManus, 30 October 2023.
6. MacStíofáin, pp. 353–4.

38. Don Carlos Haughey

1. Verrier (1983), p. 325.
2. See Burke (2022), *passim*.
3. *Ibid.*, pp. 174–5.
4. *Ibid.*, pp. 223–30.
5. Crinnion told his superiors later that people involved with the alleged Mafia organisation had taken a civil court action for defamation against the newspaper about the Mafia link and that 'the newspaper won'.
6. Crinnion to Malone, 9 May 1973.
7. *The Sunday Independent*, 24 March 1974.
8. Crinnion to Malone, 9 May 1973.
9. *Ibid.*
10. *Ibid.*
11. *Ibid.*

39. We Have a Spy in the Camp, Find Him

1. Craig (2010), pp. 141–2.
2. *Ibid.*, p. 144; see also 'Exchange of information between Garda and RUC on Control of Explosives', record of meeting, 15 August 1972, CJ 4/820, NA.
3. Crinnion to Malone, 9 May 1973.
4. Craig (2010), p. 150.
5. *Ibid.*, p. 144; DCI Rowley departed in 1973 and became a divisional head of MI6. After Maurice Oldfield retired as chief of MI6, Dick Franks succeeded him and Rowley became deputy chief of MI6. Rowley retired in 1979.
6. Urwin (2021), p. 209
7. Craig (2010), p. 146.

40. Crinnion Blames the Provisionals

1. Second Barron Report on the 1972 and 1973 Dublin bombings, p. 31.
2. Letter in my possession from Patrick Crinnion to Garda Commissioner Patrick Malone, dated 26 June 1973.

41. Offences Against the State

1. Margaret Urwin and Niall Meehan, 'The 'third man' in the case of British agent John Wyman and Garda Sergeant Patrick Crinnion, *History Ireland* magazine, May/June 2018.
2. Private interview, March 2024
3. For more details about Baker, please see Chapter 8 of Burke (2021).
4. *Sunday World*, 4 January, 1976.
5. See Burke (2021) which contains a more detailed account of Baker and Herron's relationship with British intelligence, pp. 79–81.
6. Kennedy Lindsay, *Ambush at Tully West* (Dunrod Press, Dundalk, 1980), pp. 20–22.
7. *Ibid.*
8. *Ibid.*, p. 29.
9. *Ibid.*, p. 19.
10. *Ibid.*, p. 67.
11. Murray (1990), p. 68
12. Lindsay (1980), p. 67.

42. The Long Fuse that Blew Jack Lynch out of Office

1. Cavendish (1990), p. 3.
2. Prof. Keith Jeffery, *MI6: The history of the Secret Intelligence Service, 1909–1949* (Bloomsbury, 2010); see also Nigel West, *The Friends* (Weidenfeld and Nicolson, London, 1988), pp. 33–4.
3. Urwin and Meehan have opined that 'Peck feared that the IRA might keep its "head down" in the South and thereby frustrate encouragement

of further repression. A bomb exploded in Dublin on 20 January 1973, killing another CIE employee, possibly in order, as Peck put it, to "continu[e] to concentrate Mr Lynch's mind". Before that, on 28 December 1972, two teenagers were killed in Belturbet in one of a series of explosions in the border counties of Donegal, Cavan and Monaghan. The ambassador, however much he may have approved of their political effects, may not have had prior knowledge of the bombings. They are likely to have been sponsored at some level within Britain's security apparatus.'

4. Interview with Richie Ryan.
5. See Jack Lynch interview at 36:28 via this link: https://www.youtube.com/watch?v=Suwm8YGaqjM
6. Private interview, March 2024.
7. Affidavit of Éamonn Ó Fiacháin submitted to the Hamilton Inquiry into the 1974 Dublin- Monaghan bombings (later taken over by Barron).
8. Crinnion's source was his brother-in-law, Seamus Lattimore, not a brother.
9.   Éamonn Ó Fiacháin to Liam Hamilton, 27 May 2001.
10. Second Barron Report on the 1972 and 1973 Dublin bombings, p. 22.

43. Deflection
1. Private interview, March 2024.
2. Joe Tiernan, *The Dublin and Monaghan Bombings* (Eaton Publications, Dublin, 2010), pp. 147.
3. Kevin Myers, *Watching the Door. A Memoir 1971–1978* (Lilliput, Dublin 2006), p. 151.
4. *Ibid.*, p. 174.
5. Tiernan (2010), pp. 149.

44. The Third Man
1. Urwin and Meehan, *History Ireland*, May/June 2018.
2. Private interview.
3. Keogh (2008), p. 385.
4. Urwin and Meehan, *History Ireland*, May/June 2018.
5. *Ibid.*

45. The Spy Left Out in the Cold
1. *The Irish Times*, 27 February 1973, p. 19.
2. This entry was entirely innocent. Crinnion had two sons and was in the process of purchasing a model railway for them.
3. *The Irish Times*, 27 February 1973, p. 19.
4. Crinnion to FitzGerald and others, 12 June 1973.
5. *Sunday Independent*, 24 March 1974.

46. 'I Only Knew Wyman for a Short Time'

1. *The Irish Times*, 27 February 1973, p. 19.
2. Crinnion to various religious dignitaries, 19 June 1973.
3. Crinnion to Malone, 21 March 1973.
4. *Ibid.*
5. Crinnion to Malone, 26 June 1973.
6. *The Irish Times*, 27 February 1973, p. 19.

47. Wyman the Spyman

1. *Second Barron Report on the 1972 and 1973 Dublin bombings,* p. 14., in reference to the statement of Det. Super. E. O'Dea, dated 22 December 1972.
2. Keogh (2008), p. 385.
3. Crinnion to Malone, 21 March 1973.
4. Interview with Colin Wallace, October 2023.

48. Panic inside 10 Downing Street

1. Keogh (2008), p. 384.
2. Peck was the former head of the Information Research Department (IRD). A profile of him appears in Burke (2020), pp. 105–11
3. Keogh (2008), p. 384.
4. *Ibid.*, p. 385.
5. Faligot (1983), p. 102.
6. Document in my possession entitled: 'Message number 3; number 10 to Chequers, 23 December 1973 (this should read 1972).
7. *Ibid.*
8. *Ibid.*
9. *Ibid.*
10. *Ibid.*
11. *Ibid.*

49. The Manuscript in the Governor's Safe

1. *The Irish Times* report of court proceedings, 28 February 1973, p. 15.
2. Crinnion to various religious dignitaries, 19 June 1973.
3. Wymes served as garda commissioner from September 1968 until January 1973. His successor, Patrick Malone, served January 1973 to September 1975.
4. *The Irish Times*, 13 January 1973, p. 13.
5. *Ibid.*, 17 January 1973, p. 9.
6. *Ibid.*
7. Crinnion to Costello, 27 June 1973.
8. *Second Barron Report on the 1972 and 1973 Dublin bombings,* p. 14.

50. Spies in the Dock

1. Bateman Investigations was a fabricated MI6 front. It was not listed in the telephone directory, nor was it a member of the Association of British Investigators. It was run from the home of Brian S. Bateman, a former detective-chief inspector, who had retired as head of Oxford Criminal Investigations Division in 1965. There were contradictions relating to the address it provided. Michael Gilbert stated that the firm had an address 'in Surrey' but it appeared that they operated from Long Hanborough in Oxfordshire.
2. Information supplied by a relative of Frank Martin.
3. *The Irish Times*, 2 February 1973, p. 13.
4. *Ibid.*, pp. 12–13.
5. *Ibid.*, p. 13.
6. Interview with Joe Neville.
7. *Ibid.*
8. Patrick McEntee, SC, later carried out a Commission of Investigation into certain aspects of the garda investigation into the Dublin/Monaghan bombings. His report was published in 2007.
9. Urwin and Meehan, *History Ireland*, May/June 2018.
10. *Ibid.*
11. *Ibid.*
12. Crinnion to Malone, 9 May 1973.
13. *Ibid.*

51. The Crinnion Misnomer

1. *Sunday Independent*, 24 March 1974.
2. *The Irish Times,* 27 February 1973, p. 19.
3. *Second Barron Report on the 1972 and 1973 Dublin bombings,* p. 14.
4. Interview with Seán Boyne, August 2023 Dublin.

52. Hung out on the Bleachers

1. https://www.youtube.com/watch?v=BK68yyrKUOA
2. Interview with a member of Frank Martin's family.
3. A letter in my possession from Patrick Crinnion to the Secretary-General, United Nations organisation, UN headquarters, New York, USA, dated 10 July 1973.
4. Crinnion to Malone, 21 March 1973.
5. Crinnion to various religious dignitaries, 19 June 1973.
6. *Ibid.*
7. Private interview.
8. Interim Report on the Report of the Independent Commission of Inquiry into the Dublin and Monaghan Bombings, December 2003, p. 207.
9. Deacon (1984), p. 173.

53. The Cache in the Attic

1. Crinnion to Malone, 26 June 1973.
2. The identity of the 'Contact' is known to me. I had an opportunity to discuss the Crinnion case with him.

54. MI6 Ignores and Opportunity for Black Propaganda

1. Document supplied by a former British intelligence operative.
2. Interview with Colin Wallace, 2003.
3. See sections 031–37 of my ebook, Operation Clockwork Orange' Part 1 available here: https://coverthistory.ie/ 2023/02/23/the-first-install-ment-of-covert-ireland-historys-new-30000-word-digital-pamphlet/
4. See my story on the Village website: Obit(ch)uary [Updated]: RUC Special Branch and MI5's friend in the media passes away. Journalist who cast doubt on the truth about the Kincora Boys' Home scandal has died. He once described the brutal abuse at it as 'homosexual high-jinks'.
5. Deacon (1984), pp. 173, 229 and 241.

55. Old Habits Die Hard

1. *Saor Eire* (2021), p. 11.
2. Multiple interviews with Joe Ainsworth.
3. *Sunday Times,* 2001.
4. Private information.
5. *Ibid.*
6. Interview with an individual familiar with the outcome of the negotiations between the INLA and MacStíofáin, November 2023.
7. Private interview.

56. Crinnion's Veiled Threats

1. Crinnion to Malone, 26 June 1973.
2. *Ibid.*, 21 March 1973.
3. Crinnion to Malone, 26 June 1973.
4. Crinnion to Malone, 9 May 1973.
5. *Ibid.*
6. *Ibid.*
7. *Ibid.*
8. *Ibid.*
9. *Ibid.*
10. Crinnion to the Secretary-General, United Nations, 10 July 1973.
11. *Ibid.*
12. *Ibid.*
13. *Ibid.*
14. *Ibid.*

57. C3 Hoodwinks the Press

1. *The Sunday Independent,* 10 November 1974.
2. *Ibid.*
3. *Ibid.*
4. *Ibid.*
5. *Ibid.*

58. High Flyer

1. James Lattimore was promoted to sergeant-major and retired as a major. He was awarded an MBE in 1971.
2. *The Sunday Independent,* 24 March 1974.
3. Ardmore Studios in Bray, Co. Wicklow, made nine films in the 1960s during which Crinnion could have provided security services. One of these was *The Spy Who Came in from the Cold,* starring Richard Burton. It was made in 1965.
4. *The Irish Times* report of Court proceedings, 27 February 1973, p. 19.
5. Crinnion to Malone, 21, March 1973.
6. Recollection of a solicitor who was present in the court at the time of the utterance.
7. Search in the Registry of Deeds, Ireland.
8. *The Irish Times,* 28 February 1973, p. 1.
9. *Ibid.* p. 15.
10. Private information. This comment was made by someone who knew Patrick Crinnion during this time.
11. Crinnion's love of Alsatians was a long-standing one. He had been fond of 'taking long walks well after midnight on lonely roads near his house with an Alsatian for company and a Walther pistol in his pocket' while in C3; *The Sunday Independent,* 24 March 1974.

59. The Forgotten Man

1. The late Paddy Hayes was the author of *Queen of Spies, Daphne Park, Britain's Cold War Spymaster (*Duckworth Overlook, London 2015). Discussion with Paddy Hayes, concerning John Wyman, Dublin, 26 July 2016.
2. *Ibid.*
3. See the my ebook on the Dublin and Monaghan bombings of 1974. https://coverthistory.ie/2024/05/04/returning-the-serve-the-jack-al-collusion-mi5-and-the-dublin-and-monaghan-bombings-by-david-burke/
4. Multiple interviews with Fred Holroyd.
5. Interim Report on the Report of the Independent Commission of Inquiry into the Dublin and Monaghan Bombings, December 2003, p. 207.
6. I do not wish to reveal the name Crinnion used after his return to Ireland at this time.

BIBLIOGRAPHY

Adams, Gerry, *Before the Dawn, An Autobiography* (Brandon Press, Kerry, 1996)

Anderson, Brendan, *Joe Cahill A Life in the IRA* (O'Brien Press, Dublin, 2002)

Andrew, Christopher, *The Defence of the Realm: The Authorized History of MI5* (Allen Lane, London, 2009)

Bishop, Patrick and Mallie, Eamon, *The Provisional IRA* (William Heineman Limited, London, 1987)

Bledowska, Celina (editor), *War and Order* (Junction Books, London, 1983)

Bloch, Jonathan and FitzGerald, Patrick, *British Intelligence & Covert Action*, Brandon Press, Kerry, 1983)

Boland, Kevin, *Up Dev* (Self-published 1971)

Boyer Bell, J: *The Secret Army* (Revised Third Edition Poolbeg Press, Dublin, 1998)

Bower, Tom, *The Perfect English Spy* (Heineman, London, 1990)

Boyne, Seán, *Gunrunners* (O'Brien Press, Dublin, 2006)

Brady, Conor, *The Guarding of Ireland* (Gill and Macmillan, Dublin 2014

Brady, Seamus, *Arms and the Men* (self-published, 1971)

Burke, David, *Deception & Lies, the Hidden History of the Arms Crisis* (Mercier Press, Cork, 2020)

—— *Kitson's Irish War* (Mercier Press, Cork, 2021)

—— *An Enemy of the Crown* (Mercier Press, Cork, 2022)

Cadwallader, Anne, *Lethal Allies* (Mercier Press, Cork 2013)

Callaghan, James, *A House Divided* (Collins, London, 1973)

Carlin, Willie, *Thatcher's Spy* (Merrion Press, Kildare, 2019)

Cavendish, Anthony, *Inside Intelligence* (Collins, London, 1990)

Clifford, Angela, *The Arms Conspiracy Trial* (A Belfast Magazine, March, 2009)

Collins, Stephen, *The Power Game* (O'Brien Press, Dublin, 2001)

Coogan, Tim Pat, *The I.R.A.* (HarperCollins Publisher, London, 2000)

Craig, Tony, *Crisis of Confidence* (Irish Academic Press, Dublin, 2010)

Crozier, Brian, *Free Agent: The Unseen War 1941–1991*

Deacon, Richard, *'C' A Biography of Sir Maurice Oldfield, Head of MI6* (Mac-Donald, London, 1984)

Devlin, Paddy, *Straight Left* (A Blackstaff Paperback Original, 1993)

Dillon, Martin, *The Dirty War* (Arrow; New edition, London, 1991)

Doherty, Paddy, *Paddy Bogside* (Mercier Press, Cork, 2001)

Faligot, Roger, *The Kitson Experiment* (Brandon Book Publishers Limited, Kerry, 1983).

FitzGerald, Garret, *All In A Life* (Gill and Macmillan, Dublin, 1991)

Hanley, Brian and Millar, Scott, *The Lost Revolution, The Story of the Official IRA and the Workers Party* (Penguin Ireland, Dublin, 2009).

Hayes, Paddy, *Queen of Spies, Daphne Park, Britain's Cold War Spymaster* (Duckworth Overlook, London 2015

Heney, Michael, *The Arms Crisis of 1970, The Plot That Never Was* (Head of Zeus London, 2020)

Hermon, Sir John, *Holding the Line* (Gill and Macmillan, Dublin, 1997)

Holland, Jack and McDonald, Henry, *INLA Deadly Divisions* (Poolbeg, Dublin, 1996)

Jeffery, Prof. Keith, *MI6: The history of the Secret Intelligence Service, 1909–1949* (Bloomsbury, London, 2010)

Kelly, Capt. J., *Orders for the Captain* (Kelly-Kane Limited, 1971)

Lindsay, Kennedy, *Ambush at Tully West* (Dunrod Press, Dundalk, 1980)

—— *The British Intelligence Services in Action* (Dunrod Press, Antrim, 1981)

Keogh, Dermot, *Jack Lynch: A Biography* (Gill and Macmillan, Dublin, 2008)

McManus, Fr Seán, *My Struggle for Justice in Northern Ireland* (Collins Press, Cork, 2011)

MacStíofáin Seán, *Memoirs of a Revolutionary* (Gordon Cremonisi, London, 1975)

Maguire, Maria, *To Take Arms, A Year in the Provisional IRA* (Macmillan, London, 1973)

Martin, John, *The Irish Times: Past and Present* (Belfast Historical & Educational Society Belfast 2008)

Mills, Mills, *Hurler on the Ditch* (Currach Press, Dublin, 2006)

Moloney, Ed and Pollak, Andy, *Paisley* (Poolbeg Press Ltd, Dublin, 1986)

Mulroe, Patrick, *Bombs, Bullets and the Border* (Irish Academic Press, Kildare, 2017

Murray, Raymond, *The SAS in Ireland* (Mercier, Cork, 1990)

Myers, Kevin, *Watching the Door. A Memoir 1971–1978* (Lilliput, Dublin 2006)

O'Brien, Justin, *The Arms Trial* (Gill and Macmillan, Dublin, 2000)

O'Malley, Desmond, *Conduct Unbecoming* (Gill and Macmillan, Dublin, 2014)

O'Halpin, Eunan, *Intelligence, Statecraft and International Power* (Irish Academic Press, 2006)

Pearse, Martin, *Spymaster* (Bantham Press London, 2016)

Peck, John, *Dublin From Downing Street* (Gill and Macmillan, Dublin, 1978)

Ramsey, Robin, *Ringside Seat* (Irish Academic Press, Dublin, 2009)

Rimmington, Stella, *Open Secret: The Autobiography of the Former Director-General of MI5* (Hutchinson London, 2002)

Saor Éire, The Unfinished Revolution, The Struggle for a Socialist Republic – 1967–73 (An Irish Republican & Marxists Project publication, Dublin 2021)

Smith, William Beattie, *The British State and the Northern Ireland Crisis, 1969–70. From Violence to Power Sharing* (United States Institute of Peace Press, Washington, 2011)

Sweetman, Rosita, *On Our Knees* (Pan Special, London, 1972)

Taylor, Peter, *Operation Chiffon* (Bloomsbury, London, 2023)

—— *Brits* (Bloomsbury, London, 2001)

—— *Provos, The IRA and Sinn Fein* (Bloomsbury, London, 1997)

Tiernan, Joe, *The Dublin and Monaghan Bombings* (Eaton Publications, Dublin, 2010)

Urwin, Margaret, *A State in Denial* (Mercier Press, Cork, 2016)

Verrier, Anthony, *Through the Looking Glass British Foreign Policy in an Age of Illusion* (W. W. Norton & Co. New York, London, 1983)

Walsh, Dick, *The Party, Inside Fianna Fáil* (Gill and Macmillan, Dublin, 1986)

Walsh, Liz, *The Final Beat, Gardaí Killed in the Line of Duty* (Gill & Macmillan, Dublin, 2001)

West, Nigel, *The Friends*, (Weidenfeld and Nicolson, London, 1988)

White, Robert A., *Ruairí Ó Brádaigh, The Life and Politics of an Irish Revolutionary* (Indiana University Press, Bloomington, 2006)

Whitelaw, William, *The Whitelaw Memoirs* (London, Aurum Press, 1989)

Williams, Paul, *Badfellas* (Penguin Ireland, Dublin, 2011)

Wright, Peter, *Spycatcher* (Viking Penguin Inc., New York. 1987).

INDEX